*The Charge of God's
Royal Children*

The Charge of God's Royal Children

A Narrative Analysis of the *Imago Dei* in Genesis 1–11

TIMOTHY HOWE

WIPF & STOCK · Eugene, Oregon

THE CHARGE OF GOD'S ROYAL CHILDREN
A Narrative Analysis of the Imago Dei in Genesis 1–11

Copyright © 2024 Timothy Howe. All rights reserved. Except for brief quotations in critical publications or reviews, no part of this book may be reproduced in any manner without prior written permission from the publisher. Write: Permissions, Wipf and Stock Publishers, 199 W. 8th Ave., Suite 3, Eugene, OR 97401.

Wipf & Stock
An Imprint of Wipf and Stock Publishers
199 W. 8th Ave., Suite 3
Eugene, OR 97401

www.wipfandstock.com

PAPERBACK ISBN: 979-8-3852-0969-9
HARDCOVER ISBN: 979-8-3852-0970-5
EBOOK ISBN: 979-8-3852-0971-2

05/10/24

Scripture quotations taken from the (NASB®) New American Standard Bible®, Copyright © 1960, 1971, 1977, 1995, 2020 by The Lockman Foundation. Used by permission. All rights reserved. lockman.org

Scripture quotations marked (ESV) are from The ESV® Bible (The Holy Bible, English Standard Version®), © 2001 by Crossway, a publishing ministry of Good News Publishers. Used by permission. All rights reserved.

Scripture quotations marked CSB have been taken from the Christian Standard Bible®, Copyright © 2017 by Holman Bible Publishers. Used by permission. Christian Standard Bible® and CSB® are federally registered trademarks of Holman Bible Publishers.

Scripture quoted by permission. Quotations designated (NET) are from the NET Bible® copyright ©1996, 2019 by Biblical Studies Press, L.L.C. http://netbible.com All rights reserved.

Scripture quotations marked (NIV) are taken from the Holy Bible, New International Version®, NIV®. Copyright © 1973, 1978, 1984, 2011 by Biblica, Inc.™ Used by permission of Zondervan. All rights reserved worldwide. www.zondervan.com The "NIV" and "New International Version" are trademarks registered in the United States Patent and Trademark Office by Biblica, Inc.™

Biblia Hebraica Quinta, Fascicle 1: Genesis, prepared by Abraham Tal, © 2015 Deutsche Bibelgesellschaft, Stuttgart. Used by permission.

Biblia Hebraica Stuttgartensia, edited by Karl Elliger and Wilhelm Rudolph, Fifth Revised Edition, edited by Adrian Schenker, © 1977 and 1997 Deutsche Bibelgesellschaft, Stuttgart. Used by permission.

Tables on page 34–35 are copied from *The Literary Structure of the Old Testament* by David A. Dorsey. *The Literary Structure of the Old Testament* is published by Baker Academic, a division of Baker, copyright 1999. Used by permission.

To my teachers who taught me to love the Old Testament,
Thank you.

Bing Bayer
Stephen Andrews

Gal 6:6

Contents

List of Tables | ix

Acknowledgments | xi

CHAPTER 1
The Need for a Narrative Analysis of the *Imago Dei* | 1

    Methodological Considerations | 5
        Structure | 7
        Literary Features | 9
        Textual Aims | 11
    Explanatory Power as a Measure of Success in Literary Analysis | 12
    Current State of Research on the Narrative Analysis of the *Imago Dei* in Genesis 1–11 | 16
    Conclusion | 20

CHAPTER 2
The Corpus of the Study and Critical Considerations | 21

    The Corpus of the Study | 21
    Critical Considerations | 23
        Translation and Text Critical Considerations | 23
    Genesis 1–11 as a Unit | 29
    Literary Analysis and the Text's Final Form | 39
    Literary Analysis and Historicity | 41
    Lexical Analysis of צֶלֶם and דְּמוּת | 42
        Lexical Analysis of צֶלֶם | 42
        Lexical Analysis of דְּמוּת | 47
    צֶלֶם and דְּמוּת as a Conceptual Hendiadys | 48
    The Placement of the *Imago Dei* Texts | 53
    Conclusion | 54

CHAPTER 3
A Structural Analysis of the *Imago Dei* Texts | 55

    Levels of Structural Analysis | 57
    Structural Analysis of Genesis 1:24–31 | 59
        Use of the Plural in 1:26 | 64
        Genesis 1:27 | 69
        Summary and Structural Relation to Meaning | 72
    Structural Analysis of Genesis 5:1–5 | 73
        The Relationship of Genesis 5:1–5 to Genesis 1:26–28 | 74
        Genesis 5:1–5 and Its Pericope | 77
        Use of the ב and כ Prepositions | 80
        Summary and Structural Relation to Meaning | 81
    Structural Analysis of Genesis 9:1–7 | 82
        Significance of the ב in Genesis 9:6 | 86
        Summary and Structural Relation to Meaning | 90
    Macro-Structure Analysis of the *Imago Dei* Texts | 91
    Conclusion | 92

CHAPTER 4
A Literary Analysis of the *Imago Dei* in Genesis 1–11 | 93

    Genesis 1 as a Prologue | 94
    The *Imago Dei* as an Evaluative Concept in Genesis 1 | 96
    The *Imago Dei* and the *Toledot* of the Heavens and the Earth | 99
        Genesis 2:4–25 | 99
        Genesis 3 | 118
        Genesis 4 | 123
    The *Imago Dei* and the *Toledot* of Adam | 129
    The *Imago Dei* and the *Toledot* of Noah | 135
        Genesis 6:9—9:29 | 135
        Genesis 10:1—11:9 | 140
    Conclusion | 142

CHAPTER 5
Analysis of Authorial Aims and Conclusion | 143

    The Authorial Aim of the *Imago Dei* in Genesis 1–11 | 143
    Evaluation of the Explanatory Power of the Present Study | **149**
    Areas of Further Research | 153
    Conclusion | 155

Bibliography | 157

List of Tables

1. Kikawada's and Quinn's Comparison of Genesis and Atrahasis | 33
2. Dorsey's Arrangement of the Seven Main Units of Genesis 1–11 | 33–34
3. Dorsey's Arrangement of the Fourteen Main Units of Genesis 1–11 | 35
4. Thomas's and Derouchie's Macrostructural Analysis of the *Toledot* Formulas of Genesis | 37
5. Biblical Occurrences of צֶלֶם | 44
6. Biblical Occurrences of דְּמוּת | 48–49
7. Structural Characteristics of the Days of Creation | 61
8. Structure of Genesis 1:27 | 70
9. Interpretations of the בְּ in Genesis 9:6 | 81
10. Links Between Genesis 1 and Genesis 2 | 115–116

Acknowledgments

EACH STEP OF THIS JOURNEY has many sets of footprints. My heart is full of gratitude to so many, a few of which I can name here.

First, to my family, you are my greatest earthly treasure. Valissa, you are a model of grace and grit. My heart trusts in you completely, and I lack no good thing. Words fail. Adali, Selah, and Griff, you will never know how proud I am of each of you. I love you unceasingly, and in some small way I hope to reflect to you the love of your Heavenly Father. To Alvin and Debbie, thank you for your constant support, encouragement, and love. Without your many sacrifices, this book would not exist. To Mom and Dad, thank you for raising me in a home where the word of God was cherished, and the name of God was praised.

To the people of Heritage Baptist Church, thank you for allowing me to pursue my studies while also serving as your pastor. To my fellow pastors, Jason Redick, Kevin Smith, and Caleb McClure, thank you for demonstrating Christ's love to me every day and pouring out your life for His sheep. Ministering with you all is a joy.

To my fellow doctoral students, especially Nicholas Majors and Brian Koning, I will always cherish our times together at Pizza Ranch and our many discussions birthed from a common love of the Old Testament. Nicholas, thanks for my first cup of coffee. Brian, you always score a touchdown in my book. Thank you especially to my dissertation committee, Drs. Stephen Andrews and Rustin Umstattd, whose kind corrections made me a better student and follower of Christ.

Soli Deo Gloria

Chapter 1

The Need for a Narrative Analysis of the *Imago Dei*

THE BIBLE'S TEACHING ON the *imago Dei* comes through a story of beginnings. Humanity's creation in the image of God is a foundational anthropological concept in Genesis 1–11 (1:26–28, 5:3, 9:6) and is presented as essential in understanding God's purpose for humanity.[1] This teaching has elicited nearly endless speculation and debate. Biblical scholars and theologians, Jews and Greeks, ancients and moderns, have all been captivated by this fundamental doctrine of biblical anthropology. Claus Westermann stated that "scarcely any other passage in the whole of the Old Testament has retained such interest as the verse which says that God created the person according to his image. The literature is limitless."[2] Anthony Hoekema described this doctrine as the "most distinctive feature of the biblical understanding of man."[3] Gerhard von Rad wrote, "Because of the image

---

1. Translation issues immediately arise in the claim that humanity is made "in" the image of God. The use of the *bet* in the construct בְּצַלְמֵנוּ is far from self-explanatory. For the sake of simplicity, this paper will refer to humanity being made in the image of God with the understanding that the English translation "in" is a necessary simplification. Unapologetically, this study builds upon a confessional view of the Scriptures, including beliefs regarding their ontological nature, revealed purpose, and ultimate authority for faith and practice. This includes the belief that the entirety of the Hebrew Bible and Greek New Testament constitutes the inspired, inerrant word of God for the church. Unless otherwise noted, all translations will be my own.

2. Westermann, *Genesis 1–11*, 148.

3. Hoekema, *Created in God's Image*, 11.

of God man is exalted high and above all the other creatures."[4] John Kilner claimed the doctrine "has played a liberating role in 'Christian tradition' by encouraging Christians to respect and protect the dignity and life of all human beings."[5] For millennia, readers of the Bible have seen and understood the importance of this doctrine.[6] Indeed, if the attention the *imago Dei* has received is any indication, it would be difficult to overstate the doctrine's importance.[7]

Study of the *imago Dei* spans into nearly every area related to biblical studies, including theology, lexicology, epigraphy, and archaeology. In-depth lexical studies exist on the meaning of צֶלֶם and דְּמוּת, as well as the בְּ and כְּ prepositions that modify these words in Genesis 1:26–28.[8] Archaeological and comparative studies have shed light on the ancient Near Eastern context of the image of God, particularly with reference to kings.[9] There is even considerable epigraphic evidence that has contributed to the contextual backdrop of the biblical text.[10] Of course, there is also an immense amount of theological consideration of the *imago Dei* in the realm of both biblical and systematic theology.[11]

With so much written on the *imago Dei*, there is an immediate question as to why an additional study is needed. The answer to the question is simple and straightforward. While a great amount of attention has been given to the theological significance of the *imago Dei*, grammatical and syntactic questions surrounding the pertinent Hebrew texts, and even the

---

4. Von Rad, *Theology of the Old Testament*, 145.

5. Kilner, *Dignity and Destiny*, 6. Kilner also described the grotesque consequences of distorting the doctrine of the *imago Dei*, which he refers to as the devastation of God's image. Kilner, *Dignity and Destiny*, 4. For an important recent study on the implications of the doctrine of *imago Dei* for those with severe cognitive disabilities, see Hammond, *It Has Not Yet Appeared*.

6. See Simango, "*Imago Dei* (Gen 1:26–27)"; and Gunnlaugur, *Image of God*.

7. See Kilner, *Dignity and Destiny*, for an excellent contemporary theological study. Kilner's study includes a bibliography of over one thousand sources, and he openly admits this is the tip of the iceberg.

8. See especially the study of Garr, *In His Own Image*.

9. See Clines, "Image of God"; Walton, *Ancient Near Eastern Thought*, 212; and Gentry and Wellum, *Kingdom through Covenant*, 191.

10. See Strawn, "Comparative Approaches," 117–42.

11. For a very helpful study from a biblical-theological perspective, see Gentry and Wellum, *Kingdom through Covenant*, 189–202. Gentry and Wellum demonstrated a sensitivity for the developing narrative of Genesis 1–11. For systematic theological considerations, consult any standard systematic theology.

The Need for a Narrative Analysis of the Imago Dei

historical background that culturally situates the text, relatively little attention has been given as to how, if at all, the *narrative* of Genesis 1–11 may influence the meaning of the *imago Dei*.

The investigation of this dissertation is built upon the following foundational premise: to understand the doctrine of the *imago Dei*, one must understand how the concept of the *imago Dei* functions in the narrative of Genesis 1–11. The concept of the *imago* is situated within a carefully crafted story with a discernible structure, plot, and purpose. Genesis 1–11 tells the story of a perfect creation, the fall of humanity into sin and death, a righteous judgment, and the hope of redemption.[12] By understanding the role the *imago Dei* plays within Genesis 1–11, one can best understand its significance for the greater systematic theological project. The goal of this investigation is to examine the *imago Dei* as a literary concept within Genesis 1–11.

From the very outset, the task of distinguishing between the theological concept of the *imago Dei* as it has been discussed in Christian theology and the literary concept of the image of God as it functions in the context of Genesis 1–11 is crucial. Of course, the two are integrally related to each other, but they are not exactly the same. The theological concept is what has drawn the most attention. Categories such as representation, rationality, relationality, and functionality are used to describe the systematic theological concept of what it means for humanity to be made in God's image.[13] These categories are important and informative, but they are much broader in scope than this investigation seeks to be. Additionally, lexical backgrounds and the study of ancient Near Eastern comparative materials, though necessary and informative, are not sufficient to understand the meaning of the *imago* in its narrative context. To understand the literary concept, it is necessary to use the tools of literary analysis in an effort to understand how the concept functions within its scriptural narrative. The insights produced by literary analysis can then be used to interact with systematic considerations.

Two initial observations provide a *prima facie* justification for investigating the narrative of Genesis 1–11 to fully understand the *imago Dei*. First, each of the explicit references to the *imago Dei* occurs within Genesis

---

12. For a discussion on the literary unity and theological message of the Genesis 1–11, see Keiser, "Genesis 1–11."

13. See Westermann, *Genesis 1–11*, 148–58, for a list of seven different interpretative categories regarding the meaning of the *imago Dei*. Those seven categories could be further subdivided, demonstrating the continued debate surrounding the concept.

1–11 (1:26–28, 5:3, 9:6). This observation is as important as it is conspicuous. Genesis 1–11 constitutes a coherent literary unit. By embedding each occurrence within this single narrative, it stands to reason that the author desired the concept to be understood within the context of the developing story. Because each of the references occurs within this single story, it follows that to understand the concept of the *imago* one must understand how the concept functions within Genesis 1–11.

Second, even a cursory reading reveals that the *imago Dei* is dispersed throughout the narrative of Genesis 1–11 in strategic places. Roughly, reference to humanity being made in God's image occurs in the beginning, middle, and end of the narrative unit of Genesis 1–11.[14] The state of the world is very different in Genesis 1:26–28 when the phrase first occurs than it is in Genesis 9:6 when it last occurs. Yet, in both instances the *imago Dei* plays a prominent role in God's expressed designs for humanity. This basic observation indicates the possibility that narrative development of the text plays a role in the interpretation of the *imago Dei*. Together, these two observations point to the need for a narrative investigation of the meaning of the *imago Dei* in Genesis 1–11.

With the justification for an investigation established, the following questions will be useful diagnostic tools to clarify the study. How does the concept of the *imago Dei* function within the narrative of Genesis 1–11? Are the three occurrences unrelated or related, and, if related, in what way? Is there development of the meaning of the *imago Dei* between Genesis 1:26–28 and Genesis 9:6? If so, what is the significance of this development? And how could these questions be answered in a convincing way? These are the driving questions of the investigation.

With the task established on two preliminary observations, there are also two interpretive pitfalls that are possible in a literary analysis of the *imago Dei*. The first is the imputation of preconceived theological conclusions onto the text. While this would seem to be a very obvious mistake, consideration of the *imago Dei* is particularly vulnerable to this error. The *imago Dei* is a theological idea so often and widely discussed that it is nearly impossible to approach the text without theological background noise affecting one's analysis of the text.

---

14. The significance of the placement of the *imago Dei* texts will be developed in more detail below. The first instance in Genesis 1:26–28 is the climax of the six-day creation pattern in Genesis 1. Genesis 5 is a transitional passage linking Adam to Noah and the flood. Genesis 9 is the end of the flood story and the recapitulation of God's blessings and stipulations.

The second pitfall is allowing interpretation of only one explicit reference—Genesis 1:26–28—to drive interpretation of the *imago Dei* in the subsequent occurrences. As the seminal text, it is for good reason Genesis 1:26–28 has received much attention in the discussion on the meaning of the *imago Dei*. But the assumption that the concept of the *imago Dei* undergoes no significant development as the narrative of Genesis 1–11 develops is far from obvious. If anything, the assumption is *prima facie* implausible in light of the difference in the context between the first and last occurrence. While Genesis 1:26–28 has received much attention, comparatively less attention has been given to the subsequent occurrences in Genesis 5:1–3 and 9:6. Therefore, this dissertation will seek to avoid the pitfall by asking how the subsequent occurrences may shed additional light on the meaning of the *imago Dei*.

METHODOLOGICAL CONSIDERATIONS

For the purposes of this study, a narrative analysis simply refers to an interpretation of a text whose basis is the examination of that text's literary qualities.[15] Literary qualities include structure, rhetorical aims, literary devices such as repetition, characterization, and gaps, among many other features of the text. By its very nature, a literary analysis is not scientific and therefore includes a degree of subjectivity. A narrative analysis includes the tools of the historical-grammatical method, including awareness of the ancient Near Eastern background, but it goes beyond these in carefully considering the literary features of the text and arguing for interpretive conclusions based on those observations. Thus, this investigation will seek to analyze the function of the *imago Dei* within the story of Genesis 1–11 by using the tools of literary analysis.

Literary analysis requires a methodology that can accurately discern literary markers and incorporate them into a compelling interpretive framework. The aim of this section is to develop just such a methodology that can be applied to the text of Genesis 1–11. First, however, it is necessary to situate this investigation within the current field of literary analysis.

The literary study of the Old Testament has seen a "rebirth" in recent decades.[16] This was presaged by James Muilenburg's 1969 essay "Form

---

15. Throughout the work, the author will use "narrative analysis" and "literary analysis" interchangeably.

16. See Longman, "Literary Approaches."

Criticism and Beyond," which originally appeared as the 1968 presidential address to the Society of Biblical Literature. In it, Muilenburg encouraged Old Testament scholarship in particular to branch out beyond popular critical methods.[17] In Tremper Longman's assessment, literary analysis was attractive, in part, because "the regnant historical-critical methods were yielding fewer and fewer new insights."[18] The most important catalyst in the literary study of the Old Testament is almost certainly Robert Alter's *The Art of Biblical Narrative* published in 1981.[19] Using literary analysis, scholars such as Alter were able to avoid the atomization of the text that was common among form and source critics. Alter by no means stands alone in the burgeoning field of literary analysis. Shimon Bar-Efrat, Adele Berlin, Herbert Brichto, C. John Collins, David Dorsey, John Sailhamer, and Meir Sternberg are among the many careful practitioners of what is a mixture of art and science.[20]

With regard to the literary character of biblical literature, Alter made a bold claim:

> Rather than viewing the literary character of the Bible as one of several "purposes" or "tendencies" (*megamot* in the original), I would prefer to insist on a complete interfusion of literary art with theological, moral, or historiosophical vision, the fullest perception of the latter dependent on the fullest grasp of the former.[21]

According to Alter, the meaning of the text is bound up and inseparable from its literary qualities. A text's meaning cannot be properly discerned apart from understanding the author's use of literary conventions.[22] A literary reading includes analysis of grammar, lexicology, history, epigraphy,

---

17. Muilenburg, "Form Criticism and Beyond."
18. Longman, "Literary Approaches," 97.
19. Alter, *Art of Biblical Narrative*.
20. See Bar-Efrat, *Narrative Art in the Bible*; Berlin, *Poetics and Interpretation*; Brichto, *Toward a Grammar*; Collins, *Reading Genesis Well*; Dorsey, *Literary Structure*; Sailhamer, *Pentateuch as Narrative*; and Sternberg, *Poetics of Biblical Narrative*. For a helpful introduction to the hermeneutics of Old Testament narrative, see Bechtold, "Introduction to the Hermeneutics," 51–73. Bechtold overviews the approach of Alter, Berlin, Bar-Efrat, and Brichto, and also offers some insight on the relationship between narrative art and history.
21. Alter, *Art of Biblical Narrative*, 19.
22. See Collins, *Reading Genesis Well*, 51–61, for a helpful introduction to locution, illocution, and perlocution, especially as it relates to Genesis 1–11.

and other analytic or exegetical tools, but it adds to them an awareness and analysis of the intentional artistry of the text.[23]

There is, however, an immediate problem regarding a literary analysis of Old Testament narrative. Hebrew narrative follows conventions that may be impossible for a modern reader to discern. Modern readers must bridge an enormous gap of time and culture. Current readers stand millennia removed from the authors and audience of the Old Testament. Alter faced the issue squarely:

> One of the chief difficulties we encounter as modern readers in perceiving the artistry of biblical narrative is precisely that we have lost most of the keys to the conventions out of which it was shaped. The professional Bible scholars have not offered much help in this regard, for their closest approximation to the study of convention is form criticism, which is set on finding recurrent regularities of pattern rather than the manifold variations upon a pattern that any system of literary convention elicits.[24]

Although Alter's statement is pessimistic in regard to what is inevitably lost, he was nonetheless persuaded that a careful reading of the text could elucidate much of the text's literary qualities. Significantly, Alter believed the biblical writers saw the *words themselves* as the means by which God revealed himself to the world.[25] The structure of phrases, sentences, paragraphs, and pericopes is itself part of the revelation of God.[26] While certain literary conventions may be lost on modern readers, the words of Scripture continue to anchor and communicate meaning.

Structure

Analysis of structure is an essential starting point for literary analysis. Brichto and Alter both highlight the importance of parataxis and hypotaxis in analyzing structure.[27] Hypotactic material and paratactic material are, as Brichto described, "syntactic variations that in biblical Hebrew present the

---

23. This project is not a reader's response analysis. Although the role of the reader is important, this work is built upon the belief that a legitimate literary analysis is one that seeks to discern the meaning of the author as communicated by the text itself.
24. Alter, *Art of Biblical Narrative*, 47.
25. Alter, *Art of Biblical Narrative*, 112.
26. Alter, *Art of Biblical Narrative*, 88.
27. See Brichto, *Toward a Grammar*, 16–18. Alter, *Art of Biblical Narrative*, 23–32.

author with options."[28] The significance of paratactic material is especially important to discern as the paratactic material is by definition emphatic. The emphasis could be background information, flashback, or the breaking of diachronic sequence. In every case, it bears significance. This feature of biblical Hebrew is the "richly expressive function of syntax," Alter wrote, "which often bears the kind of weight of meaning that, say, imagery does in a novel by Virginia Woolf or analysis in a novel by George Eliot. Attention to such features leads not to a more 'imaginative' reading of biblical narrative but to a more precise one."[29]

Dorsey offered a helpful paradigm in analyzing the structure of biblical narrative. He listed three steps in studying the structure of a biblical text, which he defined as its "internal organization." They are "(1) identifying the composition's constituent parts ('units'), (2) analyzing the arrangement of those parts, and (3) considering the relationship of the composition's structure to its meaning (i.e., identifying the structure's role in conveying the composition's message)."[30] The first two steps involve straightforward description. Dorsey listed several markers that help determine the parameters of a unit, as well as internal cohesion within a unit. Some of the markers focus on words and phrases (e.g., inclusio, chiasmus, and keywords), whereas others have more to do with textual circumstances and themes (e.g., sameness of time, place, or topic).[31]

Dorsey's third step is to analyze how the text's structure relates to its meaning. Dorsey claimed "a composition's layout generally reflects the author's main focus, points of emphasis, agenda, etc., and accordingly represents an important avenue to better understand the author's meaning."[32] Dorsey gave three primary ways that structure indicates meaning: "(1) the composition's overall structure, (2) structured repetition, and (3) positions of prominence."[33] Overall arrangement helps to show a work's rhetorical pattern. Structured repetition enables an author to subtly demonstrate a point by inviting the audience to compare the same word, topic, or theme occurring in two or more instances to determine if any development has taken place. The repetition could be for emphasis, or it could be for the

---

28. Brichto, *Toward a Grammar*, 17.
29. Alter, *Art of Biblical Narrative*, 21.
30. Dorsey, *Literary Structure*, 16.
31. Dorsey, *Literary Structure*, 23–24.
32. Dorsey, *Literary Structure*, 17.
33. Dorsey, *Literary Structure*, 36.

The Need for a Narrative Analysis of the Imago Dei

sake of contrast, reversal, or resolution, among other possibilities.[34] Positions of prominence include the climax or turning point of a story, or the centerpiece of a nonnarrative text.[35] Readers should pay careful attention to what occurs in climactic moments as the author uses them to indicate particularly important ideas.

Dorsey's nomenclature on structure is necessary, but he cited Bar-Efrat's caution against investing meaning in structural analysis alone.[36] Analysis of structure is necessary, but Bar-Efrat rightly recognized that structural analysis is not sufficient. He wrote, "In order to endow the proposed interpretation with a high degree of probability and convincing power it is recommendable to look for data in the text, apart from the structure, that confirm or support it."[37] Structure points to the author's meaning, but other literary features of the text play an important role in corroborating the interpretation of the structural analysis.

Literary Features

After analyzing a text's structure, the next step in a narrative analysis is to analyze the literary features of the text. These may include metaphor, simile, figures of speech, style, character, setting, time, plot development, gaps, narrative voice, time, and paranomasia. Literary analysis assumes that these features are used intentionally by an author to communicate meaning and purpose. Among these, Alter saw repetition as one of the distinctive and prominent features of biblical narrative.[38]

Alter's treatment on repetition is helpful in a number of ways, not least of which is his demonstration of how repetition is often used to emphasize *differences* in texts that seem redundant to the modern reader. When an author changes the wording of a statement previously recorded, there is potential significance. Broadly, when repetitions with significant variations occur in biblical narrative, the changes can point to an intensification, climactic development, or acceleration of the actions or attitudes initially

---

34. Dorsey, *Literary Structure*, 16.
35. Dorsey, *Literary Structure*, 40–41.
36. Bar-Efrat, "Some Observations," 154–73.
37. Bar-Efrat, "Some Observations," 173.
38. Alter, *Art of Biblical Narrative*, 88.

The Charge of God's Royal Children

represented. Or conversely, change may point to an unexpected revelation of character or plot.[39]

Alter gave his attention mainly to instances where direct verbal repetition is in view, but repetition may also include repeated reference to places, circumstances, or people. Most important for the purposes of this study is Alter's observation that repetition can highlight development within the plot. This is particularly true in cases of what Alter called "narrative analogy" by which "one part of the text provides oblique commentary on another."[40] In these instances, a repeated reference to an object, concept, or circumstance serves to juxtapose different events in the mind of the reader.

For instance, Joshua 5:13–15 sees Joshua face the commander of the hosts of Yahweh. The angelic warrior tells Joshua in verse 15, "Remove your sandals from your feet, for the place on which you are standing is holy." This is an apparent echo of Moses's encounter with the angel/messenger of Yahweh in Exodus 3:5. In that encounter, the messenger of Yahweh said to Moses, "Remove your sandals from your feet, for the place upon which you are standing, this is holy ground."[41] That both Moses and Joshua received the commandment to take off their sandals is an intentionally repetitive statement.[42] Clearly, the passage intends to evoke a parallel between Moses and Joshua, in keeping with the pattern that emerges in the early chapters in Joshua (e.g., 1:5–10; 3:1–17). God promised that his presence would go with Joshua just as God's presence had gone with Moses. For both, the presence of an angelic mediator rendered the ground holy, as indicated by the command to both Moses and Joshua to take off their sandals. The author cleverly used the device of repetition to bring the comparison of Moses and Joshua to the reader's mind.

Another important literary device, although one that receives less attention, is the element of plot. Brichto defined plot analysis as "locating a series of events (or two series of events and their convergence) in time

---

39. Alter, *Art of Biblical Narrative*, 97–98.

40. Alter, *Art of Biblical Narrative*, 21.

41. The wording of the two passages is slightly different. However, the significance of the repetition does not seem to lie in the difference of the words, but in the comparison of the two situations in which the statement was uttered. The Hebrew phrase in Joshua 5:14 is שַׁל־נַעַלְךָ מֵעַל רַגְלֶךָ כִּי הַמָּקוֹם אֲשֶׁר אַתָּה עֹמֵד עָלָיו קֹדֶשׁ, whereas Exodus 5:3 reads שַׁל־נְעָלֶיךָ מֵעַל רַגְלֶיךָ כִּי הַמָּקוֹם אֲשֶׁר אַתָּה עוֹמֵד עָלָיו אַדְמַת־קֹדֶשׁ הוּא.

42. The use of repetition in two separate texts does not necessarily imply that the texts share the same author. A second author may intentionally repeat a phrase used by a previous author.

and place in a way that suggests other meaningful relationship (such as causality) between the events and the characters who figure in them."[43] The decision to include certain events and details in the plot is a choice on the part of the author. Plot development is thus intentional, not arbitrary. Brichto's analysis is again important: "Poetical analysis cannot admit of superfluous action."[44]

The key in a literary analysis is to show how literary devices (e.g., repetition, characterization, figures of speech) relate to the plot, driving it forward and illuminating its significance beyond bare diachronic description. All character development, imagery, figurative language, or any other literary device, occur within the context of the overall plot. Plot is never less than a diachronic description of events, but it is always more.

Textual Aims

In addition to performing a structural analysis and analysis of literary devices, the reader should seek to understand an author's literary aims. Sternberg, in introducing his own methodology for approaching the Bible as literature, claimed that an awareness of the text's function is foundational in literary analysis:

> What goals does the biblical narrator set himself? What is it that he wants to communicate in this or that story, cycle, book? What kind of text is the Bible, and what role does it perform in context? These are all variations on a fundamental question that students of the Bible would do well to pose loudly and sharply: the question of the narrative as a functional structure, a means to a communicative end, a transaction between the narrator and the audience on whom he wishes to produce a certain effect by way of certain strategies. Like all social discourse, biblical narrative is oriented to an addressee and regulated by a purpose or a set of purposes involving the addressee. Hence our primary business as readers is to make purposive sense of it, so as to explain the *what's* and the *how's* in terms of the *why's* of communication.[45]

---

43. Brichto, *Toward a Grammar*, 8.

44. Brichto, *Toward a Grammar*, 8.

45. Sternberg, *Poetics of Biblical Narrative*, 1. Sternberg goes on to describe biblical narrative as a "complex, because multifunctional, discourse." Sternberg, *Poetics of Biblical Narrative*, 41. His analysis sees the discourse as having three essential functions: ideological, historiographical, and aesthetic.

Literary analysis must recognize that the text is crafted in such a way to accomplish the goals of the author. Every text has an aim, and every concept within that narrative in some way assists in communicating and performing the aim of the author. Literary devices are didactic tools. Readers analyze the author's use of these tools in order to discern the author's purpose.

Collins followed this essential insight in developing his "critically intuitive" approach laid out in his recent work *Reading Genesis Well: Navigating History, Poetry, Science, and Truth in Genesis 1–11*.[46] For Collins, a competent reader must be active, aware, and engaged with the text in order to understand the effect an author is trying to have on the reader. Awareness of literary features will clue the reader to the author's illocutionary intent—the author's desired effect—and thus the reader will be able to understand the text more accurately in light of that purpose. Within the current investigation, the reader should not only discern how the *imago Dei* functions within the story of Genesis 1–11, but how this function sheds light on the author's illocutionary purpose in writing the text.

In sum, a literary analysis begins with an analysis of structure, moves on to consider literary devices, including repetition and plot, and finally considers how these literary tools illuminate the author's aim in writing. All of these are essential components for a literary analysis.

EXPLANATORY POWER AS A MEASURE OF SUCCESS IN LITERARY ANALYSIS

One of the difficulties of literary analysis is the potential for radical subjectivity. Proposed interpretations may seem fanciful or arbitrary without criteria by which the reading can be evaluated. Of course, a literary analysis will never be empirically verifiable beyond any doubt. Interpreters must recognize the tension that often exists between the science and art of literary interpretation.

In his work *The Pentateuch as Narrative*, Sailhamer provided an important insight in explaining how a particular literary interpretation can avoid the problem of being overly subjective:[47]

---

46. Collins, *Reading Genesis Well*, 26.

47. Sailhamer, *Pentateuch as Narrative*. Sailhamer used the same basic methodology in *The Meaning of the Pentateuch*.

The Need for a Narrative Analysis of the Imago Dei

> The central concern of the large narrative unit is not always immediately apparent but usually becomes clearer with trial-and-error efforts to relate the parts to the whole. This amounts, in practice, to reading through the entire unit and formulating a general statement of the overall theme. This theme is then checked against further readings of the text. Each reading should produce a clearer idea of the whole, which in turn should cast more light on the parts or segments.[48]

Although Sailhamer's concern is the theme of the Pentateuch as a whole, the general principle applies for any investigation of the way an idea, phrase, or concept functions within a narrative. A plausible interpretation of any narrative text should shed interpretive light on the whole, which is what is meant by explanatory power. Sailhamer's approach offers valuable wisdom in regard to showing how a literary analysis could be considered successful.

Applying Sailhamer's insight to the current study, a compelling literary analysis regarding the meaning of the *imago Dei* will help the reader better understand the individual parts of the text (e.g., provide a coherent and persuasive account of the three passages referring to the image of God), as well as demonstrate a greater degree of unity of the textual unit, Genesis 1–11.

Sailhamer's insight also provides help in the development of criteria to evaluate the legitimacy of literary analyses in general. Developing Sailhamer's observation, the following five diagnostic questions are proposed in an attempt to provide as objective a framework as possible to determine the success of a literary analysis. While these questions are applicable to any biblical narrative, the discussion of their application will reference Genesis 1–11, in keeping with the purpose of this study. The questions are as follows:

(1) *Does the proposed literary analysis provide greater evidence of cohesion and unity within a given text (e.g., within Genesis 1–11)?*

This diagnostic question recognizes that an author's literary intentionality produces a unified, coherent text. In the case of Genesis 1–11, there is ample independent evidence, from its structure to its thematic content, to demonstrate that the text is intentionally crafted and coherent.[49] In light of

---

48. Sailhamer, *Pentateuch as Narrative*, 26. While Sailhamer applied this principle to the entirety of the Pentateuch, it is also true of smaller, self-contained units such as Genesis 1–11.

49. For argumentation on this point, see Keiser, "Genesis 1–11," 20–34. See also the

this observation, it seems highly unlikely that any feature within the text, such as the repetition of a word or idea, would occur randomly. Therefore, a reader is justified to ask how seemingly random features might instead be intentional.

If a proposed interpretation can be shown to harmonize with recognized evidence of coherence, it is more likely to be compelling. And, in turn, the new insight provides additional evidence for the unity of the text. In this sense, literary analysis is like examining a picture that comes into clearer focus the more one observes its features. If a literary analysis of the *imago Dei* harmonizes with and sheds additional light on the unity of Genesis 1–11, it is more likely to be convincing.

> (2) *Does the proposed literary analysis create a greater sense of unity between a textual unit and the larger text of which the unit is a part (e.g., the relationship between Genesis 1–11 and Genesis 12–50)?*

This diagnostic question points to the relationship between two distinct literary units. Any proposed literary insight should help explain not only the internal cohesion of a text's unit, but also how the entire unit relates to other units in its immediate proximity. There is not only an internal unity within Genesis 1–11, but an obvious and intentional connection between Genesis 1–11 and Genesis 12–50. If a literary analysis of the *imago Dei* in Genesis 1–11 shows greater unity between Genesis 1–11 and Genesis 12–50, it is more likely to persuade.

> (3) *Does the proposed literary reading utilize literary methods that are clearly discernible in other texts?*

This diagnostic question seeks to ensure that a proposed literary convention is not an arbitrary invention of the reader's imagination. Thus, if a literary analysis of the *imago Dei* in Genesis 1–11 is built upon well-established literary techniques (e.g., repetition), it is more likely to be compelling. Conversely, if a literary analysis is based on the observation of a purported literary feature that is not present in other texts, it is less likely to be compelling.

> (4) *Does the proposed literary analysis shed light on other grammatical, historical, or theological insights of the text?*

---

argumentation in chapter 2.

This diagnostic question highlights the interplay of narrative readings and other exegetical procedures. If a proposed literary reading completely overthrows the historical, grammatical, and theological findings of centuries of research, it is much less likely to convince. Conversely, if a proposed narrative reading illuminates independently corroborated grammatical, historical, and theological insights, it is more likely to be correct. Thus, if a narrative reading of the *imago Dei* in Genesis 1–11 helps to explain other exegetical insights of the text, it is more likely to be considered successful.

(5) *Does the proposed literary reading help explain later allusions to a text (e.g., other teaching on the* imago Dei *in the Old Testament)?*

Besides the *imago Dei* texts in Genesis 1–11, other Old Testament passages may provide commentary, as it were, that is important to consider (e.g., Ps 8). Thus, a literary analysis and the insights it might offer should be checked against potential allusions in other passages. If a deep consonance can be demonstrated between a literary reading of an Old Testament passage and other allusions within the Old Testament, the reading is more likely to be convincing. Thus, if a narrative analysis of the *imago Dei* in Genesis 1–11 can be shown to comport with other Old Testament allusions, it is more likely to be considered successful.[50]

Because literary analysis inevitably involves an element of subjectivity, these questions are intentionally designed to deal with probabilities rather than certainties. In order for any literary analysis to be convincing, it is necessary to build a cumulative case of an interpretation's probability. For instance, if a proposed narrative reading can answer only one of the above questions in the affirmative, it is less likely to be compelling.

As an example, consider a literary analysis that seems to demonstrate the internal unity of a text, but does not show how that text relates to its larger whole, is based upon a purported literary technique that has no obvious parallels and has no corroborating witness in the Old Testament or other literature. That literary reading will be much less convincing because it only fulfills one of the above criteria.

Failure to answer the above questions in the affirmative does not necessarily mean that a proposed reading is incorrect. Reasons yet undiscerned may exist that could account for the negative answers. The goal is not to

---

50. Although beyond the purposes of this study, a confessional Christian would desire to compare the results of a study of Old Testament narrative to relevant teachings in the New Testament.

prove an interpretation beyond all doubt, but rather to provide a framework by which certainty is more likely. Total certainty is all but impossible in literary analysis, but a literary reading that is able to answer in the affirmative *all* of the above diagnostic questions has a great deal of explanatory power and is therefore highly likely to be considered successful.

The diagnostic questions, therefore, are designed to provide a strong epistemic foundation for literary interpretations of the Bible. They serve to minimize subjectivity while recognizing that a certain amount of subjectivity is inevitable. Even if a narrative reading satisfies the criteria laid out by these questions, individual readers still may not find narrative interpretations convincing. Even so, the diagnostic questions can lead readers further down the epistemic spectrum of certainty: from an interpretation being improbable to possible, possible to probable, probable to highly probable, and highly probably to almost certainly true. The greater explanatory power a narrative analysis demonstrates, the more likely it is to convince other readers of its truthfulness.

CURRENT STATE OF RESEARCH ON THE NARRATIVE ANALYSIS OF THE *IMAGO DEI* IN GENESIS 1–11

Any attempt to chart recent scholarship on the *imago Dei* will face the difficulty of narrowing the scope of secondary material. For the purposes of the present study, however, the interest in literary analysis suffices to limit the corpus significantly. Indeed, there are relatively few works whose interest is a literary analysis of the *imago Dei* in Genesis 1–11.

The classic essay whose influence continues to shape the argument on the meaning of the *imago Dei* in Genesis is David J. A. Clines's "The Image of God in Man," first given as the Tyndale Old Testament Lecture in 1967. Clines's essay presented parallel ancient Near Eastern evidence to suggest that humanity's role as God's stewards over creation, particularly animals, is the most persuasive meaning of the *imago Dei* in the context of Genesis 1:26–28. Rather than being a consequence, Clines stated that dominion over animals "virtually becomes a constitutive part of the image itself."[51] Clines's argument, in one form or another, shares a near consensus in Old Testament biblical scholarship.[52] Conspicuously, however, Clines's

---

51. Clines, "Image of God in Man," 96.

52. E.g., Routledge, *Old Testament Theology*, 140; Von Rad, *Genesis*, 56–59; Wenham, *Genesis 1–15*, 29–32; and Sarna, *Genesis*, 12.

essay gave careful attention to the interpretation of Genesis 1:26–28, but very little attention to the two subsequent occurrences in Genesis 5:3 and Genesis 9:6. His discussion on the final two occurrences centers on whether or not the *imago* is retained after the fall.[53] The discussion of the retention or loss of the image is important within historical and systematic theological discussions, but it has had perhaps the unintended consequence of distracting from the development of the narrative. Clines's focus on Genesis 1:26–28 and his method of analyzing the ancient Near Eastern background, performing a lexical analysis on the relevant words and prepositions, and applying those insights to the theological discussion, has been imitated by most interpreters.

P. J. Harland's monograph, *The Value of Human Life in the Story of the Flood (Genesis 6–9)*, represents the most important work to date in the literary analysis of the *imago Dei* in Genesis 1–11.[54] He saw the *imago Dei* as an interpretive key in understanding the development of the overall plot. The cause of the flood, according to Harland, is essentially humanity's failure to live up to the kingly ideal of image-bearing.

From the perspective of the J source, as Harland identified it, Harland saw the cause of the flood as evil in man's heart, an evil that grew exponentially between Genesis 3 and Genesis 6.[55] The story of Genesis 3–6 shows "different ways in which humans can defect, from the rebellion in the garden to the evil of a whole generation."[56] The P source likewise details the evil of man, but focuses on corruption and violence.[57] He saw violence as a reference to "all violent crime, bloodshed, and oppression," and even antediluvian murder. Importantly, he tied these sins to a failure of humanity to live up to the assigned task of bearing the *imago Dei*.[58]

> The function of the *imago Dei* is corrupted, because instead of faithfully exercising his role as God's representative (צלם) and vice-gerent, man grasps at powers which are not rightfully his. Instead of using the dignity and power which is entrusted to the image at creation for the benefit of the world, humanity assumes

---

53. Clines, "Image of God in Man," 100.

54. Harland, *Value of Human Life*. Although the work focuses mainly on the flood account, Harland's analysis also considered the plot development in Genesis 1–6.

55. The author will discuss source critical issues in chapter 2.

56. Harland, *Value of Human Life*, 27.

57. Harland, *Value of Human Life*, 28–40.

58. Harland, *Value of Human Life*, 37.

an arbitrary false authority, which brings evil. The world is not just corrupt, but it is corrupted by violence. In can then be seen why the image of God is given such prominence both in the creation and in the flood. Having severed himself from God by the sin of חמס, man has made himself liable for drastic punishment by death. Humanity which commits חמס destroys itself.[59]

Cain and Lamech are prime examples of this corruption, according to Harland. Cain's violence polluted the land with the blood of his brother (Gen 4:10). Lamech and Cain's vengeance "deliberately mar[s] the image of God which is placed in all of humanity," and their angry "taking of life is an inappropriate use of the dominion which is given in Gen. 1:26ff."[60] Harland's work demonstrates how an interpreter can relate references to the *imago Dei* to the development of the plot.

Overall, Harland's work is a model of literary analysis that gives important insights regarding the *imago Dei*, the cause of God's judgment, and the role of structure and language in interpretation. The work is written, however, from a higher critical perspective that sees the interplay of source material (J and P) as creating an even deeper sense of story than one source could have done on its own. Harland's attempts to read "J and P together" are laudable, but the weakness of such an analysis is that it leads to an inevitable and unnecessary division of the story. The very coherence of the argument Harland made regarding a comprehensive interpretation of the flood from supposed different sources undermines source critical assumptions.

Jeffrey Tigay has also produced an important essay, "The Image of God and the Flood: Some New Developments," which seeks to understand Genesis 9:6 in light of the developing narrative.[61] He applied a similar understanding as Clines, relating the *imago* to its ancient Near Eastern context. More important, however, is his structural analysis that seeks to understand how the text's form impacts its meaning. His conclusion, based upon the center of the chiastic structure of Genesis 9:6, is that the text emphasizes the agency of man in executing judgment.[62]

Unlike Harland, Tigay does not give much attention to the larger plot developments that could further illuminate the structure of the text. Tigay's

---

59. Harland, *Value of Human Life*, 37–38.
60. Harland, *Value of Human Life*, 42.
61. Tigay, "Image of God."
62. Tigay, "Image of God," 174.

analysis hinges upon a direct insertion of a particular theological understanding of the image of God (e.g., functional) onto Genesis 9:6 without fully considering the unfolding narrative of Genesis 1–9, the immediately preceding verses of Genesis 9:1–5, or whether or not a functional interpretation is consistent with other teachings in the Old Testament. Thus, his argument, while important as a syntactical analysis, fails to fully consider the available evidence that bears upon the interpretation of the chiasm.

Another work that follows the same essential interpretation, although with more attention to the narrative, is "Blood Vengeance and the *Imago Dei* in the Flood Narrative (Genesis 9:6)."[63] In this essay, Stephen Wilson argued that God's allowance for retributive violence in Genesis 9:6 is essentially imitative of God's own judgment in the preceding narrative. Just as God judged humanity in the flood, humanity is authorized to judge their fellow man after the flood. Rendering judgment, Wilson argued, is a typical royal responsibility. Wilson's interpretation related the statement in Genesis 9:6 to the ancient Near Eastern background of kingship. Wilson's argument is helpful in that it seeks to situate the statement in Genesis 9:6 within the overall plot, but it suffers from a focus on the flood narrative in isolation from the preceding narrative of Genesis 1–5, as well as a consideration of how such an interpretation comports with the rest of Scripture.

Markus Zehnder's essay on the meaning of the *bet* at the center of the chiasm in Genesis 9:6 also merits attention.[64] Zehnder analyzed possible divisions of the verse, defended the traditional chiastic reading of the text, and provided an overview of how interpreters have viewed the *bet* at the center of the chiasm in Genesis 9:6. His work is not explicitly literary in nature and does not take into account the contextual factors of Genesis 9:1–5 in interpreting the *bet*, but it is notable for showing how the structure of the text plays an important role in determining meaning.

As mentioned above, works on the *imago Dei* are so numerous that is impossible to catalogue them all, much less summarize their contents. However, the works of Wilson, Tigay, and Harland are the only explicit arguments discovered thus far that highlight the literary features of Genesis 1–11 as essential in understanding the meaning of the *imago Dei* beyond its initial occurrence in Genesis 1:26–28. Thus, while this project will interact with many works that do not approach the *imago Dei* texts from a similar

---

63. Wilson, "Blood Vengeance."
64. Zehnder, "Cause or Value?"

literary perspective, the above works provide helpful models of the kind of analysis this project seeks to undertake.

CONCLUSION

Upon reviewing the previous research, relatively little attention has been given to the literary function and significance of the *imago Dei* in Genesis 1–11. Most scholarship on Genesis 1–11 tends to see each of the references to the *imago Dei* as essentially independent of the story that lies between them. The studies that give attention to literary ties operate with source critical assumptions that inevitably influence aspects of the literary analysis. While the insights of theology, lexicology, and comparative studies have proven valuable, a need remains to probe the meaning of the *imago Dei* through the lens of literary analysis. The gap in current studies on the literary significance of the *imago Dei* is what the present study will seek to fill.

Before moving on to a narrative analysis proper, it will be necessary to further define the corpus of material to be studied, as well as answer critical questions regarding the sources and unity of the text. This is the task of chapter 2. Following this, the task will be to apply the literary methodology discussed above to the textual material. This analysis will constitute the heart of the current project in chapters 3 and 4.

Once an analysis of the text is complete and an interpretation offered, it will be necessary to determine the extent to which that interpretation brings about greater clarity, greater simplicity, and greater continuity to Genesis 1–11. At that point, it will also be helpful to offer a brief discussion of how the proposed reading interacts with the greater conversation of systematic theology. The final chapter will address the relationship of the current project to systematic theological considerations. Finally, the last chapter will also briefly seek to show how the proposed narrative interpretation intersects with the life of the Christian individual and the corporate body of Christ. Indeed, the doctrine of the *imago Dei* cannot receive too much attention since Christ himself is described as the image of God (Col 1:15) and believers are called to grow in conformity to his image (Rom 8:28).

Chapter 2

The Corpus of the Study and Critical Considerations

THE CORPUS OF THE STUDY

James Barr provided a succinct and incisive statement regarding the exegetical study of the *imago Dei*: "In the past a very great amount of exegetical energy has been devoted to the understanding of the idea 'image of God'. The isolation of the phrase, combined with its highly strategic position, makes it a very debatable subject and yet at the same time one upon which very serious consequences depend."[1] With Barr's statement in mind and having established the need for a literary analysis of the meaning of the *imago Dei* in Chapter 1, it is necessary to define precisely the corpus of study and deal with introductory and critical issues pertaining to the literary exegesis of the text.

The analysis of corpus material will begin with a preliminary translation of the explicit *imago Dei* texts, including treatment of text critical questions. Following the translation, the chapter will defend the decision to read Genesis 1–11 as a coherent unit and the choice to study the final form of the text of Genesis 1–11 rather than purported textual strata. The section on critical issues will conclude with a brief consideration of the relationship between literary study and historicity.

After establishing the limits of the corpus material, the chapter will turn to a preliminary analysis of the *imago Dei* that will further clarify the

1. Barr, "Image of God," 12.

goal of the present study. At the outset, a narrative analysis of the meaning of the *imago Dei* in Genesis 1–11 must analyze all the instances where the phrase בְּצֶלֶם אֱלֹהִים occurs in Genesis 1–11. Yet, a narrative analysis is more complex and potentially more fruitful than the examination of a single phrase. The goal of a narrative analysis is to determine how a concept functions within a story, even when an explicit phrase or word may be absent.

Two examples will help show how an idea or concept might be present even when a phrase or word is absent. First, nowhere in the story of David and Bathsheba (2 Sam 11) are the words "abuse of power" or "infidelity" or "disloyalty" used. Rather, the author assumes that the reader will understand those concepts based upon the telling of the story itself. Certain concepts are fundamental to understanding narratives, yet they are not always explicitly stated. Similarly, in the New Testament parable of the prodigal son, nowhere are the words "love" or "forgiveness" found. Yet, the concepts of love and forgiveness are obviously prevalent in the story.

Similarly, many stories assume a reader will connect dots between certain concepts, whether stated explicitly or implied, and the events of the unfolding narrative. A single text may even provide an interpretive lens for a larger text. For instance, the book of Judges ends with the refrain "in those days there was no king in Israel, and each man did what was right in his eyes" (Judg 21:25). This statement seems to offer an interpretive frame through which the reader evaluates the rest of the book. The possibility here is more acute if certain texts are placed in strategic positions of emphasis, as is the case in Judges 21:15. For instance, texts presented at the beginning of narratives often set the stage for what follows.[2] As will shown briefly below and in-depth in chapter 3, the *imago Dei* texts each occur at strategic places in the development of the overall narrative of Genesis 1–11.

Therefore, the concept of the *imago Dei* may be rightly inferred by the reader in places where the phrase is not explicitly used. An interpreter may ask if the concept of the *imago Dei* is obviously identifiable within the narrative of Genesis 1–11, in the same way that love, forgiveness, or other concepts might be understood in a plot or narrative where those words are absent. Furthermore, an interpreter may ask if the *imago Dei* provides an interpretive framework through which to understand and evaluate the actions of the characters and plot.

In order to investigate this possibility, the natural place to begin is the explicit references to the *imago Dei*. Thus, this chapter will examine צֶלֶם and

---

2. See discussion in Dempster, *Dominion and Dynasty*, 45–46.

דְּמוּת, the two words used to describe humanity's creation in the *imago Dei*, in an effort to understand how the concept of the *imago Dei* might function within the narrative of Genesis 1–11. The parallel use of צֶלֶם and דְּמוּת in Genesis 1:26 and 5:1, and the reversal of the word order in Genesis 5:3, suggests that the two words function as a word pair. Therefore, the words should be examined individually as well as together. Upon the completion of a lexical analysis, the chapter will consider how the placement of the *imago Dei* texts shows their importance in interpreting the narrative as a whole. This preliminary analysis will prepare for the in-depth structural analysis of the next chapter.

CRITICAL CONSIDERATIONS

Translation and Text Critical Considerations

All translations of passages from Genesis will be based upon the fascicle of Genesis in the *Biblia Hebraica Quinta* (BHQ) published in 2015.[3] Like the *Biblia Hebraica Stuttgartensia* (BHS), the BHQ text is based upon the Leningrad Codex (e.g., B19A).[4] As the Allepo Codex does not include Genesis, the Leningrad codex provides the first complete manuscript of this section of the Hebrew Bible.[5]

Emanuel Tov concluded that the BHQ "substantially improves" on the BHS, with improvements such as additional reference to Judean scroll materials, the inclusion of more deviations of ancient versions (e.g., G and Smr), the inclusion of the Masorah magna immediately below the text, and the inclusion of text critical commentary, among other advantages.[6] Within Genesis 1–11, Abraham Tal's commentary and notes included in BHQ provide a helpful starting point in textual analysis. The sigla used for the various versions follows the usage in the BHQ.[7]

---

3. Tal, *Biblia Hebraica: Quinta Editione*.

4. Kittel and Rudolph, *Biblia Hebraica Stuttgartensia*.

5. On B19A, see discussion in Wurthwein, *Text of the Old Testament*, 39–44.

6. See Tov, *Textual Criticism*, 354–57. For a longer and more detailed interaction, see Tov, "Biblia Hebraica Quinta." The texts of Genesis found among the Judean scroll materials do not directly impact the text-critical decisions of the verses under consideration. For more information on the Judean scroll material and its relation to Genesis, see Tov, *Textual Criticism*, 94–111.

7. G stands for Old Greek, Smr for the Samaritan Pentateuch, V for the Vulgate, M for the Masoretic Text, α' for Aquila, S for Syriac, T^{ONF} for Targum Neofiti to the Pentateuch,

Ronald Hendel's volume deals at length with the textual issues in Genesis 1–11.[8] Hendel offered detailed insight into the arguments surrounding individual textual variants and offered a proposal of the relationship between M and G, in particular. In Hendel's analysis, G represents a rather literal translation of an unknown proto-M text. While Hendel recognized that much of G in Genesis 1–11 represents a tendency to harmonize syntactical or stylistic difficulties, he believed G is usually undervalued in text critical decisions.[9] Overall, Hendel's discussion of the individual variants is a helpful addition to the commentary in the BHQ.

As the following considerations will show, where the *imago Dei* texts of M differ from the other major or minor versions, the difference is almost always explicable as a facilitation or harmonization for syntactical or stylistic reasons. Tov placed harmonization or assimilation as a subset of the rule of *lectio difficilior praeferenda*.[10] Yet, as Tov cautioned in evaluation of the internal rules of textual evaluation, "to a large extent textual evaluation cannot be bound by any fixed rules."[11] For instance, while harmonization is sometimes obvious, harmonization cannot be assumed in every case where one witness adds to another.[12] While it must be recognized that the rule of *lectio difficilior praeferenda* is not without exception, the rule is the most important consideration for the text-critical decisions of this study.[13]

The translation offered here is highly literal. The below translations include the verses that explicitly reference the *imago Dei*, as well as the

---

and T^{Gnz} for manuscript fragments from Cairo Geniza.

8. Hendel, *Text of Genesis 1–11*.

9. Hendel's volume also offers a thorough discussion of the genealogies of G and M in Genesis 5 and Genesis 11. The difference in chronology represents the major difference between the M and G text of Genesis 1–11. See Hendel, *Text of Genesis 1–11*, 61–80.

10. Tov, *Textual Criticism*, 272–73.

11. Tov, *Textual Criticism*, 280.

12. Tov, *Textual Criticism*, 272–73.

13. Emanuel Tov offered a critique on using the *lectio difficilior praeferenda* as an inviolable rule in "Criteria for Evaluating Textual Readings." See Tov's argument that scribal errors by definition introduce a difficulty into the text, and therefore it is difficult to distinguish between a scribal error and other possibilities. Tov, "Criteria for Evaluating Textual Readings," 439–40. Bentzen, *Introduction to the Old Testament*, 97, argued that the rule of *lectio difficilior praeferenda* is often, but not always, sound. Tov provided a balanced conclusion: "To a large extent textual evaluation cannot be bound by any fixed rules. It is an *art* in the full sense of the word, a faculty that can be developed, guided by intuition based on wide experience." Tov, *Textual Criticism*, 280.

surrounding verses, in order to provide sufficient context for further analysis.[14] All discussion and engagement with text critical decisions will take place in the footnotes.

Genesis 1:24–31

וַיֹּאמֶר אֱלֹהִים תּוֹצֵא הָאָרֶץ נֶפֶשׁ חַיָּה לְמִינָהּ בְּהֵמָה וָרֶמֶשׂ וְחַיְתוֹ־אֶרֶץ לְמִינָהּ וַיְהִי־כֵן:

And God said, "Let the earth bring forth living creatures according to their kind: beasts and creeping animals and the creatures of the earth according to their kind." And it was so. (v. 24)

וַיַּעַשׂ אֱלֹהִים אֶת־חַיַּת הָאָרֶץ לְמִינָהּ וְאֶת־הַבְּהֵמָה לְמִינָהּ וְאֵת כָּל־רֶמֶשׂ הָאֲדָמָה לְמִינֵהוּ וַיַּרְא אֱלֹהִים כִּי־טוֹב:

And God made the living creatures according to their kind, and the beast according to its kind, and all that creeps on the ground according to their kind. And God saw that it was good. (v. 25)

וַיֹּאמֶר אֱלֹהִים נַעֲשֶׂה אָדָם בְּצַלְמֵנוּ כִּדְמוּתֵנוּ [15] וְיִרְדּוּ בִדְגַת הַיָּם וּבְעוֹף הַשָּׁמַיִם וּבַבְּהֵמָה וּבְכָל־הָאָרֶץ [16] וּבְכָל־הָרֶמֶשׂ הָרֹמֵשׂ עַל־הָאָרֶץ:

And God said, "Let us make humanity in our image, according to our likeness. And let them rule over the fish of the sea, and the birds of the

---

14. The above translations include the immediate textual units that explicitly reference the *imago Dei*, Genesis 1:24–30, 5:1–5, and 9:1–7. Genesis 1:24–30 is the entirety of the sixth day of creation. Genesis 5:1–5 includes the *toledot* formula that begins the section through the death of Adam in Genesis 5:5. Genesis 9:1–7 includes the entirety of the blessing of God in that begins in 9:1.

15. Here Smr, G, α', and V change דְמוּתֵנוּ to וכדמותנו adding a conjunctive *waw*. Tal, *Biblia Hebraica*, 5, explained the variant as a facilitation due to syntactical difficulty. S, G, and V attempt to add a slight separation between דְמוּת with צֶלֶם. As there is no reason to believe that M would have removed a *waw* if it originally existed, it is the preferred reading. The joining of the two words syntactically gives credence to the idea that they are intended as a conceptional hendiadys, an idea to be argued below.

16. The translation follows the text of M, although Hendel claimed that most commentators prefer the Syriac reading, which excludes the reference to ruling over the earth itself. Hendel also stated that a reference to ruling the earth seems odd in a zoological context. Hendel, *Text of Genesis 1–11*, 42. Hendel's argument fails to convince as verse 28 explicitly commands humanity to rule over the earth. Textually, there is no reason to prefer the Syriac reading, as Hendel conceded.

heavens, and the beasts, and over all the earth, and all the creeping animals that creep on the earth." (v. 26)

וַיִּבְרָא אֱלֹהִים ׀ אֶת־הָאָדָם בְּצַלְמוֹ ¹⁷ בְּצֶלֶם אֱלֹהִים בָּרָא אֹתוֹ זָכָר וּנְקֵבָה בָּרָא אֹתָם:

God created humanity in his image. In the image of God he created him. Male and female he created them. (v. 27)

וַיְבָרֶךְ אֹתָם אֱלֹהִים וַיֹּאמֶר לָהֶם אֱלֹהִים ¹⁸ פְּרוּ וּרְבוּ וּמִלְאוּ אֶת־הָאָרֶץ וְכִבְשֻׁהָ וּרְדוּ בִּדְגַת הַיָּם וּבְעוֹף הַשָּׁמַיִם וּבְכָל־חַיָּה הָרֹמֶשֶׂת עַל־הָאָרֶץ

And God blessed them and he said to them, "Be fruitful and multiply. Fill the earth and subdue it. And rule over the fish of the sea, and the birds of the heavens, and all the living things that creep upon the earth." (v. 28)

וַיֹּאמֶר אֱלֹהִים הִנֵּה נָתַתִּי לָכֶם אֶת־כָּל־עֵשֶׂב ׀ זֹרֵעַ זֶרַע אֲשֶׁר עַל־פְּנֵי כָל־הָאָרֶץ וְאֶת־כָּל־הָעֵץ אֲשֶׁר־בּוֹ פְרִי־עֵץ זֹרֵעַ זָרַע לָכֶם יִהְיֶה לְאָכְלָה:

And God said, "Behold, I give to you all the plants bearing seed which are on the face of all the earth, all the trees which are on it, trees with fruit that bears seeds. And they will be food for you." (v. 29)

וּלְכָל־חַיַּת הָאָרֶץ וּלְכָל־עוֹף הַשָּׁמַיִם וּלְכֹל ׀ רוֹמֵשׂ עַל־הָאָרֶץ אֲשֶׁר־בּוֹ נֶפֶשׁ חַיָּה אֶת־כָּל־יֶרֶק עֵשֶׂב לְאָכְלָה וַיְהִי־כֵן:

"And to all the living creatures on the earth, and to all the birds of the heavens, and to all that creeps on the earth which has the breath of life in it, I give all the green plants¹⁹ as food. And it was so." (v. 30)

17. G here excludes בְּצַלְמוֹ. Tal argued that the change occurred for stylistic reasons. Tal, *Biblia Hebraica*, 5. Hendel argued the variant is due to homoioarkton, whereby the scribe's eyes skipped to the second occurrence and thus the first instance was inadvertently removed. Hendel, *Text of Genesis 1-11*, 30. The textual weight falls in favor of inclusion, as inclusion preserves the apparent chiastic structure of the overall verse.

18. G and V both seem to see אֱלֹהִים as repetitive and therefore remove it. Tal argued that both instances are a facilitation of style and saw G as a harmonization with verse 22. Tal, *Biblia Hebraica*, 5. Hendel agreed that G represents a harmonization. Hendel, *Text of Genesis 1-11*, 30.

19. The exact reference to אֶת־כָּל־יֶרֶק עֵשֶׂב is unclear, but it seems that the phrase intends to include the full variety of edible vegetables, grasses, and other plant life. NASB and ESV, for instance, translated the phrase as "every green plant."

וַיַּרְא אֱלֹהִים אֶת־כָּל־אֲשֶׁר עָשָׂה וְהִנֵּה־טוֹב מְאֹד וַיְהִי־עֶרֶב וַיְהִי־בֹקֶר יוֹם הַשִּׁשִּׁי׃

And God saw all which he had made, and behold, it was very good. And there was evening, and there was morning, the sixth day. (v. 31)

Genesis 5:1–5

זֶה סֵפֶר תּוֹלְדֹת[20] אָדָם[21] בְּיוֹם בְּרֹא אֱלֹהִים אָדָם בִּדְמוּת אֱלֹהִים עָשָׂה אֹתוֹ׃

This scroll is the generations of Adam. In the day God created humanity, he made him in God's likeness. (v. 1)

זָכָר וּנְקֵבָה בְּרָאָם וַיְבָרֶךְ אֹתָם וַיִּקְרָא אֶת־שְׁמָם אָדָם בְּיוֹם הִבָּרְאָם׃ ס

Male and female he created them. And he blessed them. And he called their name, "Humanity" in the day he created them. (v. 2)

וַיְחִי אָדָם שְׁלֹשִׁים וּמְאַת שָׁנָה וַיּוֹלֶד בִּדְמוּתוֹ כְּצַלְמוֹ[22] וַיִּקְרָא אֶת־שְׁמוֹ שֵׁת׃

And Adam lived 130 years and he fathered [a son][23] in his likeness, according to his image. And he called his name Seth. (v. 3)

וַיִּהְיוּ יְמֵי־אָדָם אַחֲרֵי הוֹלִידוֹ אֶת־שֵׁת שְׁמֹנֶה מֵאֹת שָׁנָה וַיּוֹלֶד בָּנִים וּבָנוֹת׃

And the days of Adam after he fathered Seth were seven hundred years. And he fathered sons and daughters. (v. 4)

וַיִּהְיוּ כָּל־יְמֵי אָדָם אֲשֶׁר־חַי תְּשַׁע מֵאוֹת שָׁנָה וּשְׁלֹשִׁים שָׁנָה[24] וַיָּמֹת׃ ס

---

20. G translates γενέσεως. Tal claimed the change represents assimilation to the usual Hebrew usage. Tal, *Biblia Hebraica*, 13.

21. G's translation ἀνθρώπων is an interpretation of the referent as humanity in general rather than an individual. G translates the second instance of אָדָם as τὸν Ἀδάμ. While this interpretation is possible, the Hebrew text is ambiguous on this point. The above translation opts to translate the first instance as a proper name in keeping with the same pattern of the other *toledot* passages. This could be a case of intentional ambiguity.

22. Similar to Genesis 1:26, G adds καί before כְּצַלְמוֹ to separate כְּצַלְמוֹ and בִּדְמוּתוֹ.

23. Hendel saw the omission of "son" as a possible scribal error, but ultimately concluded the word son is implied. See discussion in Hendel, *Text of Genesis 1–11*, 50.

24. From ancient times, there has been an ongoing discussion about the various versions of the genealogies. See the very helpful discussion in Hendel, *Text of Genesis 1–11*,

The Charge of God's Royal Children

And all the days of Adam which he lived were nine hundred and thirty years. And he died. (v. 5)

Genesis 9:1–7

וַיְבָרֶךְ אֱלֹהִים אֶת־נֹחַ וְאֶת־בָּנָיו וַיֹּאמֶר לָהֶם פְּרוּ וּרְבוּ וּמִלְאוּ אֶת־הָאָרֶץ:[25]

And God blessed Noah and his sons and he said to them, "Be fruitful, and multiply, and fill the earth." (v. 1)

וּמוֹרַאֲכֶם וְחִתְּכֶם יִהְיֶה עַל כָּל־חַיַּת הָאָרֶץ וְעַל כָּל־עוֹף הַשָּׁמָיִם בְּכֹל אֲשֶׁר תִּרְמֹשׂ הָאֲדָמָה וּבְכָל־דְּגֵי הַיָּם בְּיֶדְכֶם נִתָּנוּ:[26]

And the fear of you, and the terror of you will be upon all living creatures on the earth, and upon all the birds of the heavens, and upon all which creeps upon the ground, and upon all the fish of the sea. They are given into your hands. (v. 2)

כָּל־רֶמֶשׂ אֲשֶׁר הוּא־חַי לָכֶם יִהְיֶה לְאָכְלָה כְּיֶרֶק עֵשֶׂב נָתַתִּי לָכֶם אֶת־כֹּל:

All moving [creeping] animals which are alive, they will be food for you. As [I gave] the green plants, I give everything to you. (v. 3)

אַךְ־בָּשָׂר בְּנַפְשׁוֹ דָמוֹ[27] לֹא תֹאכֵלוּ:

Only flesh with its life, its blood, you shall not eat. (v. 4)

61–80. The different chronologies presented in the genealogies do not obviously bear on the interpretation of the *imago Dei*.

25. G adds καὶ κατακυριεύσατε αὐτῆς in an apparent attempt to harmonize with 1:28. As there is no reason to believe this phrase would have been originally present in M and then deleted, the reading should be rejected.

26. Here, Smr uses the first person נתתי rather than נִתָּנוּ. There is little if any interpretive difference between the use of the *niphal* third person as a divine passive and God speaking in the first person. G also uses the first person, as well as T[ONF]. Textually, the reading of M is preferred as it is difficult to explain why M would have changed an original first-person speech to the third person. The change in G and Smr is explicable as an assimilation to the clear first-person speech in the following verse.

27. The apposition of life and blood has led to variant textual interpretations. G, for instance, smooths out the apposition with the rendering κρέας ἐν αἵματι ψυχῆς. As the Hebrew text creates the difficulty the other texts alleviate, M is the preferred reading.

וְאַךְ אֶת־דִּמְכֶם לְנַפְשֹׁתֵיכֶם אֶדְרֹשׁ מִיַּד כָּל־חַיָּה אֶדְרְשֶׁנּוּ וּמִיַּד הָאָדָם מִיַּד אִישׁ אָחִיו [28] אֶדְרֹשׁ אֶת־נֶפֶשׁ הָאָדָם:

What's more,[29] I will require your life blood. From the hand of all living creatures, I will require it. And from the hand of any human, from the hand of a man's brother, I will require the life of that human. (v. 5)

שֹׁפֵךְ דַּם הָאָדָם בָּאָדָם דָּמוֹ יִשָּׁפֵךְ כִּי בְּצֶלֶם [30] אֱלֹהִים עָשָׂה אֶת־הָאָדָם:

Whoever sheds the blood of humanity, by humanity his blood will be shed, for in the image of God he made humanity. (v. 6)

וְאַתֶּם פְּרוּ וּרְבוּ שִׁרְצוּ בָאָרֶץ וּרְבוּ־בָהּ: ס

Now you, be fruitful, and multiply, and spread out upon the earth, and multiply in it. (v. 7)

GENESIS 1–11 AS A UNIT

Debate rages regarding the source materials of Genesis,[31] but general agreement exists regarding the separation of the final form of Genesis into two main sections: Genesis 1–11 and Genesis 12–50. An obvious division of scope and narrative pacing separates Genesis 1–11 from Genesis 12–50. Genesis 1–11 covers the story of the creation of the cosmos and many generations of humanity from Adam to Abram. Genesis 12–50 focuses on a relatively small geographical area and covers only a few generations of

---

28. Smr, V, S, and T^{Gnz} all smooth out the awkward syntactical construction of M. Again, the difficulty of M's reading indicates its originality. Tal argued that the versions use a facilitation for stylistic reasons. Tal, *Biblia Hebraica*, 22.

29. This somewhat idiomatic translation seeks to bring out the emphatic nature of the adverb as well as the connection between verse 4 and verse 5.

30. G here does not repeat the word "humanity" but rather seems to use ἀντί as an interpretive abbreviation. V follows G in excluding a second reference to humanity. See discussion in Lust, "For Man Shall His Blood." Lust recognized that G does not preserve the chiastic structure of the Hebrew and saw the use of ἀντί as an interpretation that "eases the tensions within the context in which God reserves for himself the right to require a reckoning for the human blood that is shed." Lust, "For Man Shall His Blood," 101.

31. See, e.g., a modern critique of the documentary hypothesis in Whybray, *Making of the Pentateuch*, and a modern defense of the documentary hypothesis in Nicholson, *Pentateuch in the 20th Century*.

Abram and his descendants. Even those who accept source critical conclusions recognize a major break between Genesis 1–11 and Genesis 12–50. For instance, Claus Westermann stated, "The story of primeval events is related to the whole in a different way from the stories of the patriarchs. Accordingly, chapters 1–11 of Genesis must be regarded as a separate element of the Pentateuch, that is, as a relatively self-contained unity, and not primarily as a part of 'Genesis.'"[32] Thomas Keiser argued the thematic analyses offered by Michael Fishbane, Ellen van Wolde, and Patrick Miller all depend upon "some level of unity of Genesis 1–11 in its final form."[33] P. J. Harland's work analyzed the unity of the text as well.[34]

Exactly where the major division occurs has produced little consensus, with scholars seeing the exact division occurring at various points. As a small sample of the difference of opinion, David Cotter saw the second major division beginning in 11:10,[35] John Calvin saw the new section beginning in 12:1, as did S. R. Driver.[36] Gerhard von Rad marked the major division at 12:10, seeing 12:1–9 as a narrative link between the two sections.[37]

The most obvious and compelling textual division of the book of Genesis is the well-known תּוֹלְדוֹת formula.[38] The word תּוֹלְדוֹת derives from the *hiphil* form of ילד, meaning to father or beget.[39] Following the apparent introduction of 1:1—2:3, the תּוֹלְדֹת formula occurs eleven times in the

---

32. Westermann, *Genesis 1–11*, 2.

33. Keiser, "Genesis 1–11," 23. See Fishbane, *Text and Texture*; Van Wolde, "Facing the Earth," 22–47; Van Wolde, "Story of Cain and Abel."

34. See Harland, *Value of Human Life*, 13–19. Harland accepted the distinction between the J and P documents, but he opted for a canonical approach by which an interpreter reads the two sources first individually and then together.

35. Cotter, *Genesis*, 79.

36. Calvin, *Genesis*, 107. Driver, *Book of Genesis*, 143.

37. Von Rad, *Genesis*, 153–62.

38. For an alternative opinion on the structural components of Genesis 1–11, see Smith, "Structure and Purpose." Smith analyzed the theological structure and placed primary significance on God's blessing "be fruitful and multiply and fill the earth" in Genesis 1:28 and Genesis 9:1, 7. He also saw the curses for disobedience as an important parallel between the two main sections of Genesis. While Smith's theological insights are helpful, his failure to incorporate the תּוֹלְדֹת pattern renders his structural analysis less convincing. His is more an analysis of theological structure than textual structure.

39. Koehler et al., *HALOT*, 4:1069–1700.

THE CORPUS OF THE STUDY AND CRITICAL CONSIDERATIONS

book of Genesis.[40] Gordon Wenham provided a basic outline of Genesis based on the תּוֹלְדוֹת formula:

1:1—2:3		Prologue
(1)	2:4—4:26	History of Heaven and Earth
(2)	5:1—6:8	Family History of Adam
(3)	6:9—9:29	Family History of Noah
(4)	10:1—11:9	Family History of Noah's Sons
(5)	11:10–26	Family History of Shem
(6)	11:27—25:11	Family History of Terah
(7)	25:12–18	Family History of Ishmael
(8)	25:19—35:29	Family History of Isaac
(9)	36:1—37:1	Family History of Esau
(10)	37:2—50:26	Family History of Jacob[41]

The repetition of the formula makes it highly likely that the author is using it intentionally. Even so, the significance of the תּוֹלְדוֹת sections is not immediately clear. The goal here is not to adjudicate all of the arguments regarding the structure of Genesis or the use of the תּוֹלְדוֹת formula.[42] Rather, the more modest goal is to propose a rationale for reading Genesis 1–11

---

40. For a defense of Genesis 1:1—2:3 as an introduction to the book of Genesis, see Hart, "Genesis 1:1—2:3 as a Prologue."

41. Wenham, *Genesis 1–15*, xxii. Wenham did not count Genesis 36:9 as a separate occurrence.

42. For instance, there is debate as to whether the תּוֹלְדוֹת formula is best viewed as a colophon that ends a major section or a heading that begins one. The colophon view is defended in Wiseman, *Ancient Records*, 60–73, as well as in Harrison, *Introduction to the Old Testament*, 543–53. On this point, DeRouchie and Thomas both argued convincingly that the תּוֹלְדוֹת formula is a heading. Thomas pointed out that the named progenitors of the תּוֹלְדוֹת formula have been previously introduced in the text, which implies that the reader is assumed to be familiar with the preceding material. Thomas also saw the use of a verbless clause as most likely indicating a heading rather than a conclusion. He concluded, "A good heading provides continuity with the preceding material while presenting new material that will be the subject of the following section." Thomas, "These Are the Generations," 72–74. DeRouchie described the תּוֹלְדוֹת formulas as "transitional headings." The headings assume the reader has prior knowledge of the progenitor, but focus attention toward the future. He argued that the very nature of begetting implies a futuristic outlook. DeRouchie, "Blessing-Commission," 224–25. See also Alexander, "Genealogies, Seed."

as a literary unit that can be studied as such. To provide this rationale, the paper will consider three different structural analyses using three different methods of analysis. The first is the structural analysis of Isaac Kikawada and Arthur Quinn, based on comparison with ancient Near Eastern parallel texts. The second analysis is espoused by David Dorsey based on internal textual parallels. The final analysis is that offered by Jason DeRouchie and Matthew Thomas based on a macrostructural and syntactical analysis of the תּוֹלְדוֹת formula.[43] While the three proposals use different methods of analysis, each arrives at the common conclusion that Genesis 1–11 is a coherent textual unit.

Kikawada and Quinn argued for the unity of Genesis 1–11 based on parallels with other ancient Near Eastern texts, particularly the Akkadian version of the story of Atrahasis.[44] Their comparison of these two texts shows remarkable similarities, the most striking of which is the parallel plot structure. The parallel plots include an introductory story of creation, three threats to humanity, a flood that resets creation, and a basic resolution of the flood to a new state of equilibrium. While there is an obvious difference in the theological commitments and beliefs espoused in the two documents, the parallel plot seems too similar to be coincidental. Table 1 shows the breakdown of the text based upon these comparative similarities.

---

43. DeRouchie and Thomas offered their analyses independently, but the similarity of their arguments and conclusions justifies examining their works together.

44. Kikawada and Quinn, *Before Abraham Was*, 61. Kikawada and Quinn's work is rightly balanced in recognizing both similarity and difference between Genesis and ancient Near Eastern creation/flood stories. As one example of difference, unlike Greek and Akkadian mythic traditions where the gods are concerned with the overpopulation of earth, the Hebrew narrative presents God as commanding humanity to multiply and fill the earth. Kikawada and Quinn, *Before Abraham Was*, 36–39. As one example of similarity, the Sumerian myth of Enki and Ninmah includes a double creation of humanity.

TABLE 1
KIKAWADA'S AND QUINN'S COMPARISON OF GENESIS AND ATRAHASIS[45]

	ATRAHASIS		GENESIS
1.	Creation (I. 1–351) Summary of work of gods Creation of man	A.	Creation (1:1—2:3) Summary of work of God
B.	First Threat (I. 352–415) Man's numerical increase Plague, Enki's help	B.	Creation of man First Threat (2:4—3:24) Genealogy of heaven and earth Adam and Eve
C.	Second Threat (II. i. 1–11 v. 21) Man's numerical increase 1. Drought, numerical increase 2. Intensified drought, Enki's help	C.	Second Threat (4:1–4:26) Cain and Abel 1. Cain and Abel, genealogy 2. Lamech's taunt (in genealogy)
D.	Final Threat (II. v. 22—III vi. 4) Numerical increase Atrahasis's Flood Salvation in boat	D.	Final Threat (5:1—9:29) Genealogy Noah's Flood Salvation in ark
E.	Resolution (III. vi. 5—viii. 18) Numerical increase Compromise between Enlil and Enki, "Birth Control" Abram leaves Ur	E.	Resolution (10:1—11:32) Genealogy Tower of Babel and Dispersion Genealogy Abram leaves Ur

Kikawada and Quinn further analyzed the structural pattern of Genesis 1–11 by reviewing its narrative-genealogy pattern. Their argument here is not developed enough to fully convince. For instance, they saw a major division at 2:4, but they did not adequately explain how it relates either to the preceding material or the material that follows, calling it an "independent transitional unit."[46] Likewise, they saw 4:1–2 as a major break, calling it a "proto-genealogy."[47] Their proposal on both these points is unconvincing as 2:4 and 4:1–2 are not comparable to the other genealogies included in Genesis 1–11. Also, Kikawada and Quinn very strangely did not account for the תּוֹלְדוֹת formula in 6:9, merely including it as a part of the third threat. They are, therefore, inconsistent in seeing certain occurrences of the תּוֹלְדוֹת formula as structural markers, but seeing others as unimportant to

---

45. Kikawada and Quinn, *Before Abraham Was*, 47–48.
46. Kikawada and Quinn, *Before Abraham Was*, 60.
47. Kikawada and Quinn, *Before Abraham Was*, 60.

The Charge of God's Royal Children

the structure. Thus, the strength of their argument is in demonstrating the unity of Genesis 1–11 vis-à-vis an important ancient Near Eastern parallel.

Dorsey's treatments on the text of Genesis 1–11 dealt with internal parallels between his two proposed major sections: Genesis 1:1—6:8 and Genesis 6:9—11:26. Dorsey combined analysis of the תּוֹלְדוֹת formula with analysis of the similarity of content between the two major sections. He saw the major division in Genesis 1–11 occurring in the fourth occurrence of the תּוֹלְדוֹת formula (Gen 6:9), which marks an obvious shift to the story of the flood. Dorsey identified seven major narrative units in each of these sections in what he called a "conspicuous parallel" of a-b-c ‖ a'-b'-c' ‖ d (see table 2).[48]

Dorsey used essentially the same type of analysis to offer a second structural proposal. The second structural proposal follows the same division as the first but highlights different similarities in the text constituting the structural division. Table 3 shows the second proposal.

TABLE 2
DORSEY'S ARRANGEMENT OF THE SEVEN MAIN UNITS OF GENESIS 1–11[49]

a.	**creation:** God creates the world and humankind—a beginning (1:1—2:3)
	• <u>dry land appears</u> out of the watery chaos • animals <u>every living thing</u>, <u>birds</u>, every animal that <u>creeps</u> (*remés*) on the ground; <u>male and female</u> (*zākār ûnĕ qēbá*); <u>after their kind</u> (*lĕ mînâ*) • divine <u>blessing on animals</u>: "be fruitful and multiply upon the earth" • Yahweh <u>blesses the first people</u>: "be fruitful, multiply, fill the earth" • Instructions regarding <u>food</u> that humans may eat (plants)
b.	**humankind's degeneration:** sin and scattering of first people (Adam, Eve, Cain); non-chosen line of Adam through Cain (2:4—4:26)
	• Stories about humankind's <u>sins</u> • God deliberates in <u>first-person plural</u> over human sin (3:22) • Punishment by <u>banishing</u>, <u>scattering</u> sinner

---

48. Dorsey, *Literary Structure*, 52.
49. Dorsey, *Literary Structure*, 55.

> c. **ten generations** from Adam to Noah (5:1—6:8)
> a'. **flood:** God destroys the world and humankind—a new beginning (6:9—9:29)
>
> - Dry land appears out of the watery chaos
> - Animals: every living thing, birds, every animal that creeps (*remeś*) on the ground; male and female (*zākār ûnĕ qēbā*); after their kind (*lĕ mîna*)
> - Divine blessing on animals: "be fruitful and multiply upon the earth"
> - Yahweh blesses the new first people: "be fruitful, multiply, fill the earth"
> - instructions regarding food that humans may eat (now they may eat animals)
>
> b'. **humankind's degeneration:** sin and scattering of new first people (Noah's descendants); non-chosen lines of Noah's sons (10:1—11:9)
> - Story about humankind's sin
> - God deliberates in first-person plural over human sin (11:7)
> - Punishment by banishing, scattering sinners
>
> c'. **ten generations from Shem to Abraham** (11:10-26)
> d. **conclusion:** Abram (11:27-32)

TABLE 3
DORSEY'S ARRANGEMENT OF THE FOURTEEN MAIN UNITS OF GENESIS 1-11[50]

> **Section 1: Genesis 1:1—6:8**
> a **creation story:** first beginning, divine blessing (1:1—2:3)
> b sin **of Adam:** nakedness, seeing/covering nakedness; curse (2:4—3:24)
>   c younger righteous son **Abel murdered** (no descendants) (4:1-16)
>   d descendants of sinful son **Cain** (4:17-26)
>   e descendants of chosen son **Seth** (5:1-32)
>   f divine judgment on unlawful (?) unions (6:1-4)
>   g brief introduction of **Noah**, through whom God will bless humankind (6:5-8)

> **Section 2: Genesis 6:9—11:26**
> a' **flood story:** reversal of creation, new beginning, divine blessing (6:9—9:19)
> b' sin **of Ham:** nakedness, seeing/covering nakedness; curse (9:20-29)
>   c' descendants of younger righteous son **Japheth** (10:1-5)
>   d' descendants of sinful son **Ham** (10:6-20)
>   e' descendants of chosen son **Shem** (10:21-32)
>   f' divine judgment on human attempt to stay together (11:1-9)
>   g' brief introduction of **Noah**, through whom God will bless humankind (11:10-26)

Dorsey's comparison provides insights into similar language, themes, and patterns within the individual pericopes of Genesis 1-11; yet, his

---

50. Dorsey, *Literary Structure*, 55.

proposal is not without weaknesses. As an example, the story of the flood does bear some clear similarities to the story of creation in 1:1—2:3, but the differences are also marked enough to question whether a formal parallel was intended. For instance, the creation story is characterized by a high prosaic craftsmanship and rhythm that is not true of the flood narrative. Neither of Dorsey's proposals recognized this difference or the possibility that Genesis 1:1—2:3 might function as a prologue. Rather, both assume that Genesis 1:1—2:3 is intended to parallel Genesis 6.

Dorsey's proposals face other difficulties as well. For example, Dorsey's first proposal did not in any meaningful way account for the narrative element of Genesis 6:1–8, simply referring to it as "ten generations from Adam to Noah." He sought to remedy this weakness in his second proposal by noting the similarity in divine judgment in Genesis 6:1–4 and Genesis 11:1–9. In sum, while Dorsey's analysis highlighted important similarities and recapitulations in different stories, it also flattened the differences between those stories. Overall, one gets a sense of a degree of subjectivism in Dorsey's structural proposals.[51] The parallel structure he proposed is based on interpretive parallels rather than a strictly textual pattern.[52]

Despite certain weaknesses, one particularly helpful insight Dorsey offered is the concept of pearling, the intentional linking of a narrative unit with the text to follow. This concept rightly sees the ability of transitional elements such as the תּוֹלְדוֹת formula to retain contact points at both ends of a structural division. The lines between different units often should not be seen as hard and fast, but rather as crafted seams that weave different sections into a whole. He saw, for example, the תּוֹלְדוֹת formulas in Genesis 2:4, 5:1, and 11:27 as examples of pearling.[53]

DeRouchie and Thomas both analyzed the תּוֹלְדוֹת formula from a macrostructural perspective. Of the eleven occurrences in Genesis, five are asyndetic and six are preceded by a conjunctive *waw*. Both DeRouchie and Thomas argued that the תּוֹלְדוֹת occurrences that begin with the conjunctive *waw* are subordinate to the asyndetic תּוֹלְדוֹת occurrences. Following

---

51. Dorsey, *Literary Structure*, 52.

52. See also the argument in Garrett, *Rethinking Genesis*, 121–25. He concluded that Genesis 1–11 can be considered an "ancestor epic" in which a major theme is alienation. Garrett's conclusions on the division of Genesis 1–11 are the same Dorsey's. See also Kaiser, "Literary Form of Genesis 1–11," 48–65, who sees the תּוֹלְדוֹת formula as the primary structural component of Genesis 1–11.

53. Dorsey, *Literary Structure*, 49–54.

this analysis, DeRouchie and Thomas identified five major divisions of the book, as identified in table 4.

TABLE 4
THOMAS'S AND DEROUCHIE'S MACROSTRUCTURAL ANALYSIS OF THE TOLEDOT FORMULAS OF GENESIS[54]

Prologue	1:1—2:3
First Division	תּוֹלְדוֹת of the Heavens and Earth (2:4—4:26)
Second Division	תּוֹלְדוֹת of Adam/Humanity (5:1—6:8)
Third Division	תּוֹלְדוֹת of Noah (6:9—11:9) And the תּוֹלְדוֹת of Noah's Sons (10:1—11:9)
Fourth Division	תּוֹלְדוֹת of Shem (11:10—37:1) And the תּוֹלְדוֹת of Terah (11:27—25:11) And the תּוֹלְדוֹת of Ishmaal (25:12—18) And the תּוֹלְדוֹת of Isaac (25:19—35:29) And the תּוֹלְדוֹת of Esau (36:1—8 and 36:9—37:1)
Fifth Division	תּוֹלְדוֹת of Jacob (37:2—50:26)

Both DeRouchie and Thomas argued that the function of the major divisions is to create a narrowing effect that progressively focuses the reader's attention from Adam to the line of promise in Jacob at the end of the book.[55] DeRouchie contended that the key to interpreting the significance of the divisions is in Genesis 1:28 where God commanded humanity to be fruitful and multiply. The remainder of the book, according to DeRouchie, functioned to show the multiplication of humanity in adherence to this command, as well as the narrowing of the salvific line. Thus, he placed the split between the major sections at 11:9 rather than 11:27, saying, "The Shem *toledot* serves to introduce the Patriarchal Cycles rather than to close what has been termed the Primeval History."[56]

The proposal of Thomas and DeRouchie is attractive because it provides an objective, textual criterion for division. Yet, the division at 11:9 does not fully satisfy since it does not account for the major shift in scope and narrative pace that occurs with the introduction of the Abrahamic narrative in chapter 12. From a literary perspective, Dorsey's concept of

---

54. Adapted from DeRouchie, "Blessing-Commission," 233.

55. Thomas, "These Are the Generations," 122—27. DeRouchie, "Blessing-Commission," 225.

56. DeRouchie, "Blessing-Commission," 234.

pearling is helpful here, as it reminds the reader that textual divisions should not be seen as walls that separate sections, but rather as bridges that join them. As such, a hard division between sections may serve to obscure the author's purpose rather than illuminate it. DeRouchie acknowledged, for instance, that distinguishing between chapters 1–11 and Genesis 12–50 is not "fully without merit" given the incredible difference between the narrative pace in Genesis 1–11 versus Genesis 12–50.[57] Furthermore, DeRouchie identified the תּוֹלְדוֹת formula function as "transitional headings" that incorporate and link previous material to the material that follows.[58] If this is true on a microscale in a heading, why is it not also possible that an entire genealogy could function in the same way, especially in introducing the main narrative focus of the book in Genesis 12?

Accounting for these insights, two conclusions follow. First, while Kikawada and Quinn, Dorsey, Thomas, and DeRouchie each analyzed the textual division using different methods, each reached similar conclusions about the basic structural division. Despite slight disagreement about the borders, each saw Genesis 1–11 as a unit. Thus, their analyses justify the study of Genesis 1–11 as a coherent whole. Second, their combined work shows that the תּוֹלְדוֹת formula plays an important role in determining not only the structure of the text, but also the relationship of the genealogical material to the narrative material. An essential part of understanding the structural purpose of Genesis 1–11 is accounting for the relationship between the narrative and genealogical material. This study will further develop this in chapters 3 and 4, which will provide a more in-depth analysis of the structure of the *imago Dei* texts and the individual pericope units of Genesis 1–11.

The conclusion of Kikawada and Quinn regarding the overall unity of Genesis 1–11 is thus sound:

> The evidence commonly used to show that Genesis 1–11 is a literary patchwork does in our opinion—when closely examined and put in proper context—support the view that Genesis 1–11 is a literary masterpiece by an author of extraordinary skill and subtlety. So much so, that when we think we find this author napping we had better proceed very carefully.[59]

---

57. DeRouchie, "Blessing-Commission," 234.
58. DeRouchie, "Blessing-Commission," 224.
59. Kikawada and Quinn, *Before Abraham Was*, 83.

Indeed, the craftsmanship is so masterful that the seams connecting Genesis 1–11 to Genesis 12–50 are difficult to identify with certainty. The above considerations, combined with the assumption that it is methodologically sound to let the textual markers define structure, render the תּוֹלְדֹת formula the most compelling division for literary analysis.[60]

LITERARY ANALYSIS AND THE TEXT'S FINAL FORM

While source critical studies have consumed much attention since the time of Julius Wellhausen, literary criticism has brought attention again on the final form of the text. Rather than dissecting the text its into composite parts, the starting point of literary analysis is an assumption of basic unity. At least three reasons validate the decision to study the final form of the text rather than the purported sources.[61] First, studying the final form of the text allows the interpreter to see larger patterns that may be missed in source critical considerations. On this point, Leland Ryken wrote, "The

---

60. Of the proposals considered, DeRouchie's and Thomas's is the most convincing with the caveat that the genealogy of Genesis 11:10–26 and Genesis 11:27–32 uses a pearling effect to tie together the major sectional divisions that begin in Genesis 11:9. The introduction of new narrative material in Genesis 12 marks the end of the transition point between the new sections.

61. In *Making of the Pentateuch*, 129–32, Whybray listed a number of critiques of the documentary hypothesis, the following of which are but a summary that directly relates to the necessity and legitimacy of literary analysis: (1) The documentary hypothesis rests upon a deficient view of the evolutionary development of religion. This view, based on the Hegelian dialectic, saw a gradual development over time in the making of the Pentateuch. This same view of religious development (e.g., primitive to more advanced) led scholarship to overlook aspects of the text's advanced literary qualities. (2) The supposed "constants" that mark the style and theological perspective of each document have been shown to be invalid. This critique emphasizes the arbitrary determinations of what style (e.g., word choice) could be attributed to which document. (3) Repetitions could be used for aesthetic or didactic purposes. This point has been brought to the fore through literary analyses that provide explanations for intentionality of repetition that were not considered by advocates of the documentary hypothesis. (4) Whybray's fourth point is especially important: "The authors of the documents are credited with a consistency in the avoidance of repetitions and contradictions which is unparalleled in ancient literature (and even in modern fiction), and *which ignores the possibility of the deliberate use of such features for aesthetic and literary purposes*" (emphasis added). Whybray, *Making of the Pentateuch*, 130. Whybray's critique reaches to the heart of the matter for literary analysis. The rise of literary analysis has shown that interpretations based upon the documentary hypothesis may not have as much explanatory power as interpretive methods that view the text as a literary unit. See also the arguments in Rooker, *Leviticus*, 31–39.

literary approach to the Bible, by contrast [to source criticism], accepts the biblical text in its final form as the focus of study. It assumes unity in a text. The resultant ability to see the overall pattern of a story or poem is one of the greatest gifts that a literary approach confers."[62]

Second, literary analysis of the text's final form has come in concert with the arguments of canonical critics such as Brevard Childs. Childs pointed out that the issue of a text's underlying sources is an entirely different question than the study of its reception: "The study of the history of Hebrew literature in the context of the ancient Near East is a different enterprise from studying the form and function of the Pentateuch in the shape accorded it by the community of faith as its canonical scriptures."[63] In order to understand how the text functioned for the believing communities that treat it as canon, it is unnecessary to uncover the various sources, strata, or documents behind the text. To do such would be to treat the text in a fundamentally different way than the communities by whom the text was received and preserved. Because the final form of the text (e.g., canonical form) is the received canon of Scripture, it is worthy of analysis for that reason.

Third, from the perspective of literary analysis, the goal of analysis is to discover the enduring significance of a text as it has been received. Benjamin Sommer argued, "Literature that endures for millennia does so precisely because it transcends its setting, because it presents insights into the human condition that remain relevant long after the historical or social conditions from which it emerged have disappeared."[64] Even if one cannot be certain of the history of the text's composition and compilation, one can be certain of the text's reception as a unit. Therefore, it is epistemologically and methodologically sound to examine the unit as it has been received—a coherent unit of literature. In sum, a literary analysis is rightly more concerned with the final form of the text than by any single source the text may contain because it is the received, final form of the text that has had a lasting literary impact. Studying the final form of the text involves the least amount of conjecture and provides the greatest opportunity to discern the overall message of the text. Therefore, the final form of the text is the necessary object of literary study.

---

62. Ryken, *How to Read the Bible*, 30. See also the discussion in Alter, *Art of Biblical Narrative*, 131–54.

63. Childs, *Introduction to the Old Testament*, 128.

64. Sommer, "Dating Pentateuchal Texts," 106.

THE CORPUS OF THE STUDY AND CRITICAL CONSIDERATIONS

LITERARY ANALYSIS AND HISTORICITY

Because the present investigation seeks to understand the literary significance of the text itself and not the historical events it describes, the question of the text's historical reference is not a governing concern. Even so, a brief consideration of the matter is necessary to situate the present investigation within the overall context of the study of Genesis.

With regard to the intention of the authors of biblical narrative to record historical events, the evidence points strongly in the affirmative.[65] Artistic telling of events, however, does not preclude literal or historical reference. Along with artistry, the biblical authors have a high regard for historical details (e.g., locations, times, and written records), and there is no evidence to suggest that they felt the freedom to invent stories in the writing of sacred history.[66] Indeed, there is ample evidence, both biblical and otherwise, to show that the first readers believed in the historicity of the events portrayed in biblical narratives. While it is true that a faithful reader must determine the level of referentiality that is required by the genre of a text, an artistic telling of a story does not in any way preclude historicity.[67] The conclusion of William Bechtold, following Meir Sternberg, is sound: "However we may define history, there can be little doubt that the authors of the narrative material considered what they were writing to be based in actual events and especially actual saving events of God."[68]

The present study assumes that the events described in Genesis 1–11 were intended to be understood as events in space and time. However, the need remains to distinguish between the question of the referential *intention* of the text and the question of the historicity of the events the text describes. Sternberg wrote of "the difference between truth value and truth claim."[69] The latter is a legitimate question to ask in a literary analysis; the former is a question for the field of biblical apologetics. The goal of a literary analysis is not to engage directly the question of the text's historical claims, but rather to discern how the author's crafting of the story illuminates the text's meaning. Whatever conclusions one may come to about the

---

65. See the brief but convincing discussion in Bechtold, "Introduction to the Hermeneutics," 62–63.
66. Bechtold's list quotes Waltke and Yu, *Old Testament Theology*, 96.
67. See discussion in Collins, *Reading Genesis Well*, 89–106.
68. Bechtold, "Introduction to the Hermeneutics," 63.
69. Sternberg, *Poetics of Biblical Narrative*, 25.

historicity of the events described in the text, it is not a major factor in the literary analysis of the text itself.

LEXICAL ANALYSIS OF צֶלֶם AND דְּמוּת

The following section will seek to offer a preliminary examination of the meaning of the *imago Dei* by performing a lexical analysis of צֶלֶם and דְּמוּת. While a lexical analysis is not sufficient to fully understand the meaning of the *imago Dei*, it is a necessary starting point in order to establish a strong foundation for literary analysis. Subsequent chapters will build upon and further refine the lexical analysis offered below.

Lexical Analysis of צֶלֶם

The word צֶלֶם occurs seventeen times in a total of fifteen verses of biblical Hebrew (Gen 1:26, 27a, 27b; 5:3; 9:6; Num 33:52; 1 Sam 6:5a, 5b, 11; 2 Kgs 11:18; 2 Chr 23:17; Ps 39:6 (7), 73:20; Ezek 7:20; 16:17; 23:14; Amos 5:26). The word also occurs seventeen times in biblical Aramaic.[70] צֶלֶם likely is related to the Arabic ṣalama meaning "to chop off, hew, cut, to carve." Francis Brown, Samuel Driver, and Charles Briggs affirmed this, suggesting that צֶלֶם refers to "something cut out."[71] Both Barr and Wenham referred to צֶלֶם as "opaque," meaning that neither the etymology nor the verbal form of the word provides the reasoning behind its biblical usage.[72] The clearest nominal cognate is the Akkadian ṣalmu, which is used to describe statues and

---

70. These references include Dan 2:31 (2x), 32, 34, 35; 3:1, 2, 3 (2x), 5, 7, 10, 12, 14, 15, 18, and 19.

71. Brown et al., *BDB*, s.v. "צֶלֶם."

72. Wenham, *Genesis 1–15*, 29. Barr, "Image of God," 17. Barr's tactic in determining the significance of the word צֶלֶם in Genesis 1–11 was to examine other lexical possibilities he believed were available to the author and the nuance each alternative word carries. He then reasoned inductively why the author might have chosen one word rather than another. Barr analyzed words with conceptual correspondence to צֶלֶם (e.g., *pesel*, *masseka*, and *semel* each describe physical representations of objects) or words with textual linkages to צֶלֶם and דְּמוּת (e.g., the parallel use of *dᵉmut* and *mar'e* in Ezek 1:26). Barr concluded that the choice of *ṣelem* in Genesis is tied to its ambivalent moral status when compared with alternatives such as *tᵉmuna* or *masseka*. Both *tᵉmuna* or *masseka* are used negatively to describe the evil of graven images and idols. Comparatively speaking, *ṣelem* is not consistently associated with idolatry or idol-making, which makes it useful as a word to describe the positive relationship between humanity and the Creator.

images of gods and kings.[73] Westermann represented a standard position in seeing the meaning of צֶלֶם as "concrete representation."[74] Numbers 33:55, for instance, refers to metallic images of foreign gods. First Samuel 6:5 refers to golden images of tumors and mice. Second Kings 11:18 refers to the Israelites smashing into pieces the images of Baal.[75] In addition, each reference in biblical Aramaic refers to either a statue, a dream of a statue, or a facial expression.[76]

The LXX uses mostly εἰκών ("image") to translate צֶלֶם, but also uses τύπους ("image," Amos 5:26), εἴδωλον ("idol," Num 33:52; 2 Chr 23:17), and ὁμοίωμα ("figure," 1 Sam 6:5).[77] Basic glosses for the word include "image," "statue," and "idol."[78]

Two references in the Psalms show that צֶלֶם may not, in certain circumstances, entail physicality.[79] The instances occur in Psalm 39:6 (7) and Psalm 73:20. The immediate context of Psalm 39 shows that human transience is in view. Compared to an eternal God, verse 5 describes the life of humanity as nothing but a handbreadth (טְפָחָה) and breath (הֶבֶל). Verse 6 then states that humanity walks around as a צֶלֶם, usually translated as "shadow" or "phantom." While the exact meaning here is unclear, the term clearly relates to humanity walking, which means that even the metaphorical or poetic usage of the word still assumes a physical backdrop. Psalm 73:20 refers to God's eventual judgment against the prosperous wicked. In the present, the wicked experience pleasure (vv. 2–12), but God will eventually mete out judgment. God will awake (עוּר) as from a dream, and in that moment despise (בזה) their images (צַלְמָם). Thus, the wicked are derided as "shadows" or "phantoms" that will not last. These usages in the Psalms led H. Wildeberger to observe that a "remarkable flexibility characterizes the term."[80] The word's flexibility, while notable, is explicable given the poetic nature of the Psalms. Table 5 examines each occurrence.

---

73. Merrill, "Image of God," 442.

74. Westermann, *Genesis 1–11*, 146.

75. Using the *piel* form of שבר.

76. Each of the Aramaic references occurs in Daniel where the image of Nebuchadnezzar is in view.

77. Stendebach, "צֶלֶם, ṣelem," 12:385–96.

78. Koehler et al., *HALOT*, 3:1028–29.

79. This has even led some to postulate the word used in the Psalms is a homonym of צֶלֶם that derives from a different root. See the discussion in Barr, "Image of God," 21; Stendebach, "צֶלֶם, ṣelem," 12:388.

80. Wildeberger, "צֶלֶם, ṣelem, image," 1081. Wildeberger argued against those who

TABLE 5
BIBLICAL OCCURRENCES OF צֶלֶם

Occurrences of צֶלֶם	Translation	Significance
Gen 1:26	"in our image"	Relation of man to God
Gen 1:27 (2x)	"in his image," "in the image of God"	Relation of man to God
Gen 5:3	"after his image"	Relation of Adam to Seth
Gen 9:6	"image"	Relation of man to God
Num 33:52	"images"	Foreign idols
1 Sam 6:5 (2x), 11	"images," "images"	Models of tumors, models of mice
2 Kgs 11:18	"images"	Idols depicting Baal (and possibly other gods)
2 Chr 23:17	"images"	Idols depicting Baal (and possibly other gods)
Ps 39:6	"shadow" or "phantom"	Significance unclear, possibly reference to transience on earth
Ps 73:20	"form" or "shadow" or "phantom"	Significance unclear, term is related to "dream"
Ezek 7:20	"images"	Crafted idols
Ezek 16:17	"images"	Crafted idols, described as male
Ezek 23:14	"images" or "depictions"	Physical depictions (of the Chaldeans)
Amos 5:26	"images"	Idols of Sikkuth and Kiyyun

In addition to this lexical data, it is necessary to consider the word's conceptual associations as evidenced by the way images were understood in the environs surrounding Israel. While a comprehensive survey of the vast body of literature that exists on this subject is impossible, scholarship of the ancient Near East has largely accepted the notion that kingship lies behind the reference to humanity being made in God's image.[81] Catherine McDowell pointed to Johannes Hehn as the first to bring ancient Near Eastern parallels to bear on the exegesis of the *imago Dei*.[82] Von Rad followed

---

saw a separate root in the two instances of צֶלֶם in the Psalms.

81. See Gunnlaugur, *Image of God*.
82. McDowell, *Image of God*, 130. Hehn, "Zum Terminus 'Bild Gottes,'" 36–52.

this vein.[83] W. H. Schmidt documented much of the primary evidence that has been used and expanded by other scholars.[84] Among these, the work of David J. A. Clines has been especially influential over the course of the last half century.[85]

Examining the parallel evidence from the ancient Near East, links with royal imagery and the *imago Dei* exist in Mesopotamian, Egyptian, and Caananite contexts.[86] Clines, for instance, pointed to two letters where Esarhaddon, the seventh-century Assyrian king, is described as the image (*ṣalmu*) of a god. One letter describes him as the image of Bel and the other as the image of Shamash.[87] Clines likewise pointed to several examples in Egyptian literature of Pharaohs being referred to as "begotten or created by the god whose image he is."[88] Amosis I is described as "a prince like Re, the child of Qeb, his heir, the image of Re, whom he created, the avenger (or the representative), for whom he has set himself on earth."[89] The god Amon calls Amenophis III "my living image, creation of my members, whom Mut bare to me."[90] Likewise, Amon-Re tells Amenophis III, "You are my beloved son, who came forth from my members, my image, whom I have put on earth. I have given to you to rule the earth in peace."[91] These considerations led Clines to the following conclusion:

> The application of the phrase "image of God" to a human person in the foregoing texts enables us to conclude, with particular reference to Egypt, that: It is the king who is the image of God, not mankind generally. The image of the god is associated very closely

---

83. Von Rad, *Genesis*, 55–59.

84. Schmidt, *Die Schöpfungsgeschichte der Priesterschrift*.

85. Clines, "Image of God in Man."

86. Merrill, "Image of God," 442. See also the discussion in Stendebach, "צֶלֶם, ṣelem," 12:389–92. Stendebach asserted that linking the image of God with kingship faces certain problems, including the fact that Mesopotamian and Egyptian parallels do not reference the creation of all humanity in the image of God. Yet, this critique is based upon the incorrect assumption that the conceptual connection must be parallel in every regard. There seem to be important similarities and differences between the Israelite conception of the *imago Dei* and those of their neighbors.

87. Clines, "Image of God in Man," 83.

88. Clines, "Image of God in Man," 83. Clines drew the references for the Egyptian passages from Schmidt, *Die Schöpfungsgeschichte der Priesterschrift*, 139.

89. Clines, "Image of God in Man," 85.

90. Clines, "Image of God in Man," 85.

91. Clines, "Image of God in Man," 85.

with rulerhood. The king as image of the god is his representative. The king has been created by the god to be his image.⁹²

Peter Gentry and Stephen Wellum concurred with the conceptual association of image and kingship. They wrote, "The epithet or descriptive title of the Egyptian king as a 'living statue of such and such a god' was common in Egypt from 1630 BC onward and therefore was well known to the Israelites."⁹³ Gentry and Wellum also noted the association of being made in the image of the gods and conquering in battle. They cited the following inscription from the Karnak temple, which describes the victory of Thutmose III in 1460 BC:

> I came to let you tread on Djahi's chiefs,
>   I spread them under your feet throughout their lands;
>   I let them see your majesty as lord of light,
>   so that you shone before them in my likeness.⁹⁴

Likewise, they pointed to the thirteenth-century BC example of Ramesses II hewing his image on a rock at the mouth of the Kelb River as a visible sign of his dominion. Gentry and Wellum concluded, "In the ancient Near East, since the king is the living statue of the god, he represents the god on earth. He makes the power of the god a present reality."⁹⁵

Brent Strawn gave specific examples of the link between the image of God and kingship in a Neo-Assyrian setting.⁹⁶ Like its Egyptian counterpart, the Neo-Assyrian examples link the image of the gods with kingship and military victory. While Strawn recognized similarity, he also contrasted the biblical depiction and that of the Neo-Assyrian culture. The biblical image seems to be devoid of any connotation of violence, unlike its Neo-Assyrian counterpart.⁹⁷

While there is much less evidence available in the Syria-Canaanite tradition, the bilingual Tell Fakhariye inscription shows correspondence between images and kingship.⁹⁸ The inscription, which includes both an

---

92. Clines, "Image of God in Man," 85.
93. Gentry and Wellum, *Kingdom through Covenant*, 191.
94. Gentry and Wellum, *Kingdom through Covenant*, 191, citing Lichtheim, *Ancient Egyptian Literature*, 36–37.
95. Gentry and Wellum, *Kingdom through Covenant*, 191.
96. Strawn, "Comparative Approaches," 130–33.
97. Strawn, "Comparative Approaches," 134–35.
98. For more on the Tell Fakhariye inscription, see Garr, "Image and Likeness."

Akkadian and Aramaic text, translates the single Akkadian word *ṣalam* with the Aramaic words *ṣlm* and *dmwt*.[99] The inscription itself is in reference to the king Hadad-Yithi who ruled in the ninth century BC.

In sum, the word צֶלֶם, usually translated as "image" or "idol," is used primarily to refer to statues or physical representations of people or objects. In poetic contexts, צֶלֶם can refer to non-physical entities as well. Conceptually, the association of "the images of gods" was common throughout the ancient Near East and seems to be tied closely to kingship.

Lexical Analysis of דְּמוּת

דְּמוּת occurs a total of twenty-five times in twenty-one verses of biblical Hebrew. דְּמוּת is related to a cognate verb, דָּמָה, which in the *qal* means "be like, resemble."[100] The noun דְּמוּת, often translated "likeness," can be used elastically to describe a detailed physical description (e.g., an altar in 2 Kgs 16:10) or metaphorically as an untranslated particle of comparison (e.g., "like" venom in Ps 58:4).[101] דְּמוּת is used most often in Ezekiel (sixteen times) where it expresses similarities between the appearance of physical objects (e.g., men, animals, and thrones) to what Ezekiel sees in his visions.[102] The examples in Ezekiel establish close similarity between two objects, but also maintain distinction between those objects. W. Randall Garr noted that most of the occurrences in Ezekiel occur in theophanic contexts, describing similarities with God, God's throne, or beings in the heavenly throne room.[103]

LXX renderings of דְּמוּת include ὁμοίωμα ("likeness," fourteen times), ὁμοίωσις, ("likeness" or "similarity," five times), εἰκὼν ("image," once in Gen 5:1), ἰδέα ("appearance," once in Gen 5:3), and ὅμοιος ("resemblance," once in Isa 13:4).[104] The most concrete usage in Genesis 1–11 occurs in Genesis 5:3, where Adam is said to beget Seth in his likeness. Table 6 provides a comprehensive list of the term's usage and translation in the Hebrew Bible, as well as a brief statement of significance.

99. Merrill, "Image of God," 442.
100. Koehler et al., *HALOT*, 1:226.
101. Francis et al., *BDB*, s.v. "דְּמוּת."
102. Preuss, "דָּמָה, *dāmāh*; דְּמוּת, *demûth*," 260–65. Jenni and Westermann, *Theological Lexicon*, 339–42.
103. Garr, *In His Own Image*, 122–25.
104. Preuss, "דָּמָה, *dāmāh*; דְּמוּת, *demûth*," 234.

The Charge of God's Royal Children

In sum, דְּמוּת is used elastically to describe both physical and metaphorical similarity, correspondance, or likeness. The word is used almost exclusively to describe the similarity between two objects or persons and can refer to either physical or metaphorical similarities.

צֶלֶם AND דְּמוּת AS A CONCEPTUAL HENDIADYS

Many argue that within Genesis, צֶלֶם and דְּמוּת essentially function as synonyms based on their apparent collocation and parallelism in Genesis 1:26–28 and Genesis 5:1–3. Eugene Merrill, for instance, referred to דְּמוּת as an "explanatory synonym" of צֶלֶם.[105] Barr argued that דְּמוּת was used as a limitation on צֶלֶם, but that by using the two terms together, it became possible to "use one of the two alone subsequently without risk of confusion."[106] E. W. Bullinger claimed the two nouns form a hendiadys meaning "in the likeness of our image," but he did not comment on the possible nuances of each word within the hendiadys.[107]

TABLE 6
BIBLICAL OCCURRENCES OF דְּמוּת

Occurrences of דְּמוּת	Translation	Significance
Gen 1:26	"likeness"	Relation of humanity to God
Gen 5:3 (2x)	"likeness" "likeness"	(1) Relation of humanity to God (2) Relation of Adam to Seth
2 Kgs 16:10	"likeness" or "detailed physical description"	Description of an altar
2 Chr 4:3	"figures" or "models"	Description of oxen under the bronze sea
Ps 58:4 (5)	"like" or untranslated word of comparison	Comparing anger of wicked to venom of cobra
Isa 13:4	"like" or untranslated word of comparison	A sound like the voice of many people
Isa 40:18	"likeness" or (lack of) physical resemblance	Comparison of God to an idol (impossible!)

---

105. Merrill, "Image of God," 442.
106. Barr, "Image of God," 24.
107. Bullinger, *Figures of Speech*, 659.

The Corpus of the Study and Critical Considerations

Occurrences of דְּמוּת	Translation	Significance
Ezek 1:5 (2x)	"likenesses" or "figures" "likeness" or "appearance"	Vision of four living creatures Similarity of physical appearance
Ezek 1:10	"appearance"	Similarity of physical appearance (faces)
Ezek 1:13	"appearance"	Similarity of physical appearance (creatures)
Ezek 1:16	"appearance" or "form"	Similarity of physical appearance (wheels)
Ezek 1:22	"likeness" or untranslated comparison	Similarity of physical object (firmament)
Ezek 1:26 (3x)	"like" or "resembling" "like" or "resembling" "like"	Similarity of physical object (2x throne) Similarity of physical appearance (man)
Ezek 1:28	"likeness"	Similarity of environment (glory of God)
Ezek 8:2	"likeness"	Similarity of physical appearance (fire)
Ezek 10:1	"like" or "resembling"	Similarity of physical object (throne)
Ezek 10:10	"appearance" or "likeness"	Similarity of physical objects (wheels)
Ezek 10:21	"likeness" or "appearance"	Similarity of physical attributes (hands)
Ezek 10:22	"likeness" or "appearance"	Similarity of physical attributes (faces)
Ezek 23:15	"like" or "resembling"	Similarity of physical appearance (like the sons of Babel)
Dan 10:16	"like" or "resembling"	Similarity of physical appearance (like a son of man)

Horst Preuss, Ernst Jenni, and F. J. Stendebach all see a basic synonymity.[108]

---

108. Preuss, "דָּמָה, dāmāh; דְּמוּת, demûth," 2:259. Stendebach, "צֶלֶם, ṣelem," 12:394. Jenni and Westermann, *Theological Lexicon*, 341.

The Charge of God's Royal Children

In his extensive study of both terms, Garr challenged the basic framework of synonymity. While the lexical analysis shows דְּמוּת is used mainly for purposes of comparison, Garr noted that the usage of דְּמוּת within Genesis is "uniformly associated with human genealogy."[109] Garr's observation stems from the association of דְּמוּת with Adam and Seth in Genesis 5. Genesis 5 describes Adam's creation in the likeness of God (v. 1), and then describes Adam fathering Seth in the likeness of Adam (v. 3). The reference suggests that God's creation of humanity is analogous to human fathering of children. Humanity mirrors this procreative role in the passing on of likeness from generation to generation. Based on this text, Stephen Dempster made the following observation:

> By juxtaposing the divine creation of Adam in the image of God and the subsequent human creation of Seth in the image of Adam, the transmission of the image of God through this genealogical line is implied, as well as the link between sonship and the image of God. As Seth is a son of Adam, so Adam is a son of God. Language is being stretched here, as a literal son of God is certainly not in view, but nevertheless the writer uses an analogy to make a point.[110]

Gentry joined Dempster and Garr in his conclusion.[111] Gentry pointed out that the early Greek and Latin translations most often used separate words to translate צֶלֶם and דְּמוּת, indicating a degree of distinction. Likewise, Gentry analyzed the bilingual Tell Fakhariye inscription where he believed a distinction was evident. As mentioned above, the Tell Fakhariye inscription depicts king Hadad-Yithi and invokes both cognate Aramaic terms for image and likeness to describe the statue dedicated in the king's honor. The statue itself includes two different inscriptions: one for an original dedication and one for a later rededication. While both words are used twice each to describe the statue, Gentry argued that the term *dmwt'* was used to describe the quality of the original statue's resemblance to the king, as well as the quality of the rededicated statue's likeness to the original statue. Thus, Gentry argued that the references to the *dmwt'* are a reference of physical resemblance or likeness, what he called the relationship of the copy to the original. Conversely, the reference to the statue as the *ṣlm* of the

---

109. Garr, *In His Own Image*, 126.
110. Dempster, *Dominion and Dynasty*, 58.
111. Gentry, "Humanity as the Divine Image."

king emphasizes not the copy's likeness to the original image or person, but rather the king's presence in the world. He drew the following conclusion:

> So both occurrences of *dmwt'* focus on the relationship of the copy to the original and emphasize the vertical relationship of the king to his god while the term *ṣlm* corresponds to the emphasis in the rededication section on the horizontal relationship of king to his subjects—the majesty and power of the king in relation to his world.[112]

Gentry believed this analysis provides additional evidence for seeing distinction between the two words in Genesis. Gentry also cited Ezekiel 23:14–15, which is the only other biblical text to use צֶלֶם and דְּמוּת in close proximity. Ezekiel 23:14–15 describes artwork that is said to have elicited lust from the inhabitants of Jerusalem and Samaria. In Ezekiel 23:14, the text described the artwork as "images of the Chaldeans" (צַלְמֵי כַשְׂדִּיִים) carved on the wall, and in verse 15 the text described the artwork as depicting the "likeness of sons of Babel" (דְּמוּת בְּנֵי־בָבֶל כַּשְׂדִּים). Gentry saw a distinction between צֶלֶם and דְּמוּת in this context similar to the one he saw in the Tell Fakhariye inscription.[113] Based on these observations, Gentry concluded, "The adverbial modifiers 'in our image,' and 'according to our likeness' indicate a vertical relationship between humans and God that can be described as obedient sonship and a horizontal relationship between humans and all creation that can be characterized as servant kingship."[114]

McDowell reached a similar conclusion and described the *imago Dei* as an expression of correspondence, kind, and kinship.[115] McDowell argued that there is a similarity between humanity's creation in the *imago Dei* and the description of animals reproducing according to their kind. McDowell related Genesis 1:26–27 to Genesis 5:1–3 saying, "To be created in Adam's likeness and according to his image means that Seth was created according

---

112. Gentry, "Humanity as the Divine Image," 62.

113. Gentry, "Humanity as the Divine Image," 60. He wrote, "The term *dĕmut* focuses on the relationship of the copy to the original. The term *ṣelem*, however, focuses on how the physical figures or images in bas-relief impacted those who saw them, i.e., the relationship of the copy to the larger world. The impact and power of the images is that they excited lust in the eyes of the beholder so that they sought political alliances with the Chaldeans. This is metaphorically pictured as fornication by Ezekiel." Also notable is that דְּמוּת is used in direct connection with the *sons* of Babel.

114. Gentry, "Humanity as the Divine Image," 68.

115. McDowell, "In the Image of God," 35.

The Charge of God's Royal Children

to Adam's kind."[116] Adam, being made in God's kind, in turn, entails a kinship with God, as evidenced by the father-son relationship between Adam and Seth. McDowell cited several Old Testament texts that describe Yahweh as a father (e.g., 2 Sam 7:14; Ps 2:7; Jer 3:19; Exod 4:22–23; Isa 66:12–13). She also cited ancient Near Eastern texts that describe a connection between a king being made in the image of the gods and the sonship of the king.[117] These include a hymn from the Tukulti-Ninurta Epic, a Tenth Dynasty Egyptian wisdom text called *The Instructions for Merikare*, and the introduction to the Enuma Elish.[118] Each of these texts describes humanity as both the offspring *and* image of the gods.

Given the lexical differences between the two words, as well as the analysis offered by Garr, Barr, Gentry, McDowell, and others, it seems that the words carry different and important nuances. Yet, the parallelism of the two words, evidenced most poignantly by the reversal of order in the parallelism between Genesis 1:26 and Genesis 5:3, shows the words are connected in the context of Genesis 1–11. Furthermore, the reversal of the words and the modifying prepositions in Genesis 5:3 suggest that דְּמוּת is not merely an explanatory synonym of צֶלֶם, but that both nouns are equally important within the hendiadys.[119]

Therefore, while it is possible to distinguish between the words, the text of Genesis makes it impossible to separate them conceptually. The two words function as a conceptual hendiadys, a single and coherent idea within the context of Genesis 1–11. Within the two poles of the conceptual hendiadys, צֶלֶם seems to be linked to the idea of physical representation and kingship, where דְּמוּת is concerned with likeness and similarity between God and humanity that is concretely associated with sonship. McDowell's designation of "royal sons" is an apt summary of the hendiadys.[120]

In light of these considerations, the present study will view the *imago Dei* as a concept that encompass both ideas of sonship and kingship, or "royal sons," and seek to understand how this concept relates to the narrative

---

116. McDowell, "In the Image of God," 35.

117. McDowell, "In the Image of God," 40–43.

118. See the descriptions in McDowell, *Image of God*, 134–36. See also the arguments in Crouch, "Genesis 1:26–27 as a Statement," and Ortlund, "Image of Adam."

119. Against Bullinger, who identified the occurrence in Genesis 1:26 as a hendiadys, but suggested that דְּמוּת is subordinate to צֶלֶם. Bullinger, *Figures of Speech*, 659. Bullinger did not comment on the occurrence in Genesis 5:3, which reverses the order of the two nouns, as well as the modifying prepositions.

120. McDowell, *Image of God*, 131.

of Genesis 1–11.¹²¹ As McDowell suggested, and Gentry alluded to, humanity being made as royal sons of God comes "with all the responsibilities and privileges sonship entails."¹²²

THE PLACEMENT OF THE *IMAGO DEI* TEXTS

As discussed throughout, the explicit references to the *imago Dei* occur in Genesis 1:26–28, 5:1–3, and 9:6. Following the criteria of literary analysis established in Chapter 1, a competent reader can ask the following questions: Is the placement of the *imago Dei* strategic? If so, what is the significance?

The evidence regarding strategic placement points strongly in the affirmative. First, these three texts roughly correspond to the beginning, middle, and end of Genesis 1–11. References to the *imago Dei* at the beginning, middle, and end of the narrative indicate its importance in understanding the characters and intervening events. Second, the references to the *imago Dei* occur at strategic places within their own pericopes. The first reference to the *imago Dei* (Gen 1:26–28) comes at the climax of the six-day creation pattern. As the next chapter will show, the attention given to the sixth day of creation gives it a place of prominence in the overall scheme of creation. The second reference (Gen 5:1–3) comes at the head of a major unit and a new pericope. Genesis 5:1–3 echoes the first occurrence and shows a continuation of the importance of the *imago Dei* in understanding the story. The final reference (Gen 9:6) comes at the culmination of the flood narrative and the introduction of the postdiluvian world. Each of these texts comes at a major transition point in the plot and sets the stage, as it were, for the events that follow. The next chapter will consider the structural relationship of the *imago Dei* texts in more detail, but even a cursory analysis reveals their importance in their immediate contexts and in the narrative as a whole. Therefore, it seems possible that analyzing the *imago Dei* may require more than attention to the explicit references. Those references may provide the reader an interpretative lens through which to understand and evaluate the characters and the events of the plot.

---

121. The conclusion offered here is consonant with Kline, *Kingdom Prologue*, 45–46.
122. McDowell, "In the Image of God," 30.

CONCLUSION

The current chapter has sought to discuss the critical questions relevant to the study, including a preliminary translation of the *imago Dei* texts and a defense of reading Genesis 1–11 as a literary unit. While the exact division between Genesis 1–11 and Genesis 12–50 is difficult to determine with precision, various structural analyses show general agreement that Genesis 1–11 is a textual unit. As an object of literary study, the final form of the text is the necessary object of analysis.

The chapter then sought to establish a framework for understanding the *imago Dei* by performing a lexical study of צֶלֶם and דְּמוּת, both individually and together. When used in Genesis 1–11, the two words form a conceptual hendiadys that emphasizes slightly different aspects of what it means for humanity to be made in the *imago Dei*. צֶלֶם seems to emphasize physical representation and kingship and דְּמוּת seems to emphasize similarity that is best illustrated by the relationship between father and son. Taken together, the text's claim that humanity is made in the *imago Dei* is aptly captured in the phrase "royal sons." While the next chapter will discuss the structure of the *imago Dei* texts, a cursory survey of the placement of the *imago Dei* texts shows that God's creation of humanity as "royal sons" likely plays a significant role in understanding the characters and events of Genesis 1–11.

Chapter 3

A Structural Analysis of the *Imago Dei* Texts

As described in Chapter 1, a literary analysis includes the exposition of a text's structure, literary elements, and rhetorical aims. Structural analysis provides a foundation for understanding the author's purposes in writing. David Dorsey defined structure as a text's "internal arrangement,"[1] and Shimon Bar-Efrat defined structure as "the network of relations among the parts of an object or a unit."[2] A text's structure helps to reveal the author's emphases and aims, and therefore communicates meaning. Gary Smith pointed to the necessary task of studying structure to ascertain the author's purposes:

> The relationship of structure to meaning, which is recognized in the syntactical study of language, is also to be recognized as significant in the conscious and unconscious development of longer portions of oral and written forms of communication. The linguist derives the meaning of language from a careful study of individual words as well as from an analysis of syntactical patterns. In a similar manner, the exegete discovers the meaning of the text from a study of individual verses as well as from the larger structural context of which they are a part. In order to comprehend the purpose of a text, one must make use of every clue the author provides.[3]

1. Dorsey, *Literary Structure*, 15.
2. Bar-Efrat, "Some Observations," 155.
3. Smith, "Structure and Purpose," 307.

The Charge of God's Royal Children

Dorsey provided a conspicuous but necessary insight regarding structural analyses: "The goal of structural analysis is to identify the units that the biblical author *designed and intended* as units, rather than to impose artificial schemes on the text."[4] A structural analysis assumes that a text's structure reflects intentional decisions on the part of the author, and those decisions communicate meaning. While it is impossible to reproduce the internal state of mind of an author, structural markers can provide insight into what an author considered most important or wanted to emphasize.

Whereas structural analysis is an important part of the overall task of literary analysis, Bar-Efrat offered caution saying that analysis of a text's structure is necessary, but the relationship between a text's structure and the text's meaning is often subjective. For an interpretation to be convincing, therefore, "it is recommendable to look for data in the text, apart from the structure, that confirm or support it."[5] Michael Fishbane argued the same:

> For it must be stressed that stylistic conventions allow the voice of a text to speak on its own terms and according to its own arrangement. The more conscious a reader is of these conventions, the less

---

4. Dorsey, *Literary Structure*, 21 (emphasis added). Structural analysis thus looks for textual markers that may include beginning markers of texts, end markers of texts, and other techniques for creating what Dorsey called "internal cohesion" within a given unit. This internal cohesion, for Dorsey, consisted of "sameness" within a text. A few examples included sameness of time, place, participants, topic, genre, narrative techniques, syntactic forms, and key words. Dorsey, *Literary Structure*, 23–24. Dorsey believed these elements come together to form a "complete, independent, self-contained 'package.'" Dorsey, *Literary Structure*, 23. These self-contained packages then relate to one another as part of a larger structure of a textual unit.

5. Bar-Efrat, "Some Observations," 173. Bar-Efrat described four different elements of structure: (1) the verbal level, (2) the level of narrative technique, (3) the level of the narrative world, and (4) the level of the conceptual content. Bar-Efrat, "Some Observations," 157. Each of these layers, according to Bar-Efrat, should be analyzed independently of the others. The verbal level consists of words and phrases, but in such a way that highlights the "large-scale relations among the main and possibly distant parts." Bar-Efrat, "Some Observations," 158. Thus, it is possible to distinguish structural analysis from syntactical analysis, according to Bar-Efrat, although the latter is related to the former. Syntactical analysis is a necessary part of structural analysis, but structural analysis seeks to relate syntactical findings to a larger passage. Bar-Efrat included analysis of metaphors, similes, and unusual constructions at the verbal level. The structural level of narrative technique focuses on what Bar-Efrat called "narrative method," a broad term that encompasses the choice of dialogue, scenery, pace, narration, explanation, and commentary. The third level, the narrative world, focuses on characters and events. The fourth level, conceptual content, focuses on broad themes that connect a unit. Structure, in turn, "serves to express or accentuate meaning." Bar-Efrat, "Some Observations," 157–72.

likely will he be to subjectivize a text irresponsibly; the more likely will his reading tend towards a disciplined freedom: spontaneity within necessity.[6]

Thus, a proper structural analysis must seek to analyze the structural markers of the text itself to understand how structure communicates meaning. Furthermore, structural analysis is a necessary starting point in literary analysis, but is not sufficient to bear the full weight of interpretive conclusions apart from other literary considerations.

LEVELS OF STRUCTURAL ANALYSIS

Analysis of a text's structure occurs at various levels; indeed, at every level of composition. Structure functions at the micro level of syllables and words all the way to the macro level of the compositional strategy of an entire canon. An author may use structure to emphasize part of a phrase or sentence or may use structure to emphasize one paragraph, pericope, or unit within an entire work. Fishbane correctly observed that "stylistic structuring . . . affects the formation of single texts and larger literary cycles."[7] Bruce Waltke and Cathi Fredricks, building on the work of J. P. Fokkelman, suggested "twelve levels in the biblical text, moving from smallest to largest."[8]

12. book/composition
11. sections/cycles
10. acts or phases
9. scenes or episodes
8. scene parts or incidents
7. frames/speeches
6. sentences
5. clauses
4. phrases
3. words
2. syllables
1. sounds

The author arranges these "levels of signification," and the goal of the interpreter, as Waltke suggested, is "to uncover the layers of meaning within

---

6. Fishbane, *Text and Texture*, xii–xiii.

7. Fishbane, *Text and Texture*, xii.

8. Waltke with Fredricks, *Genesis*, 31, quoting and adapting from Fokkelman, *Narrative Art and Poetry*, 4.

the text."⁹ Thus, a structural analysis must examine a text at various levels to determine how the author uses structure to illuminate meaning.

As the above levels of signification suggest, it is possible to divide and analyze a text according to very small or very large units. In performing a structural analysis, an interpreter must determine at what level to begin a structural analysis. While it would be tempting to begin at the bottom of the structural ladder, as it were, and simply work up the rungs step by step, the task is unfortunately not so simple. For instance, since Genesis 1:24–31 comes at the end of a highly structured unit (Gen 1:1—2:3), the structural patterns, words, phrases, and emphases of Genesis 1:24-31 relate to the other days of creation. Conversely, Genesis 5:1–5 stands at the head of a new division within Genesis 1–11. Thus, analysis of its structure must consider the patterns of other introductions, as well as how references in later texts relate to references in prior texts (e.g., Gen 1:26–28). Finally, Genesis 9:1–7 occurs at the end of a long story (e.g., the flood narrative). An interpreter, therefore, must take into account its place at the conclusion of a narrative and how that conclusion sets the stage for the events that follow. Because texts function differently in given contexts, the starting point of structural analyses will necessarily look different. As a facet of literary analysis, structural analysis is a mixture of science and art.

Even with the awareness that structural analyses will have different starting points, this chapter will seek to follow a systematic approach to examine each of the explicit references to the *imago Dei* in Genesis. The order will vary depending on each case, but each analysis will (1) provide a basic outline of the *imago Dei* texts, (2) place each of the explicit references to the *imago Dei* within the context of its pericope, and (3) analyze pertinent structural markers at the levels of words, phrases, and internal echoes of the passages that reference the *imago Dei*.

Finally, the chapter will conclude with a brief macrolevel examination of the *imago Dei* texts within Genesis 1–11 as a whole. The conclusion will consider the structural relationship of the pericopes within Genesis 1–11 and consider how the *imago Dei* texts function within the larger flow of Genesis 1–11.

---

9. Waltke and Fredricks, *Genesis*, 33.

A Structural Analysis of the Imago Dei Texts

STRUCTURAL ANALYSIS OF GENESIS 1:24–31

The first reference to humanity's creation in the *imago Dei* occurs in Genesis 1:26–27, which is part of the sixth day of creation in Genesis 1:24–31. Given the obvious structural features of the creation account, a natural starting point in analyzing Genesis 1:24–31 is to analyze the structure of the pericope as a whole and the place of day 6 within this pattern.

Genesis 1:1—2:3 is a story of compositional beauty and universal scope.[10] Umberto Cassuto rightly argued that Genesis 1 must be read in comparison and contrast with other ancient Near Eastern creation accounts and theogonies, and he powerfully described its polemical value over and against its competitors.

> Then came the Torah and soared aloft, as on eagle's wings, above all these notions. Not many gods but One God; not theogony, for a god has no family tree; not wars nor strife nor the clash of wills, but only One Will, which rules over everything, without the slightest let of hindrance; not a deity associated with nature and identified with it wholly or in part, but a God who stands absolutely above nature, and outside of it, and nature and all its constituent elements, even the sun and all the other entities, be they ever so exalted, are only His creatures, made according to His will.[11]

The most obvious structural feature of Genesis 1:1—2:3 is the seven-day pattern of creation. The creation order follows an a-b-c || a'-b'-c' || d pattern, with day 1 corresponding to day 4, day 2 corresponding to day 5, day 3 corresponding to day 6, and day 7 standing alone.[12] Since the *wayiqtol* mainline begins in verse 3, 1:1–2 is likely introductory, paratactic material.[13] The following structural breakdown follows the text's use of the *wayiqtol* mainline, beginning in verse 3.

---

10. For arguments regarding the division of the text at Genesis 2:3 rather than Genesis 2:4, see chapter 2.

11. Cassuto, *Genesis, Part One*, 8.

12. Many commentators have noted this pattern. E.g., Collins, *Genesis 1–4*, 42–43; Dorsey, *Literary Structure*, 48–49; Cassuto, *Genesis, Part One*, 13–19; Waltke and Fredricks, *Genesis*, 56–57.

13. Scholars debate the relation of Genesis 1:1–2 to the days of creation. Cassuto, *Genesis, Part One*, 19–25, argued that Genesis 1:1 constitutes an introduction and that Genesis 1:2 belongs with Genesis 1:3–6. Westermann, argued that Genesis 1:1 and Genesis 1:2 both function as introductory verses, but each verse functions in a slightly different way. Westermann, *Genesis 1–11*, 102. For arguments regarding Genesis 1:1 as the first act of creation, see Poythress, "Genesis 1:1," and Chambers, "Genesis 1.1."

The Charge of God's Royal Children

Outline of Genesis 1:1—2:3

Introduction to creation: (vv. 1–2)
Day 1: Creation and division of light and darkness (vv. 3–6)
Day 2: Creation and division of the firmament (vv. 7–8)
Day 3: Creation of land (vv. 9–13)
Day 4: Creation of the sun, moon, and stars (vv. 14–19)
Day 5: Creation and blessing of the fish and birds (vv. 20–23)
Day 6: Creation of land animals and humans (vv. 24–31)
    Creation of land animals (vv. 24–25)
    Creation and blessing of humanity (vv. 26–28)
    Provision of food for humanity and animals (vv. 29–30)
    God's final evaluation of creation (v. 31)
Day 7: Sabbath rest (2:1–3)

Both similarity and distinction mark the first six days of creation. First, each of the six days begins with the refrain, "And God said" (וַיֹּאמֶר אֱלֹהִים). Second, each of the days ends with the statement, "And there was evening and there was morning, day [x]" ([x] וַיְהִי־עֶרֶב וַיְהִי־בֹקֶר יוֹם). Beyond these universals, each day differs slightly in its pattern. For instance, days 1–3 each record God naming a part of creation, whereas days 4–6 do not include divine naming.[14] Conversely, days 4–6 each include a divine blessing, whereas days 1–3 do not. Each day except day 2 includes God's evaluation of creation.[15]

Table 7 uses the categories of divine speech, divine naming, divine evaluation, divine blessing, fulfillment (i.e., וַיְהִי־כֵן, "and it was so"), and the concluding evening/day formula to show the structural similarities and differences between each day of creation.

---

14. The act of divine naming perhaps ties into Genesis 2 where God gave Adam the authority to name the creatures created on days 5 and 6.
15. The evaluation of day 1 breaks slightly from the pattern of days 3–6. On day 1, God saw that the light was good (וַיַּרְא אֱלֹהִים אֶת־הָאוֹר כִּי־טוֹב), whereas on days 3–6 the narrator used the evaluative phrase "and God saw that it was good" (וַיַּרְא אֱלֹהִים כִּי־טוֹב).

A Structural Analysis of the Imago Dei Texts

TABLE 7
STRUCTURAL CHARACTERISTICS OF THE DAYS OF CREATION

	Divine Speech	Divine Naming	Divine Evaluation	Divine Blessing	Fulfillment	Concluding Formula
Day 1	x	x	x	Ø	Ø	x
Day 2	x	x	Ø	Ø	x	x
Day 3	x (2x)	x	x (2x)	Ø	x (2x)	x
Day 4	x	Ø	x	Ø	x	x
Day 5	x	Ø	x	x	Ø	x
Day 6	x (4x)	Ø	x (2x)	x	x	x
Day 7	Ø	Ø	Ø	x	Ø	Ø

Table 7 shows several patterns. First, and perhaps most importantly, no two days follow exactly the same pattern. Thus, while there is a high degree of coordination and even repetition between the days, each day also has a unique structural quality. The uniqueness of days keeping with what Cassuto described as a "basic principle of Biblical narrative prose not to repeat a statement in identical terms."[16] The similarity between the days of creation, yet the uniqueness of each individual day, is an indication of the intentionality and beauty of the text's composition.

The description of the days undergoes a clear development. The days move from short and simple to longer and more complex. Waltke described the story as consisting of "billowing detail and movement. With crescendo the narrator devotes more time and space to each day until the climactic apex of creation, when motion ceases and God rests."[17] Dorsey also noted the compositional strategy of progressively longer days:

> The story is designed so that the description of the creative days grows progressively longer. The first two days are briefly recounted (with 31 and 38 words respectively). The next three days (days 3, 4, and 5) are approximately double that length (69, 69, and 57 words, respectively); and the account of the final creative day (day 6) is doubled again (149 words). This structuring technique conveys the impression of ever-increasing variety and profusion.[18]

---

16. Cassuto, *Genesis, Part One*, 16.
17. Waltke and Fredricks, *Genesis*, 57.
18. Dorsey, *Literary Structure*, 49.

Given this structural pattern, the author seems to be building up to the prominence of the sixth day. Beyond mere length, the sixth day also has a unique fourfold description of divine speech, a twofold evaluation of the goodness of creation, a blessing from God after the creation of humanity, and the unique designation at the end of the day that creation was "very good" (טוֹב מְאֹד). Thus, from a structural perspective, the reader recognizes that day 6 represents a climax to God's creation. The structure of Genesis 1 punctuates the events of day 6, including the description of humanity's creation in the *imago Dei*. The sixth day of creation can be divided as follows:

The Structure of Day 6 of Creation (Genesis 1:24–30)

    God's first pronouncement:
        God's command to the earth to bring forth living things according to their kind (v. 24)
        Record of completion (v. 24b)
        Statement of God's creation of animals according to their kind (v. 25)
        Record of approval (v. 25b)
    God's second pronouncement:
        God declares his intention to create humanity (v. 26)
            Description of humanity created in his image and after his likeness (v. 26a)
            Description of purpose of humanity's creation (e.g., dominion over creatures) (v. 26b)
            Record of completion (v. 27)
        God's blessing and commission of humanity (v. 28)
            Commandments (v. 28a)
            Description of scope of dominion (v. 28b)
        God's provision of food for man and animals (vv. 29–30)
    Final record of completion and approval (v. 31)
        God's assessment and pronouncement of all he had made (v. 31a). God pronounced it was *very* good.
        Evening/day Formula (v. 31b)

Within day 6, there are three clear divisions marked by divine speech and a fourth division marked by divine evaluation. In the first section, Genesis 1:24 begins with the divine speech, indicating the beginning of a new day. Genesis 1:24–25 then describes the detailed creation of all land animals according to their kinds. Genesis 1:25 provides an initial evaluation, "and God saw that it was good" (וַיַּרְא אֱלֹהִים כִּי־טוֹב). Following the pattern of day 3 in Genesis 1:11, an initial divine evaluation gives way to another divine speech and another creative act in Genesis 1:26. As shown in table 1, only days 3 and 6 feature more than one divine speech.

Genesis 1:26 begins with the second divine speech of day 6, which in turn marks a new creative event. Similar to the repetition in Genesis 1:24–25, Genesis 1:26–28 describes God's pronouncement before creating humanity, the creation of humanity, and the blessing and commissioning of humanity. Genesis 1:26–28 uses a paneling effect that follows an a | b | a pattern of pronouncement-fulfillment-blessing. The verb repetition (רדה), as well as the repetition of the list of animals, tie Genesis 1:26 and Genesis 1:28 together so that they act as bookends to the fulfillment in Genesis 1:27. By framing Genesis 1:27 between the panels of Genesis 1:26 and Genesis 1:28, the structure suggests that Genesis 1:27 is emphatic.

A. v. 26—God's declaration of his intent to make humanity (pronouncement)

B. v. 27—God's act of creation of humanity (fulfillment)

A. v. 28—God's blessing and commission of humanity (blessing)

God's blessing in Genesis 1:28 includes a direct fivefold command to be fruitful, multiply, fill the earth, subdue it, and rule over the fish of the sea and birds of the heavens. God spoke again in Genesis 1:29 and provided the necessary provision of food to both humanity and animals. God's provision for humanity gives way to God's final divine evaluation of creation: "And God saw all which he had made, and behold, it was very good" (וַיַּרְא אֱלֹהִים אֶת־כָּל־אֲשֶׁר עָשָׂה וְהִנֵּה־טוֹב מְאֹד). God's evaluation not only closes the sixth day of creation, but also serves as a capstone evaluation for the entire creation week. Following the six-day pattern, the seventh day finishes the sequence in relative brevity and simplicity. God ceased from his work.

As the reader considers the structure of Genesis 1, a few observations rise to the fore. First, this pericope is highly structured from beginning to end. From the numerical harmony to the correspondence in form and content of the days of creation, Genesis 1 displays a high degree of intentional structuring. Second, the structural pattern of Genesis 1 suggests that the sixth day of creation plays a climactic role in the narrative. The length and unique features of day 6 signify its importance. Third, the composition of Genesis 1:26–28 shows its prominence within the sixth day, as evidenced by its unique linguistic features (e.g., the use of the divine plural, the description of humanity made in the image and likeness of God, and the chiastic/poetic nature of 1:27), as well as the divine evaluation following this section that creation is "very good" (טוֹב מְאֹד).[19] If day 6 is the climactic day, 1:26–28 is the climactic moment within that day. As the interpreter considers these structural features, the conclusion follows that the creation of humanity in the *imago Dei* is the pinnacle of the creation narrative of Genesis 1. Indeed, it is difficult to conceive how the author could have more skillfully or emphatically described the creation of humanity in the *imago Dei*.

Having considered the overall six-day pattern of creation and its emphasis upon the creation of humanity, it is now necessary to examine certain structural features of Genesis 1:26–28 at the level of words and phrases to further understand the emphases of the text.

Use of the Plural in 1:26

Genesis 1:26 famously states, "And God said, 'Let us make humanity in our image, according to our likeness'" (וַיֹּאמֶר אֱלֹהִים נַעֲשֶׂה אָדָם בְּצַלְמֵנוּ כִּדְמוּתֵנוּ). God's use of the plural cohortative (נַעֲשֶׂה) is unique within this pericope. As much attention as this verse has received, the interpretation of the use of the plural in Genesis 1:26 remains a difficult problem without an entirely satisfactory solution.

Several structural observations are clear. First, both day 3 and day 6 record multiple instances of divine speech, so the fact that God spoke again in Genesis 1:26 is not unusual, but rather continues the pattern. Yet, the use of a plural form in Genesis 1:26 presents a marked difference between day 3 and day 6. Second, the use of the plural in Genesis 1:26 breaks with the pattern not only of day 3 and day 6, but with the other days of creation as well. The uniqueness of the structure leads the reader to see that the content of the speech and the creative act to follow is highly important. Third, while God's address in Genesis 1:26 uses a plural form of the verb,

---

19. Although God's final evaluation occurs in Genesis 1:31 and not immediately after Genesis 1:26–28, God's "very good" evaluation is clearly tied to the creation and blessing of humanity in the *imago Dei*.

all other descriptions of creation, including reference to the creation of humanity in Genesis 1:27 and Genesis 5:1–3, use singular verbs with God as the sole subject of the verb. These descriptions also use singular possessive pronouns to describe God.[20] Only God's speech in Genesis 1:26, not the actual acts of the creation, uses a plural verb form. Thus, for an interpretation of the divine plural to convince, it must account for both God's plurality of speech as well as the singularity of God's activity in creation.

Fourth, within day 6, both preceding and following the creation of humanity, the text uses singular verbs to describe God's other actions.[21] No matter how an interpreter understands the referent of the plural verb, its unique use to describe God's intention for creating humanity marks the act as eminently important within the sixth day. Fifth, in the final statement of approval given in Genesis 1:31, the text records that God saw all that he had made, again using a singular verb and singular subject, saying, "And God saw what all which he had made. And behold, it was very good" (וַיַּרְא אֱלֹהִים אֶת־כָּל־אֲשֶׁר עָשָׂה וְהִנֵּה־טוֹב מְאֹד). Thus, the unique use of the divine plural in Genesis 1:26, and its correspondence to the unique evaluation of Genesis 1:31, sets apart the creation of humanity in the *imago Dei* as a climactic act within day 6, as well as within the creation week as a whole.

David Clines identified six possible interpretations for the use of the divine plural, including (1) an unassimilated fragment of myth, (2) address to creation, (3) plural of majesty, (4) address to the heavenly court, (5) self-deliberation or self-summons, (6) duality within the Godhead.[22] In Cline's view, the list follows "an ascending order of probability."[23] Gerhard Hasel provided a similar list, but he preferred the term "plural of fullness" rather than "duality within the Godhead."[24]

Gerhard von Rad represented a standard position of those who argue that the divine plural refers to a heavenly court. Von Rad wrote, "God includes himself among the heavenly beings of his court and thereby conceals himself in this majority. That, in our opinion, is the only possible

---

20. Genesis 1:27 uses the singular verb form וַיִּבְרָא, "and *he* created," as well as the singular pronominal suffix, בְּצַלְמוֹ, "in *his* image."

21. E.g., Genesis 1:28 uses a singular verb in the phrase "and God blessed them" (וַיְבָרֶךְ אֹתָם אֱלֹהִים). Genesis 5:1b uses a singular verb in the phrase "in the likeness of God he made him" (בִּדְמוּת אֱלֹהִים עָשָׂה אֹתוֹ).

22. Clines, "Image of God in Man."

23. Clines, "Image of God in Man," 63.

24. Hasel, "Meaning of 'Let Us.'"

explanation for this string stylistic form."[25] Randall Garr defended the same view and presented perhaps the most detailed defense.[26] As many interpreters pointed out, other biblical passages refer to God's angelic counselors, and therefore God taking counsel with a heavenly court is not unprecedented.[27]

Despite the popularity of this view and consonance with ancient Near Eastern and even Israelite conceptions of the heavenly court, the position fails to reckon with the basic tension presented by the text itself. The text clearly indicates that whomever the plurality refers to, God referred to their involvement in the *act of creation* itself. Yet, the text just as clearly says that God *alone* is the one who created humanity in his image. Just as the verb and pronouns are plural in Genesis 1:26, the verbs and pronouns are singular in Genesis 1:27. Similarly, the echo of the creation account in Genesis 5:1 uses a singular verb (עָשָׂה) to describe God's creation of humanity. Furthermore, God's statement in Genesis 6:6 says that *he* regretted he had made humanity (וַיִּנָּחֶם יְהוָה כִּי־עָשָׂה אֶת־הָאָדָם בָּאָרֶץ) and he was grieved to *his* heart (וַיִּתְעַצֵּב אֶל־לִבּוֹ).[28] The text does not refer to any kind of outside influence, agency, or partnership in the act of creation. Thus, the interpreter must recognize and preserve the tension between God's plural speech and God's sole act of creation.

Here, Clines's critique was convincing:

---

25. Von Rad, *Genesis*, 57.

26. Garr, *In His Own Image*.

27. E.g., Hasel, "Meaning of 'Let Us,'" 62, pointed to 1 Kings 22:19, Job 1:6–12, 2:1–6, and 38:7. See also the extensive and helpful treatment of Oseka, "History of the Jewish Interpretation."

28. Oseka, "History of the Jewish Interpretation," 7. Apart from the inability of the heavenly court view to account for the tension in the text, Garr's view is internally problematic. He saw the "sons of God" in Genesis 6:1–4 as angelic or divine beings; indeed, the same angelic beings with whom God took counsel elsewhere in the primeval narrative (Gen 3:22–24a; 11:7–9). Garr wrote, "The emergency depicted in this text is incompatible with divine consultation. Yahweh can not consult those who're violating the cosmic order that he established. He can not productively take counsel from those who defy him.... Absent a cooperative partner in this instance, Yahweh acts unilaterally. He acts on his own behalf." Garr, *In His Own Image*, 61. Garr's assertion that members of the angelic courts are at times "cooperative partners" who are involved in the decisions and actions of God, yet at other times the object of divine punishment due to their rebellion, is unconvincing. Such interpretation is indicative of the larger problem of seeing the angelic court in view; namely, it raises more questions than it answers. Thus, while it is true the angelic court makes appearances in other places in Scripture, and that angelic beings exist within the book of Genesis (e.g., Gen 16:7–11; 22:15), there is no immediate textual indication that the angelic court is in view.

A Structural Analysis of the Imago Dei Texts

The force of the further objection, that the *elohim* would be said to have shared in man's creation, is seldom recognized by those scholars who see the heavenly court here. The Old Testament quite consistently represents creation as the act of Yahweh alone, and we cannot evade the force of "let us" by explaining it as a mere consultation before the work of creation begins.[29]

In addition to the multiple descriptions of God's role in the creation of humanity, the interpreter must consider the singularity of God's work in creation in days 1–5. The author describes God alone as the agent of creation in days 1–5. Therefore, it seems highly unlikely that God worked alone to create the entire rest of the cosmos, whereas the creation of humanity involved a collaborative process. Does it make sense to claim angels were involved or consulted in the creation of humanity and nothing else?[30]

Scholars often reject that Genesis 1:26 uses a "plural of majesty" or a "plural of self-reference" because there are arguably no comparative examples in other texts.[31] While it is possible that the uniqueness of the creation account in Genesis 1 calls for a kind of declaration that is without parallel, the relative lack of evidence renders this proposal dubious.

While no solution is wholly satisfactory, Clines's proposal regarding a duality in the Godhead seems to comport best with the inherent tension of the textual data. In Genesis 1:2, the author describes the Spirit of God hovering over the waters.[32] While falling short of providing a description of

---

29. Clines, "Image of God in Man," 67.

30. Clines provided the comical example of a rabbinic interpretation that suggested the angels were offered the chance to participate in the creation of humanity but declined. The example fails to answer the obvious question as to why God would offer angels the opportunity to participate in the creation of humanity and nothing else. Clines, "Image of God in Man," 66.

31. See the discussion in Joüon, *Grammar of Biblical Hebrew*, 469–70, 136 d–f. While the examples provided there refer exclusively to nouns, there is no conceptual hindrance for God to use a form of the plural of majesty, especially given the climactic nature of the creation of humanity within the narrative. On this point, Oseka, "History of the Jewish Interpretation," 12, quoted Saadia Gaon's contention that the plural in Genesis 1:26 is similar to the singular subjects which combine with plural nouns in Numbers 22:6, Judges 13:15, and Daniel 2:36.

32. Wenham, *Genesis 1–15*, 16, catalogued the "deep disagreement" between scholars regarding the meaning of רוּחַ אֱלֹהִים in Genesis 1:2. Wenham noted that all other occurrences of רוּחַ אֱלֹהִים refer to the "Spirit or Wind of God," and he concluded "the phrase must be taken to involve some manifestation of God, whether as wind, spirit, or breath." Wenham, *Genesis 1–15*, 17. Westermann pointed out that nowhere else does רוּחַ אֱלֹהִים occur with the verb רחף, and therefore a unique interpretation of the phrase may be

personhood, the Spirit does seem to be an active agent and could easily be the coreferent of God's speech. Indeed, considering only the text itself, no other alternatives are obvious.

Given these considerations, seeing the reference in Genesis 1:26 as some kind of plurality within the Godhead offers two main advantages. First, the interpretation rests solely upon the textual data and, second, the interpretation does not hypothesize about extra-textual entities.[33] Furthermore, this position reserves the creation of humanity for God alone, a point which the text seems to emphasize in both Genesis 1:27–28 and Genesis 5:1–3. Thus, while not answering every question, the view that Genesis 1:26 refers to some kind of plurality within the Godhead is the option that best accounts for the tension in the textual data.[34]

At the very least, the use of the plural represents a unique variation from the previously established pattern. John Calvin here saw a powerful rhetorical effect that set apart the creation of man from other acts of creation. He wrote:

> But he chose to give this tribute to the excellency of man—that he would, in a manner, enter into consultation concerning his creation. This is the highest honor with which he has dignified us. *Moses uses this language in order to draw our attention to this.* For God is not now first beginning to consider what form he will give to man and with what endowments it would be fitting to adorn

---

appropriate. Westermann, *Genesis 1–11*, 107. Even considering Westermann's argument, a rendering such as "mighty wind" or "breath of God" does not solve the interpretive difficulties. Waltke noted than in every other occurrence in Genesis 1, אֱלֹהִים is a personal reference to God, not a superlative adjective. Waltke and Fredricks, *Genesis*, 60. Hamilton observed that the Spirit/wind of Genesis 1:2 operates as a "beneficent force" that participates in the creative work, rather than a passive, brute, or destructive force. Hamilton, *Genesis*, 114. Overall, the interpretations that render רוּחַ אֱלֹהִים as a "mighty wind" or imply that the Spirit/wind is an inanimate force fail to account for the normal meaning of the phrase and the constructive role of the רוּחַ in Genesis 1. Furthermore, other passages in the Old Testament affirm the impression of the Spirit's active involvement in creation. Clines, "Image of God in Man," 69, cited Job 33:4, Psalm 104:30, and Ezekiel 37 as examples.

33. In Genesis 1–11, the introduction of new characters into the narrative is highly strategic (e.g., Gen 3:1). Thus, it would be irregular for the author to include characters, especially at the climax of the creation account, without having previously introduced them into the text.

34. Of course, many Christians from ancient times saw these statements as references to the Trinity. While beyond the purview of this paper, such an interpretation is valid from a redemptive-historical framework.

him; nor is he pausing as over a work of difficulty. But just as the creation of the world was spread over six days for our sake, so that our minds might more easily concentrate on God's deeds, now, for the purpose of commending to our attention the dignity of our nature, he, in taking counsel concerning the creation of man, testifies that he is about to undertake something great and wonderful.[35]

Calvin's observation regarding the text's rhetorical purpose and uniqueness of the language is valid regardless of how one interprets the reference to plurality. The uniqueness of God's plural speech points to the uniqueness of the moment of humanity's creation in the *imago Dei*, and thus lifts it above and separates it from the other acts of creation in Genesis 1.

Genesis 1:27

Several structural features are evident in Genesis 1:27. First, Genesis 1:26 shifts from direct discourse back to narration in Genesis 1:27.[36] Second, Genesis 1:27 displays a tricolon arrangement. The first two lines form a chiasm, and the third line parallels the second line in both structure and content. Given the highly structured nature of the chiasm, as well as the parallelism, Waltke described Genesis 1:27 as "the first poem in the Bible."[37] Third, there is a conspicuous threefold use ברא, with the verb occurring once in each colon. Fourth, the pronouns in the verse alternate between singular and plural. Examination of these four structural features is thus necessary for interpretation.

First, the switch from divine speech to direct narrative follows a similar pattern in days 1–5. The use of the plural in Genesis 1:26 is unique in the creation narrative to this point, creating a sense of weightiness and suspense to what follows. Genesis 1:27 then flows back into the narrative sequence, but the use of ברא to describe God's creation of humanity indicates its importance relative to the rest of creation.[38]

Second, even as the perspective shifts back to narrative fulfillment, the poetic structure of Genesis 1:27 sets it apart from other fulfillments in Genesis 1. Genesis 1:27 features a neat chiasm in 27a and 27b. The center point of the chiasm is the dual description of humanity's creation in the

---

35. Calvin, *Genesis*, 25 (emphasis added).
36. Hamilton, *Genesis*, 138.
37. Waltke and Fredricks, *Genesis*, 67.
38. Waltke and Fredricks, *Genesis*, 67.

imago Dei, as shown in table 8. Taken together with Genesis 1:26, the text three times describes the creation of humanity in the *imago Dei*.

TABLE 8
STRUCTURE OF GENESIS 1:27

Structure of Genesis 1:27	
וַיִּבְרָא אֱלֹהִים ׀ אֶת־הָאָדָם בְּצַלְמוֹ	A. And God created humanity b. in his image
בְּצֶלֶם אֱלֹהִים בָּרָא אֹתוֹ	b.' In the image of God A.' he created him
זָכָר וּנְקֵבָה בָּרָא אֹתָם׃	B. Male and female he created them.

Genesis 1:27c follows the chiasm of Genesis 1:27a and Genesis 1:27b and parallels Genesis 1:27b. The question is, in what sense does Genesis 1:27c relate to the description of Genesis 1:27a and Genesis 1:27b? Phyllis Bird argued that Genesis 1:27c constitutes progressive parallelism, emphasizing the difference between humanity and God. She saw Genesis 1:27c as contrasting Genesis 1:27a and Genesis 1:27b and linked Genesis 1:27c with God's command to be fruitful and multiply in Genesis 1:28.[39] J. Richard Middleton endorsed the same view.[40] Bird wrote, "The two parallel cola contain two essential and distinct statements about the nature of humanity: *adam* is created *like* (i.e., resembling) God, but *as* creature, and hence male and female. The parallelism of the two cola is progressive, not synonymous. The second statement adds to the first; it does not explicate it."[41] While Bird referred to this parallelism as progressive, she saw 1:27c as an intentional *contrast* to the statements in 1:27a and 1:27b.

Bird's interpretation on this point fails to convince. First, there is no structural indication Genesis 1:27c introduces an antithesis. Bird based her interpretation in part on the basic difference between the dominion mandate of Genesis 1:26 and the procreative mandate of Genesis 1:28.[42] Yet, Paul Niskanen convincingly showed that the themes of dominion and procreativity are complementary and commensurate, not contradictory.[43] Furthermore, the connection between the *imago Dei* and human

---

39. Bird, "Male and Female," 146–50.
40. Middleton, *Liberating Image*, 49–50.
41. Bird, "Male and Female," 149–50.
42. Bird, "Male and Female," 134, 150–54.
43. Niskanen, "Poetics of Adam," 429–34.

procreation is evident in Genesis 5:1–2, which explicitly quotes Genesis 1:27c. Second, Bird's interpretation failed to grapple with the structural relationship of Genesis 1:27 as a whole, as well as the relationship of Genesis 1:26 to Genesis 1:28. God proclaimed his intention for humanity in Genesis 1:26, accomplished his intention in Genesis 1:27, and blessed humanity in Genesis 1:28. The author presents a plain and linear progression from proclamation to fulfillment and blessing. Thus, rather than seeing Genesis 1:27c as disconnected, it is much better to see Genesis 1:27c as a "bridge" that "identifies who exactly bears the image of the divine."[44] The commands of Genesis 1:28 link to the original proclamation of God in Genesis 1:26.

The third structural feature of Genesis 1:27, the threefold use of ברא, provides an important clarification regarding the relationship of the three lines. Rather than pointing to a contrast between the first two lines and the third line, the use of the same verb in each line suggests a unity of purpose. Furthermore, the threefold use of ברא in this context adds an aesthetic balance and quality to the text that again points to its coherence rather than contrast. The continuity of Genesis 1:27 is an important feature to the reader, especially given the switch from the masculine singular pronoun in Genesis 1:27b and the masculine plural pronoun in Genesis 1:27c. To further add to the aesthetic balance, the threefold use of ברא matches the threefold description of humanity as made in the *imago Dei*.

Fourth, Genesis 1:27 features a variation between singular and plural pronouns, both in relation to God and humanity. With reference to God, Victor Hamilton suggested that the use of the singular pronoun in Genesis 1:27 might be the narrator's way of clarifying that God alone, and not a divine council, is in view.[45] With reference to humanity, Von Rad argued, "the plural in v. 27 ('he created them') is intentionally contrasted with the singular ('him') and prevents one from assuming the creation of an originally androgynous man."[46]

Niskanen offered an intriguing argument that the variation of pronouns in Genesis 1:27 plays on the ambiguity inherent in אָדָם.[47] He noted the use of the definite article in reference to אָדָם in Genesis 1:27a, as well as the variation between singular and plural pronouns in Genesis 1:27b and

---

44. Hamilton, *Genesis*, 139.
45. Hamilton, *Genesis*, 138.
46. Von Rad, *Genesis*, 58.
47. Niskanen, "Poetics of Adam," 417–36.

Genesis 1:27c, respectively.[48] Given the poetic context, as well as the similar ambiguity that exists in Genesis 5:1–2, the author may be pointing forward to the story of Adam's creation *as well as* affirming the universal creation of humanity, male and female, in God's image. Niskanen argued that at the very least the singular pronoun in Genesis 1:27b functions in an attributive sense (e.g., in the image of God he created *each one*), but he left open the possibility of a direct reference to Adam's creation.[49] Niskanen's argument for a double reference makes sense of the variation of the pronouns.

In sum, the structural features of Genesis 1:27 all accentuate the creation of humanity in the *imago Dei*. The unusual use of the divine plural in Genesis 1:26 heightens the anticipation for humanity's creation and sets it apart as unique. The creation of humanity in the *imago Dei* constitutes the center of the chiasm of Genesis 1:27a and Genesis 1:27b, and thus the structure punctuates the importance of humanity's creation in the *imago Dei*. Genesis 1:27c parallels Genesis 1:27b and further clarifies that the creation of humanity in the *imago Dei* includes both male and female. That Genesis 1:27c continues the thought of Genesis 1:27ab is evidenced by the parallel form of Genesis 1:27b and Genesis 1:27c, the use of ברא in each colon, and the linear flow of Genesis 1:26–28. The variation of pronoun in Genesis 1:27 is possibly an intentional play on the ambiguity of the word אָדָם, as one might expect in a poetic text and as likely exists in Genesis 5:1–2. Overall, Genesis 1:27 is a highly structured and beautifully crafted description of God's creation of humanity in the *imago Dei* and the importance of this act in the overall account of Genesis 1.

Summary and Structural Relation to Meaning

In summary, the structural analysis of Genesis 1:24–31 shows that the creation of humanity in the *imago Dei* is the climactic event within the climactic day of God's creation. The days of creation build to a climax in day 6, and the unique structural features of Genesis 1:26–28 (e.g., use of the plural, unique language, chiasm in 1:27, use of ברא, final divine evaluation) show that the creation of humanity in the *imago Dei* is the crowning jewel of God's creative acts. As God's image bearers, God blessed humanity and provided for them all they would need to live out their vocation as his royal sons and daughters.

---

48. Niskanen, "Poetics of Adam," 424–29.
49. Niskanen, "Poetics of Adam," 426–29.

A STRUCTURAL ANALYSIS OF THE IMAGO DEI TEXTS

STRUCTURAL ANALYSIS OF GENESIS 5:1–5

A number of initial observations are possible regarding the structural arrangement of Genesis 5:1–5. First, the section begins with an asyndetic תּוֹלְדֹת formula, which, as argued in chapter 2, marks a major new section in the book of Genesis.[50] The reference to the תּוֹלְדֹת of Adam connects Genesis 5 to the preceding narrative, as well as sets the stage for a new major section. Second, Genesis 5:1–2 breaks the *wayiqtol* pattern that then resumes in Genesis 5:3, indicating that the two verses constitute an introductory unit to the entire pericope.[51] Third, Genesis 5:1–2 flows seamlessly into Genesis 5:3–5. References to the name Adam (Gen 5:1, 3), humanity being made in the likeness of God (Gen 5:1), and Adam fathering a son in his image and likeness (Gen 5:3) tie together Genesis 5:1–2 and Genesis 5:3–5. Thus, the analysis here includes Genesis 5:1–5. Fourth, in several ways Genesis 5:1–2 echoes Genesis 1:26–28.

Outline of Genesis 5:1–5

    Introductory תּוֹלְדֹת formula of Adam (5:1a)
    Temporal marker of humanity's creation (5:1b–5:2)

---

50. See table 4 in chapter 2. The תּוֹלְדֹת formula in Genesis 5 is unique. Genesis 5:1 literally reads, "This is the book of the generations of Adam." Wiseman argued that the reference to the scroll or book most likely refers to tablets whose named subjects were the author and/or owner. Wiseman, *Ancient Records*, 67–73, 86–97. Von Rad hypothesized the existence of an original "toledoth book" consisting of "genealogies, lists, and at the most quite brief theological remarks." Von Rad, *Genesis*, 63. Genesis 5:1, according to Von Rad, preserved the title of the ancient work, and the current biblical (e.g., priestly) document was built on this "oldest foundation." Sarna stated that Genesis 5:1 "is most likely the title of an ancient genealogical work that served as the source for the data provided in the present chapter, in 11:10–17, and possibly in other genealogical lists as well." Sarna, *Genesis*, 41. Wenham reached a similar conclusion in *Genesis 1–15*, 126. Westermann disagreed, citing the arguments of O. Eissfeldt, and saw Genesis 5:1 as an introduction to the chapter itself rather than a separate, independent document. Westermann argued the reason Genesis 5:1 is described as a ספר, whereas other תּוֹלְדֹת occurrences are not, is that Genesis 5 represents a true genealogy or list, whereas the other occurrences merely introduce narratives. Westermann, *Genesis 1–11*, 355. Westermann's argument is dubious because Genesis 6:1–8 is a narrative included in this תּוֹלְדֹת section. See also Carr, "Biblos Geneseōs Revisited," who, in a similar vein as Von Rad, argued that the תּוֹלְדֹת divisions grew over time to include extensive narratives.

51. For an argument against seeing Genesis 5:1–2 as a unit of independent composition, see Hamilton, *Genesis*, 255.

Description of humanity's creation (5:1b–5:2a)
    Humanity created in God's likeness (5:1b)
    Humanity created male and female (5:2a)
Description of God's blessing/naming (5:2b–5:2c)
    God blesses humanity (5:2b)
    God names humanity (5:2c)
Temporal marker of humanity's creation (5d)
The line of Adam
    Statement of Adam's age (5:3a)
    Description of son (5:3b–5:3c)
        In his likeness (5:3b)
        After his image (5:3c)
    Naming the son Seth (5:3d)
    Description of Adam's life after the birth of Seth (5:4)
        Length of Adam's days (5:4a)
        Birth of other sons and daughters (5:4b)
    Statement of Adam's total lifespan (5:5)
        Statement of length of days (5:5a)
        Statement of death (5:5b)

The above observations fall into two main points of analysis: (1) the function of Genesis 5:1–5 as the head of a pericope unit and (2) the structural relationship between Genesis 5:1–5 and Genesis 1:26–28. As the individual connections with Genesis 1:26–28 help clarify the role of Genesis 5:1–5 as the head of its pericope, it is the best point of departure for analysis.

The Relationship of Genesis 5:1–5 to Genesis 1:26–28

That Genesis 5 connects with Genesis 1:26–28 is widely recognized, although the strength of the connection seems under appreciated.[52] The texts

---

52. For instance, Hamilton noted the reference to blessing and divine image bearers, but he did not comment on the threefold use of ברא in both passages or the similar use of pronominal suffixes in both passages. Hamilton, *Genesis*, 254-55. Cassuto pointed out the similar ambiguity between the use of אָדָם and the pronominal suffixes in both texts, but he did not comment on the threefold use of ברא. Cassuto, *Genesis, Part One*, 273-78. Westermann followed the same pattern as most other commentaries, seeing

correspond in the following ways: (1) Genesis 5:1 references the "day" God created humanity; (2) Genesis 5:1, 3 references the creation of humanity in the image and likeness of God; (3) Genesis 5:1–2 quotes nearly verbatim the creation of humanity as male and female; (4) Genesis 5:1–2 uses a form of ברא three times, just as Genesis 1:27; (5) Genesis 5 records God's blessing of humanity, just as Genesis 1:28; (6) Genesis 5 uses אָדָם in a similarly ambiguous way as Genesis 1:26–28; and (7) Genesis 5 uses singular and plural pronouns in a similar way to Genesis 1:26–28. Each of these observations merits closer examination.

First, Genesis 5:1 refers to the "day God created humanity" (בְּיוֹם בְּרֹא אֱלֹהִים אָדָם). At first glance, this might seem to be a general formula to identify temporal sequence and thus bear no relation to the days of creation described in Genesis 1. Yet, in the context of Genesis 5 as a new תּוֹלֵדֹת heading, and thus a new beginning, the reference likely echoes back to the previous תּוֹלֵדוֹת heading in Genesis 2:4. Genesis 2:4 similarly states, "On the day he created them, the Lord God made the earth and the heavens" (בְּהִבָּרְאָם בְּיוֹם עֲשׂוֹת יְהוָה אֱלֹהִים אֶרֶץ וְשָׁמָיִם). Both Cassuto and Wenham highlighted the structural similarity between Genesis 5:1–2 and Genesis 2:4.[53] Since both Genesis 5 and 2:4 constitute a major תּוֹלֵדוֹת heading, it is likely their similarity in structure is an intentional linking of the two passages. Given the proximity of the days of creation in Genesis 1:1—2:3, the reference to the "day" God created the heavens and the earth in Genesis 2:4 is almost certainly intentional.[54] And given this linkage between Genesis 2:4 and Genesis 5:1, it seems highly likely that Genesis 5:1 alludes to the original days of creation as well.

---

obvious connection points between the passages, but not enumerating them beyond basic phraseology and content. Westermann, *Genesis 1–11*, 355–56.

53. Wenham argued that both Genesis 2:4 and Genesis 5:1–2 follow a ABCCBA chiastic pattern that "pair 'making' and 'creating' at the midpoint (CC) of the construction." Wenham, *Genesis 1–15*, 126. Wenham's argument, however, did not account for the differences (e.g., the blessing and naming of humanity in Genesis 5 that has no parallel in Genesis 2:4). Cassuto likewise saw both texts following a chiastic pattern, although he did not delineate the pattern in the same way as Wenham. Cassuto, *Genesis, Part One*, 274.

54. The connection between the texts is even stronger if one considers Genesis 2:4 as the conclusion of the creation narrative rather than the beginning of a new section. If Genesis 2:4 is an ending to the previous section, there can be no doubt regarding the correlation of the days of creation and the reference to the "day" God created the heavens and the earth. As argued above, however, it is best to see Genesis 2:4 as a heading that connects two passages rather than a conclusion to a single passage.

Second, Genesis 5:1 explicitly references the creation of humanity in the "likeness" of God (בִּדְמוּת אֱלֹהִים עָשָׂה אֹתוֹ). Genesis 5:3 states that Seth is made in the image (צֶלֶם) and likeness (דְּמוּת) of Adam, using the same words as Genesis 1:26. The reference to humanity's creation in the *imago Dei* in Genesis 5 links it closely to Genesis 1:26–28.

Third, Genesis 5:2 provides a near verbatim quote from Genesis 1:27: "male and female he created them."[55] This intertextual quotation relates to the role of both male and female in reproduction, obviously essential to the genealogy that follows. Especially given the preference to include slight variations within similar narratives, the decision to directly quote Genesis 1:27 explicitly shows that the relationship between the two texts is direct and highly intentional.

Fourth, both Genesis 1:26–28 and Genesis 5:1–2 use a form of ברא three times to describe the creation of humanity.[56] The rarity of the word, combined with the choice to use the near synonyms עשה in Genesis 5:1b and Genesis 1:26, shows that the threefold use or ברא was intentional, with the exact number of uses in each text likely chosen for stylistic and aesthetic reasons. Again, the fact that both Genesis 1:26–28 and Genesis 5:1–2 both use this word the exact same number of times shows not only a similarity in general content, but also a similarity of composition and an intentional connection between the two texts.

Fifth, following the creation of humanity as male and female, Genesis 5:2 records God's blessing of humanity (וַיְבָרֶךְ אֹתָם), an exact echo of God's original blessing of humanity in Genesis 1:28 (וַיְבָרֶךְ אֹתָם). God's blessing ties the passages together and also links the procreative mandate in Genesis 1:28 to its fulfillment in the genealogy of Genesis 5.

Sixth, both Genesis 1:27 and Genesis 5:1–2 seem to play on the ambiguity inherent in the collective noun/personal name אָדָם. While Genesis 5:3 obviously refers to the first man, Adam, it is not obvious whether Genesis 5:1 refers to the first human or to humanity. Just as Genesis 1:27 may play on the inherent ambiguity of the word אָדָם, so here in Genesis 5:1. Genesis 5:2 seems to revert to the collective usage as evidenced by the reference to male and female and the use of the plural pronominal suffix. This stylistic

---

55. Only a slight difference exists between the construction of Genesis 1:27 (זָכָר וּנְקֵבָה בָּרָא אֹתָם) and Genesis 5:2 (זָכָר וּנְקֵבָה בְּרָאָם). The presence of the direct object marker in Genesis 1:27 versus the pronominal suffix in Genesis 5:2 is a negligible difference.

56. Interpreters seem to overlook this connection between the two passages, perhaps because two of the uses of ברא in Genesis 5:1–2 occur in the infinitive construct (i.e., the *qal* form בְּרֹא in Genesis 5:1 and the *niphal* form הִבָּרְאָם in Genesis 5:2).

variation is similar to Genesis 1:27. Thus, Genesis 5:1–3 uses אָדָם in both the individual and generic sense.

Seventh, and closely tied with the sixth point, Genesis 1:27 and Genesis 5:1–2 use both singular pronouns and plural pronouns to refer to humanity's creation.[57] This further highlights the author's use of both senses of אָדָם.

When the interpreter considers the similarities between Genesis 1:26–28 and Genesis 5:1–3, it is difficult to imagine a stronger intertextual relationship. These texts are a model of narrative repetition. Genesis 5:1–3 does not merely reference, quote, echo, or allude to Genesis 1:26–28. The composition of both texts is intentionally crafted and interwoven in a way that suggests they should be read coreferentially. That is, the reader understands that Genesis 1:26–28 is crucial for the interpretation of Genesis 5:1–3, but because the reading of Genesis 5:1–2 so closely relates to Genesis 1:26–28 in the mind of the author, Genesis 5:1–3 likely provides further clarification on the intention of Genesis 1:26–28. Furthermore, with the points of similarity so methodically reproduced, the author alerts the interpreter to search for *differences* in the texts that may provide interpretive keys for Genesis 5. Having considered the structural similarities between the two texts, it is now possible to consider more accurately the role Genesis 5:1–5 plays as the head of its pericope unit.

Genesis 5:1–5 and Its Pericope

Given the similarities between Genesis 5:1–3 and Genesis 1:26–28, the question arises, why does the author so strongly tie together the two passages? To pose the question as Hamilton did, "Why does the narrative regress? Why another reference to the creation to the first human beings as the blessed and divine image bearers?"[58] Cassuto offered a direct answer: "The details that are duplicated here are precisely those that have a special importance for the main theme of our chapter, which is the continued existence of the human race, created in the Divine image, and its dispersion

---

57. Genesis 1:27 uses a singular pronoun to refer to the creation of humanity as a whole (אֱלֹהִים בָּרָא אֹתוֹ) and plural pronouns to describe the creation of humanity as male and female (זָכָר וּנְקֵבָה בָּרָא אֹתָם). Similarly, Genesis 5:1 uses a singular pronoun to describe the creation of humanity in the likeness of God (בִּדְמוּת אֱלֹהִים עָשָׂה אֹתוֹ) and a plural pronoun in Genesis 5:2 to describe humanity's creation as male and female (זָכָר וּנְקֵבָה בְּרָאָם).

58. Hamilton, *Genesis*, 255.

upon the face of the earth."⁵⁹ Cassuto's thesis seems a reasonable answer, and the interpreter can test it by examining the differences between Genesis 5:1–5 and Genesis 1:26–28.

Genesis 5:1—6:8 resets the stage, as it were, taking the reader back to the line of Adam through Seth. The pericope begins with God creating humanity in his likeness and moves from Adam through Seth all the way to Noah at the end of the pericope in Genesis 6:8. As shown above, the similarities between Genesis 5:1–5 and Genesis 1:26–28 are striking. Yet, in keeping with the pattern of Hebrew narrative to use repetition and difference to connect yet advance narratives, the differences between the two texts may help explain the function within the pericope.

Just as several similarities are evident between Genesis 1:26–28 and Genesis 5:1–3, so also two main differences are apparent. First, Genesis 5:3 reverses the order of the operative nouns (דְּמוּת and צֶלֶם) that describe the creation of humanity in the *imago Dei*. Both nouns occur in both texts, but in Genesis 1:26–28, צֶלֶם occurs three times and דְּמוּת occurs only once, whereas in Genesis 5:1–3 דְּמוּת occurs twice and צֶלֶם only once. Second, not only are the operative nouns used differently, but their governing prepositions (בְּ and כְּ) are reversed in Genesis 5:3. Given the extent and intentionality of the similarities outlined above, including the fact the author gives a near exact echo of Genesis 1:27 in the previous verse, it is highly unlikely that use of the nouns and the reversal of their prepositions is incidental.

As argued in chapter 2, the two nouns צֶלֶם and דְּמוּת form a conceptual hendiadys meaning "royal sons." Since each word relates to a slightly different shade of meaning within the hendiadys, the emphasis on one word over another may better serve the author's purpose in a given context. In the case of Genesis 5:1–3, the emphasis on דְּמוּת in Genesis 5:1 and the reversal in the order of nouns between Genesis 1:26 and Genesis 5:3 may be a subtle indication that the author desired to emphasize the idea of sonship within the hendiadys.

If this were the case, one would expect the author to confirm the connection to sonship and parentage in other ways, which is in fact what occurs. Speaking of the creation of humanity, Genesis 5:2 says that God "called their name אָדָם on the day he created them" (וַיִּקְרָא אֶת־שְׁמָם אָדָם בְּיוֹם הִבָּרְאָם). The reference to God naming humanity is conspicuously absent from the account in Genesis 1:26–28, and thus it stands out by its difference. Like God, Adam named his son Seth in Genesis 5:3 (וַיִּקְרָא אֶת־שְׁמוֹ

---

59. Cassuto, *Genesis, Part One*, 274.

שֵׁת).⁶⁰ Cassuto saw a connection between God and Adam here and pointed out that all of the other patriarchs were named by their parents.⁶¹ Thus, he said, "it was appropriate to state here who named Adam."⁶² Again, we see here a linkage between humanity's creation in the *imago Dei* and divine parentage.⁶³ The same pattern of a father naming a child occurs near the end of the genealogy in Genesis 5:28 when Lamech fathers and names Noah. Thus, the genealogy begins and ends with a parent fathering and naming a child. The human examples follow the example of God's original act of fathering and naming humanity. As many noted, Adam's parentage of Seth indicates that God's blessing of humanity to be fruitful and multiply is actively being fulfilled.⁶⁴

Thus, the emphasis on דְּמוּת in Genesis 5 likely intends to highlight the divine parentage of humanity and the continuation that occurs in the passing on of likeness from one generation to the next. Occurring at the head of the pericope, this idea of divine parentage of humanity likely is intended to govern the interpretation of the events within the pericope. God created humanity as sons and daughters of God, those made in his likeness, and those who pass on his likeness to future generations.

---

60. Interestingly, the immediately preceding verses, Genesis 4:26–27, also draw a connection between the act of naming and parentage. Eve named Seth in 4:26, and Seth named his son Enosh in 4:27. Thus, both male and female parents participate in the act of naming, just as God made both male and female in the *imago Dei*.

61. Cassuto, *Genesis, Part One*, 276.

62. Cassuto, *Genesis, Part One*, 276.

63. For additional arguments on God as a divine parent, see Crouch, "Genesis 1:26–27 as a Statement," and Ortlund, "Image of Adam, Son of God," 678–80. Ortlund provided an excellent textual examination of the connection between the *imago Dei* and divine parentage. See also the argument in Lemma, "Noachic Blessing and Covenant," 184–99. Lemma offers a cogent defense of the importance of divine parentage in understanding the *imago Dei*, and even suggests that the royal responsibility of humanity derives from and is subordinate to humanity's sonship to God. His arguments regarding the primacy of sonship over royal imagery, however, are not fully convincing, in part because the word pair צֶלֶם and דְּמוּת occur together in both Genesis 1:26–28 and Genesis 5:1–3 and thus the ideas are inextricably tied together.

64. Hamilton, *Genesis*, 255. Waltke and Fredricks, *Genesis*, 113–14. Wenham, *Genesis 1–15*, 126. Westermann, *Genesis 1–11*, 348.

Use of the ב and כ Prepositions

Speculation continues regarding the meaning of the ב and כ prepositions that govern the nouns דְּמוּת and צֶלֶם, both in Genesis 5:1–3 and in Genesis 1:26. Some interpreters see them as essentially synonymous in Genesis 1:26, 5:1, and 5:3. The reasoning is straightforward: the preposition-noun combinations in Genesis 1:26 are reversed in Genesis 5:3. Genesis 1:26 describes the creation of humanity in (ב) the image (צֶלֶם) of God, after (כ) his likeness (דְּמוּת). Genesis 5:3 describes the creation of humanity in (ב) the likeness (דְּמוּת) of God, after (כ) the image (צֶלֶם). The use of both prepositions with both nouns, with no obvious intended change in meaning, would seem to indicate a basic synonymity.

Garr offered the strongest cases against the synonymity of the prepositions. Garr's analysis shows that the ב preposition most commonly carries a "locative-proximate" quality, whereas the כ often has a "similative-separative" element.[65] Garr described the significance in this way: "In sum, Gen 1:26a is tantamount to a double comparison or double-barreled relationship between humanity and the gods: in two similar ways, the human creatures will be very much like, yet somewhat unlike, God and the gods."[66] Peter Gentry concurred with Garr's arguments and conclusion.[67] Clines argued that the ב in Genesis 1:26 is a ב *essentiae,* citing Exodus 6:3 as comparable example.[68] Interestingly, Clines recognized that this interpretation likely requires interpreting the כ in Genesis 1:26 as a כ *essentiae* since the prepositions seem to function in such a similar way.[69]

Attempts to distinguish between the two prepositions are not fully convincing, in part because they cannot account for the reversal between Genesis 1:26 and Genesis 5:3. Aware of this problem, Gentry argued that the reversal of the prepositions in Genesis 5:3 is explicable in the following way: "Seth shares precisely in the matter of generation and sonship but is only similar and not identical in the representation of his father's image to the rest of the world."[70] This interpretation is dubious, however, for it is unclear why Genesis 5:3 would intend to lessen or distance Seth's role

---

65. Garr, *In His Own Image,* 113.
66. Garr, *In His Own Image,* 115.
67. Gentry, "Humanity as the Divine Image," 64.
68. Clines, "Image of God in Man," 74–75.
69. Clines, "Image of God in Man," 77.
70. Gentry, "Humanity as the Divine Image," 64.

as a representative of his father. In what sense would Seth have continued to represent his father in some way, but in a way that was not identical? Gentry's argument fails to consider the use of the בּ in Genesis 9:6, where the text seems to imply that humanity's creation in the *imago Dei* is not mitigated or lessened by generational separation from Adam.

A simpler solution is possible. The בּ preposition may not indicate a stronger statement of identity, but rather may indicate the author's emphasis in a given context. In both Genesis 1:26 and Genesis 5:3, the בּ occurs at the beginning of the prepositional phrase. This interpretation incorporates the insights of Garr and Gentry; namely, that the בּ tends to carry with it a greater degree of similitude than the כּ, yet it also recognizes that within the conceptual hendiadys, either preposition might be appropriate, depending on the author's purpose. In the case of Genesis 5:3, the reversal in the order of the nouns, and the use of the בּ in conjunction with דְּמוּת, highlights the difference with Genesis 1:26 and emphasizes sonship. The author's point is not that Seth does not represent Adam in some way, but that the emphasis in Genesis 5:3 is on sonship rather than royalty. This interpretation also alleviates the need to see either the בּ or the כּ as *essentiae*.

In sum, there is a not a fully persuasive argument to view the prepositions as essentially different in meaning. Furthermore, the reversal of the prepositions with the nouns they govern supports the idea that the noun-preposition combinations function as a conceptual hendiadys in which it is possible to distinguish between the concepts of royalty and sonship, but not separate them. Both prepositions emphasize similitude, yet difference. Given the consistency of the בּ's connection to the primary nouns in each instance, it is possible that the בּ preposition is slightly more emphatic. The switch between the prepositions and the nouns encourages the reader to focus on the nouns and warns the reader against pressing the significance of the prepositions too far.

Summary and Structural Relation to Meaning

In summary, the structural analysis of Genesis 5:1–5 shows that the text is carefully crafted to harken back to Genesis 1:26–28, yet with a slightly different emphasis. Genesis 5:1–5 focuses on humanity's divine parentage and the call of humanity to be fruitful and multiply. The author communicates this through the many similarities between Genesis 5:1–5 and Genesis 1:26–28, the choice and order of the operative words, and possibly even the order of the prepositions. Indeed, Genesis 5:1–5 as the head of a new section serves to recapture and continue God's call for humanity to live as royal sons. While both poles of the conceptual hendiadys still apply, the focus in Genesis 5:1–3 is on sonship.

STRUCTURAL ANALYSIS OF GENESIS 9:1–7

Genesis 9:6 contains the last explicit reference to the *imago Dei* in Genesis 1–11, and it occurs at the end of the larger narrative of the flood. The story of the flood begins in Genesis 6:9 and consists of several episodes. The immediate unit of Genesis 9:6, Genesis 9:1–7, occurs after God's command for Noah to disembark from the ark (Gen 8:15) and Noah's act of building an altar to the Lord and offering a sacrifice (Gen 8:20). The Lord responded to Noah's sacrifice in an interesting self-address, "And God said to his heart" (וַיֹּאמֶר יְהוָה אֶל־לִבּוֹ), after which God promised that he would never curse the ground because of humanity's sin (Gen 8:20–22). The scene then shifts back to Noah and his sons, whom God addressed with a blessing and a command. Genesis 9:1 and 7 form an inclusio that begins and ends with God's command to be fruitful and multiply. Genesis 9:1–7 outlines as follows.

Outline of Genesis 9:1–7

    God's blessing of Noah and his sons (9:1)
        Pronouncement of blessing (9:1a)
        Three-part commandment of blessing (9:1b)
    God's description of the postdiluvian world (9:2–6)
        Fear and dread of humanity will be upon all animals (9:2)
            God's provision of food from both animals and plants (9:3)
        God's prohibition on eating lifeblood (9:4b)
    God's protection of humanity's lifeblood (9:5)
        Requirement of life from all living things (9:5a)
        Requirement of life from fellow man (9:5b)
        Requirement of life from brother (9:5c)
    God's statement of requirement (9:6)
        Whoever sheds the blood of man (9:6a)

A Structural Analysis of the Imago Dei Texts

By man his blood shall be shed (9:6b)

For in the image of God he made man (9:6c)

God's blessing and commands to be fruitful, multiply, and spread over the earth (9:7)

As with Genesis 5, Genesis 9:1–7 clearly references previous texts, and therefore the interpretation of Genesis 9:1–7 depends largely on how one understands the relationship between Genesis 9:1–7 and the texts it references. Indeed, the main structural pattern that emerges is the relationship between Genesis 9:1–7 and prior texts. Thus, as with Genesis 5:1–5, it is necessary to analyze both similarities and differences between Genesis 9:1–7, Genesis 1:24–31, and Genesis 5:1–5.

First, God's blessing and command to be fruitful and multiply in Genesis 9:1, 7 is a direct parallel to Genesis 1:28. The commands are a verbatim quotation, the only difference being the recipient of the blessing, as shown below:

Genesis 9:1

וַיְבָרֶךְ אֱלֹהִים אֶת־נֹחַ וְאֶת־בָּנָיו וַיֹּאמֶר לָהֶם פְּרוּ וּרְבוּ וּמִלְאוּ אֶת־הָאָרֶץ

Translation: And God blessed Noah and his sons, and he said to them, "Be fruitful, multiply, and fill the earth."

Genesis 1:28

וַיְבָרֶךְ אֹתָם אֱלֹהִים וַיֹּאמֶר לָהֶם אֱלֹהִים פְּרוּ וּרְבוּ וּמִלְאוּ אֶת־הָאָרֶץ

Translation: And God blessed them, and God said to them, "Be fruitful, multiply, and fill the earth."

While both texts begin with the same three commands, Genesis 1:28 includes two commands that are noticeably absent in Genesis 9; namely, the command for humanity to subdue (כבש) the earth and rule (רדה) over the animals. Again, just as in Genesis 5, both the similarities with Genesis 1:26–28 and the differences provide insights for interpretation. Considering the absence of a command to rule over the animals, the content of Genesis 9:2–4 provides a stark contrast to Genesis 1:28.[71] Rather than humanity exercising dominion over the animals, as in Genesis 1:28, God stated that

---

71. Hamilton, *Genesis*, 313.

The Charge of God's Royal Children

the fear (מוֹרָא) and dread (חַת) of humanity will be upon the animals. Wenham noted that the same combination of "fear and dread" is associated with military terminology pointing to Deuteronomy 1:21, 11:25, and 31:8 as parallels.[72] God's statement implies that the relationship of perfect harmony between humanity and animals in Genesis 1:28 has fallen into a new state, or what Hamilton called a "deteriorated situation."[73] Genesis 9:2 provides the familiar list of animals that is similar to Genesis 1:28, although in an alternate order (e.g., birds, creeping things, fish).[74] Whereas Genesis 1:29 describes God giving (נתן) all green things to both animals and humans, Genesis 9:2 says that God has now given (נתן) animals into the hand of humanity.

The statement of the animals being given into the hands of Noah and his sons is an apparent reference to humanity's continued authority over them, yet the description "into your hands they are given" (בְּיֶדְכֶם נִתָּנוּ) differs from the statement in Genesis 1:28. Wenham suggested that the phraseology of God giving animals into the hands of humanity "implies that man has the power of life and death" as is evident from parallel statements in Deuteronomy 19:12 and 20:13.[75] In Genesis 9:3, God explicitly connected the new arrangement between humanity and animals with the original arrangement in Genesis 1:29–30. In Genesis 9:3, God gives the animals to humanity for food just as he had given green plants in Genesis 1:29–30. God's statement is in clear contrast to Genesis 1:29–30, where God had given the green plants and the fruit of trees to both humanity *and* animals. As Derek Kidner noted that the new gifts echoed the original, but "sin has darkened the scene."[76]

---

72. Wenham, *Genesis 1–15*, 192.

73. Hamilton, *Genesis*, 314.

74. Cassuto made an interesting suggestion regarding the difference in order in Genesis 9:2. He stated, "Since the fear of mankind is spoken of here, there are first mentioned, in order to show how far it reached, those kinds of creatures that naturally have less reason to be afraid than other kinds, namely, the beasts of the earth, which are strong and fierce, and the flying creatures of the air, which can wing their way on high above the sphere of human life. It seems as though Scripture meant to say: Even the savage animals and the birds that soar aloft in the sky will fear you." Cassuto, *Genesis, Part Two*, 125.

75. Wenham, *Genesis 1–15*, 192. Deuteronomy 19:12, speaking of the elders of a city handing over a murderer to the blood avenger, states, "And they shall give him into the hand of the redeemer" (וְנָתְנוּ אֹתוֹ בְּיַד גֹּאֵל). Deuteronomy 20:13 describes God giving enemy cities over to the Israelites, saying, "When the Lord God gives it into your hand" (וּנְתָנָהּ יְהוָה אֱלֹהֶיךָ בְּיָדֶךָ).

76. Kidner, *Genesis*, 100. Curiously, Cassuto viewed humanity's permission to

A Structural Analysis of the Imago Dei Texts

Genesis 9:4 continues to provide clarity on the parameters of consuming animals, but God gave a firm stipulation that flesh with its life blood in it is forbidden for food. This prohibition is appropriate at this juncture given God's new permission for humans to eat animals. Whereas green plants do not have the breath of life or lifeblood in them, animals do. Thus, God stated in emphatic terms (אַךְ) that humanity is not to eat the flesh of animals while the lifeblood remains.

Genesis 9:5 records an additional stipulation regarding the punishment of any animal or human who takes the lifeblood of a human being. God explicitly stated that he will require the lifeblood of any living creature or man that sheds the lifeblood of a man. The latter half of the verse presents a statement that likewise echoes back to previous narratives. Genesis 9:5b states, "From the hand of any human, from the hand of *his brother*, I will require the life of that man" (וּמִיַּד הָאָדָם מִיַּד אִישׁ אָחִיו אֶדְרֹשׁ אֶת־נֶפֶשׁ הָאָדָם). First, the reference to the hand of "his brother" reminds the reader that all human beings share the same lineage. This assumes the reality of Genesis 5:1–2; namely, that all human beings descend from Adam, who is himself a son of God. Additionally, at this point in the narrative God is addressing Noah and his sons directly, thus the reference to the blood of your brother is appropriate. As such, there is a universal brotherhood of humanity that makes taking the life of another human particularly reprehensible.

As with the other echoes of the passage, the reference to demanding the blood of a brother seems to harken back to the story of Cain's murder of Abel. The key link is the reference to "brother," which is a major feature of the Cain and Abel narrative. Genesis 4:1–16 refers to Cain as Abel's brother seven times. As in Genesis 9:5, the story of Cain and Abel emphasizes brotherhood as well as the shedding of a brother's blood (Gen 4:10).[77] In the case of Cain, God *does not* require the life of a brother who takes his brother's life. Yet, Genesis 9:6 seems to authorize exactly such a punishment. The shift in Genesis 9:5–6 seems to be a reversal of God's previous policy, in a similar way to the reversal God has already indicated in all humans to consume animals.

---

consume animals as a kind of reward for rescuing the animals from the flood. Cassuto, *Genesis, Part Two*, 126.

77. Genesis 4:10 reads, "He [God] said 'What have you done? The voice of your brother's blood is shouting out to me from the ground!'" (מֶה עָשִׂיתָ קוֹל דְּמֵי אָחִיךָ צֹעֲקִים אֵלַי מִן־הָאֲדָמָה). For a helpful survey of interpretations of the Cain and Abel narrative, see Byron, *Cain and Abel*.

This leads to Genesis 9:6 and the explicit reference to the *imago Dei*. In a continuation of direct speech, God said, "Whoever sheds the blood of humanity, by humanity his blood shall be shed, for in the image of God he made humanity" (שֹׁפֵךְ דַּם הָאָדָם בָּאָדָם דָּמוֹ יִשָּׁפֵךְ כִּי בְּצֶלֶם אֱלֹהִים עָשָׂה אֶת־הָאָדָם).

Three structural considerations of Genesis 9:6 are important. First, the first half of the verse forms a tight chiasm. Each word in the first half of the chiasm is repeated in the second. Scholars almost universally recognize and accept the chiastic structure of Genesis 9:6, and those who argue against the chiasm must account for an alternative interpretation of the ב at the center of the verse. Westermann wrote extensively regarding the chiastic structure and believed that the verse represents an extended development of an originally shorter apodictic law such as "kill and be killed."[78] Reference to a former version, however, is unnecessary for literary considerations that look to the final form of the text. Second, the ב preposition stands at the center of the chiasm and thus is in the emphatic position. A proper interpretation of the ב is key to understanding the verse. The significance of the ב is a matter of great debate and will be discussed in detail below. Third, the כי clause comes after the completion of the chiasm and is best understood as a rationale and explanation for the previous statement. Because the interpretation of the ב is crucial for understanding the explanation, the significance of the כי clause depends in large part upon the meaning of the ב. Since all three of the main structural considerations relate to the function of the ב, it is necessary to give it careful consideration.

Significance of the ב in Genesis 9:6

Table 9 lays out the various interpretations of the ב in Genesis 9:6, including the few that argue the chiastic reading is mistaken and the phrase בָּאָדָם should be included with the first half of the verse.[79]

---

78. Westermann, *Genesis 1–11*, 467–68.

79. See the arguments presented in Lust, "For Man Shall His Blood." Lust's article provided reasoning and representatives for each position of table 9. For instance, Lust pointed to Targum Pseudo-Jonathan, as well as Targum Onkelos, as examples of reading a ב of location where witnesses are in view. Lust likewise cited the Midrash Genesis Rabbah, which offered a list of possibilities for ב, including the ב of location representing the location of the womb (i.e., within a human), the ב of agency referencing mercenary murder (i.e., by another man), as well as the ב of location involving the presence of witnesses. The translator of the Septuagint seems to prefer the ב *pretii*, as indicated by its use

The first three (both ב‎s of location and the ב‎ of agency) depend upon the reader ignoring the chiastic structure of the text. While a non-chiastic division of the text is grammatically possible, each of these renderings creates interpretive problems. First, the only reason to reject a chiastic reading when a chiasm is obviously present would be that the chiastic structure does not render an intelligible interpretation.

TABLE 9
INTERPRETATIONS OF THE ב‎ IN GENESIS 9:6

Interpretation	Translation	Significance
ב‎ of Location	"Whoever sheds the blood of man in man's presence, his blood shall be shed."	Indicates the requirement of witnesses present in order to execute capital punishment
ב‎ of Location	"Whoever sheds the blood of man within a man, his blood shall be shed."	Prohibits the shedding of blood of a pregnant woman (e.g., murder of the baby or abortion)
ב‎ of Agency	"Whoever sheds the blood of man by means of another man, his blood shall be shed."	Prohibits the use of mercenaries/agents to kill another man
ב‎ of Agency	"Whoever sheds the blood of man, by [the testimony of/the decision of] one man his blood shall be shed."	Allows for punishment based upon the witness of one person or one judge
ב‎ *Pretii*	"Whoever sheds the blood of man, for the price of man his blood shall be shed."	Indicates the price required given the loss of life (e.g., *lex talionis*)
ב‎ *Instramenti*	"Whoever sheds the blood of man, by man his blood shall be shed."	Humanity is the instrument by which punishment is meted out

Second, each of the non-chiastic options faces serious interpretive difficulties on its own terms. The first ב‎ of location interpretation does fall in line with later laws concerning witnesses and murder (Deut 17:6,

---

of ἀντί in place of the ב‎. Lust, "For Man Shall His Blood," 95–96.

19:15), but a statement about the presence of witnesses in Genesis 9:6 is out of place, especially since the only people in the immediate context were members of Noah's immediate family. The second ב of location interpretation, while expressing a true statement of the value of life within the womb, suffers from a sense of special pleading. Again, there is no reason to believe that the author would lead one to consider such a specific circumstance surrounding the shedding of blood. The first ב of agency interpretation likewise is too narrow to be convincing. Why would there be a need to condemn mercenary murder, especially since no such mercenary murder had been recorded in the Genesis narrative up to that point? The second ב of agency interpretation likewise does not fit the context and runs afoul of later laws requiring multiple witnesses for capital punishment (e.g., Deut 17:6, 19:15).

If the chiastic pattern is the correct reading, two possible options emerge with regard to the ב. The first is a ב *pretii*, which would indicate that bloodshed is the *price* for punishment.[80] This interpretation would render the verse "whoever sheds the blood of man, *for the price of* man shall his blood be shed." Some interpreters opt for this translation because it reflects the established principle of *talion*, where the punishment for the crime exactly reflects the crime itself.[81] The ב in Deuteronomy 19:21 functions this way, and in Deuteronomy 19:21 the use of the *talion* is beyond question.[82] The second possibility is that the ב is used in an instrumental sense that expresses the authorization of the agency of humans in exacting punishment.[83] This interpretation would render the verse "whoever shed the blood of man, *by man* shall his blood be shed." In favor of this rendering is the fact the *niphal* stem often uses the ב to indicate agency, and in most cases a ב *pretii* attaches to an abstract noun rather than a person.[84] The use of the *niphal* with the ב preposition could also be an intentional indication of double agency, as Markus Zehnder concluded. Zehnder suggested that the passive voice could point to "a direct human agent who is in fact

---

80. Joüon, *Grammar of Biblical Hebrew*, 486.
81. See also Zehnder, "Cause or Value?" 82.
82. Lust, "For Man Shall His Blood," 94.
83. Waltke and O'Connor, *Introduction to Biblical Hebrew Syntax*, 385.
84. Zehnder, "Cause or Value," 84. Zehnder further distinguished between the possibility of a ב *causae* and a ב *instrumenti*, although the distinction between the two is negligible. In the end, both are forms of human agency.

executing his action on behalf of the divine commissioner."[85] In support of this idea of double agency, Genesis 9:5 records God saying *I* will require (אֶדְרֹשׁ) the life of anyone who sheds blood in murder.[86]

As mentioned above, the significance of the כי clause directly relates to the reader's understanding of the ב. Whether one interprets the ב as indicating instrumentality or the price for bloodshed, the כי functions as an explanation of the preceding phrase.[87] If the ב *pretii* is in view, the phrase "for in the image of God he made the man" most naturally indicates humanity's inherent value. The punishment of the *talion* is legitimate because of humanity's value as those made in the *imago Dei*. If, however, the instrumental ב is in view, the כי clause explains the legitimacy of humanity's agency in taking human life. The phrase "for in the image of God he made man" explains why humanity can legitimately exercise authority to shed the blood of other humans.

Against the ב *pretii* interpretation, if the required price is in view in the first half of the verse, the explanation that humanity is made in the *imago Dei* is somewhat superfluous. A simple and natural correlation exists between the act of shedding blood and the punishment of having one's own blood shed as a punishment. The rule of *talion* would apply whether or not humanity is made in the *imago Dei* in the same way that eye for eye and tooth for tooth is not dependent upon humanity being made in the *imago Dei*. So, while the statement of humanity's value is certainly true, it is not clear how the statement of humanity's creation in the *imago Dei* would advance the statement of the *talion* in the first part of the verse.

If, however, agency is in view, the purpose of the explanation becomes clearer. In humanity's original commission, they are given dominion over the land and animals, but not over their fellow humans. In the story that

---

85. Zehnder, "Cause or Value," 87.

86. Numbers 35:9–34 provides additional context to the idea described in Genesis 9:6. The text addresses cities of refuge and the laws that govern murder. Numbers 35:19 translates, "The redeemer of the blood, he will kill the murderer. When he meets him, he will/must kill him" (גֹּאֵל הַדָּם הוּא יָמִית אֶת־הָרֹצֵחַ בְּפִגְעוֹ־בוֹ הוּא יְמִיתֶנּוּ). Human agency is clearly in view in Numbers 35:9–34.

87. See the arguments in Aejmelaeus, "Function and Interpretation of כי," who pointed out that in any given context, "the tightness and directness or looseness and indirectness of causality correlates positively with the dependence of the clauses on one another." Aejmelaeus, "Function and Interpretation of כי," 202. In Genesis 9:6, the כי clause clearly and directly relates to the preceding clause in an explanatory causal relation. See also the discussion in Muilenburg, "Linguistic and Rhetorical Usages," 150–51, where Muilenburg discussed the use of כי in legal contexts.

most directly parallels the statement of Genesis 9:5–6, the Cain and Abel narrative, God explicitly forbade the taking of one life for another. Given the absence of dominion over fellow humans in Genesis 1, and given God's prohibition of retribution in Genesis 4, the reader might wonder how in Genesis 9:6 it is legitimate for God to use human agents to carry out his retribution. The possible answer: human beings are commissioned as God's agents in creation as those made in the *imago Dei*. Just as the original commission of humanity changed with reference to animals (Gen 9:1–4), so here God changes the original commission of humanity with reference to one another. Whereas syntactical and structural considerations allow for either the ב of agency or the ב of price, the overall flow of the narrative seems to point the reader toward agency.

In sum, the כי clause (כִּי בְּצֶלֶם אֱלֹהִים עָשָׂה אֶת־הָאָדָם) functions as a rationale for the previous statement. The phrase neatly translates "for in the image of God he made humanity." The rationale may indicate the high value of humanity as those who bear God's image. The rationale could indicate the new authority that God has now bestowed upon mankind as his image bearers. Of course, the rationale may imply both.

Genesis 9:7 ends with the repeated command for Noah and his sons to be fruitful and multiply and adds God's command for them to populate and multiply on the earth. The emphasis of Genesis 9:7 seems to be geographical dispersion, which presents a clean transition to the following narratives where descendants multiply and nations arise. Furthermore, the command to be fruitful and multiply creates an inclusio between Genesis 9:1 and Genesis 9:7, thus indicating the parameters of the immediate unit.

Summary and Structural Relation to Meaning

In summary, the structural analysis of Genesis 9:1–7 shows that the text intentionally harkens back to Genesis 1:26–28 and other texts, yet Genesis 9:1–7 presents major differences. Genesis 9:1–7 still reflects the blessing of God given in Genesis 1:28 and repeated in Genesis 5:1. Humanity's dominion and God's provision are still in effect (Gen 9:2–6). Yet, the scene and nature of humanity's dominion changed drastically between Genesis 1 and Genesis 9. The explicit reference to humanity's creation in the *imago Dei* is either a tragic reminder of humanity's value in the face of those who would seek to destroy human life (ב *pretii*), an endorsement of a new kind of authority given to humanity as those who now can exact capital punishment (ב *instrumenti*), or both. Genesis 9:1–7 preserves the reality of humanity's authority, responsibility, and blessing to live as royal sons, but in a world that is far distant from its original glory. Yet, even after the flood, God's blessing and commission of humanity continues (Gen 9:7).

MACRO-STRUCTURE ANALYSIS OF THE *IMAGO DEI* TEXTS

Having considered the *imago Dei* texts individually, it is now possible to consider macrostructural patterns.[88] The *imago Dei* texts each occur in very different places in the narrative of Genesis 1–11 and function differently in each of those places. Genesis 1:24–31 constitutes the climax of the creation account. The structural patterns suggest that the creation of humanity in the *imago Dei* is of utmost importance to the author. Indeed, the creation of humanity in the *imago Dei* is the climactic event of the climactic day of creation. With the creation of humanity in the *imago Dei* comes God's divine blessing, as well as his commission and command to be fruitful and multiply on the earth. Genesis 5:1–5 relates very closely to Genesis 1:24–31 and in one sense seems to be a recapitulation of it. The emphasis of Genesis 5:1–5 relates to the sonship of humanity and the role humanity plays in fulfilling the procreative mandate as those made in the likeness of God. Thus, the relationship between Genesis 1:26–28 and Genesis 5:1–5 is both recapitulation and continuation. The relationship, blessing, and commands of God continue even after sin has entered the world. Genesis 9:1–7 once again echoes back to the original statement in Genesis 1:26–28 in its reference to the blessing of God, the command to be fruitful, and the scope of humanity's dominion as those made in the *imago Dei*. Yet, the scene shifts starkly from a glorious climax of creation in Genesis 1:24–31, to recapitulation and continuation in Genesis 5:1–5, to continuation yet alteration in Genesis 9:1–7. Genesis 9:6 reaffirms the creation of humanity as the *imago Dei*, but the world in which humanity lives out its calling and commission is far from the harmonious paradise of God's original intent.

Importantly, each one of the references to the *imago Dei* occurs at pivotal points within the story of Genesis 1–11. Genesis 1:24–31 sets the stage for humanity in God's perfect creation. Genesis 5:1–5 sets the stage for humanity after the fall, yet before the flood. And Genesis 9:1–7 resets

---

88. As plot analysis is the main consideration of chapter 4, this discussion here is brief.

the stage of creation, as it were, after the utter wickedness of humanity made the flood necessary. As the story of Genesis 1–11 unfolds, reference to the *imago Dei* comes at crucial turning points in the narrative. From a macrostructural standpoint, the *imago Dei* is a constant bond that ties together the story of Genesis 1–11 from its majestic beginning to its tragic conclusion. Considered as a whole, the compositional connection of the texts, despite the drastic changes that take place in the intervening narrative, is the most striking structural feature. This feature, in turn, suggests that understanding how the *imago Dei* functions within the story is crucial to understanding the significance of the story of Genesis 1–11 as a whole.

CONCLUSION

This chapter has sought to perform a structural analysis of the *imago Dei* texts whereby the interpreter understands the text first within their own contexts (e.g., pericopes), as well as in their relation to one another and Genesis 1–11 as a whole. The analysis has demonstrated that each of the *imago Dei* texts functions differently in its own context, with Genesis 1:26–28 functioning as the climactic act of creation, Genesis 5:1–5 harkening back to the glory of the original creation as God's royal sons and daughters multiply and fill the earth, and Genesis 9:1–7 showing that humanity's call continues yet changes in the starkly different postdiluvian world. The structural analysis has shown that the texts are intentionally crafted to reference one another and build on one another with both similarities and differences, creating a sense of continuation amidst the dramatic shift from Genesis 1 to Genesis 9.

CHAPTER 4

A Literary Analysis of the *Imago Dei* in Genesis 1–11

To this point, this work has sought to establish a methodology for literary analysis in chapter 1, answer critical issues regarding the text of Genesis 1–11 and perform a lexical analysis of צֶלֶם and דְּמוּת in chapter 2, and analyze the structural patterns and signficance of the *imago Dei* texts in chapter 3. Chapter 4 will continue the application of the proposed methodology by considering how other literary elements of Genesis 1–11 illuminate the meaning of the *imago Dei*. Particularly, this chapter will examine the narrative development of Genesis 1–11 and analyze how the concept of the *imago Dei* relates to the unfolding plot.

As discussed in chapter 2 of this dissertation, Genesis 1–11 constitutes a unified and coherent literary unit. As such, Genesis 1–11 contains an internal narrative logic and flow. Genesis 1–11 is an unfolding story consisting of many smaller stories or episodes. To understand the overall flow, an interpreter must seek to understand how the stories relate to one another.

Also as outlined in chapter 2 of this dissertation, the structural division of Genesis 1–11 consists of a prologue (Gen 1:1—2:3) and five *toledot* sections. Following the macrostructural analysis of Matthew Thomas and Jason DeRouchie, the five *toledot* sections fall into four major divisions: (1) the *toledot* of the heavens and the earth (Gen 2:4–4:26); (2) the *toledot* of Adam/humanity (Gen 5:1–6:8); (3) the *toledot* of Noah (Gen 6:9–11:9) with the *toledot* of Noah's sons (Gen 10:1–11:9) as a subordinate *toledot*;

and (4) the *toledot* of Shem (Gen 11:10—37:1).[1] The final *toledot* functions as a transition, tying together the story of the primaeval world with the story of Abram.

An examination of all the exegetical and literary features of Genesis 1–11 would require a library of books. As such, the following analysis does not attempt to interact with every argument or position, or even identify every literary feature. Rather, this investigation will seek to provide enough context to show that the overall exegetical investigation is considerate and sound. The aim is to examine the specific role the *imago Dei* plays in the unfolding narrative of Genesis 1–11.

GENESIS 1 AS A PROLOGUE

Several pieces of evidence indicate that Genesis 1:1—2:3 serves as prologue to Genesis 2–11. First, the style of Genesis 1:1—2:3 differs drastically from the texts that follow. Gordon Wenham stated that the creation narrative "stands apart from the narratives that follow in style and content and makes it an overture to the whole work."[2] Claus Westermann likewise said "the narrative of Gen 1 is characterized by its onward, irresistible and majestic flow that distinguishes it so clearly from the drama narrated in Gen 2–3."[3] Bruce Waltke and Cathi Fredricks noted that Genesis 1 is a "highly sophisticated presentation, designed to emphasize the sublimity (power, majesty, and wisdom) of the Creator God and to lay the foundations for the worldview of the covenant community."[4] This book outlined the structural features of Genesis 1 in chapter 3, including the rhythmic and structural pattern evident in the composition of Genesis 1. The dramatic difference in style in Genesis 1 sets it apart from the narrative texts of Genesis 2:4–11:9.

Second, Genesis 1:1—2:3 precedes the structural *toledot* formula that marks the major sections of the rest of the book. By not beginning the work with a *toledot* heading, yet choosing to use a *toledot* heading for every

---

1. Thomas, "These Are the Generations," 111–12; DeRouchie, "Blessing-Commission," 233. See the argument in chapter 2 of this dissertation for viewing Genesis 11:10–32 as an example of narrative pearling whereby the conclusion of one major section connects with the beginning of another major section.

2. Wenham, *Genesis 1–15*, 5.

3. Westermann, *Genesis 1–11*, 80.

4. Waltke and Fredricks, *Genesis*, 56.

subsequent division, the author distinguishes and offsets Genesis 1:1—2:3 from the other sections.

Third, Genesis 1:1—2:3 provides the setting, concepts, and categories that later texts reference and develop. Ian Hart's work, for instance, showed how the theme of humanity's work in creation, as evidenced by the six-day creation pattern, the creation of humanity in the *imago Dei*, and the Sabbath, weaves its way through the text of Genesis 1–11 and, indeed, the rest of Genesis.[5] The six-day pattern of Genesis 1, and the description of God resting on the seventh day in Genesis 2:1–3, are a "pattern of work to follow."[6] Hart likewise tied humanity's creation in the *imago Dei* with a royal responsibility to exercise dominion through work.[7] He showed how the theme of work unfolds in the curses of Genesis 3, the sacrifices brought by Cain and Abel in Genesis 4:1–16, the development of new skills in Genesis 4:17–22, and Noah's planting of a vineyard in Genesis 9:20.[8]

In addition to the theme of work identified by Hart, many other ideas present in Genesis 2–11 find their origin in the account of Genesis 1:1—2:3. For instance, Genesis 1:1—2:3 describes the creation of animals and their relationship to humanity. Genesis 2 elaborates upon this relationship, describing God as bringing animals to the man to see what he would name them (Gen 2:19). In addition, humanity's stewardship of the animals is a clear part of God's directive to Noah to bring into the ark two of all living creatures (Gen 6:19–20). God also spoke about the relationship of humanity to animals in the postdiluvian world (Gen 9:1–5).

Another idea that originates in Genesis 1:1—2:3 and undergoes development in the subsequent chapters is the relationship of male and female. Genesis 1:27 explicitly states that God created both male and female in his image, thus distinguishing humanity from the rest of creation. Genesis 2 follows the same timeline, describing the creation of woman as the final event of creation. The man responded to God's creation of the woman by naming her אִשָּׁה, an apparent reference to the sameness she shares with the man, who is called אִישׁ. The fundamental similarity of man and woman vis-à-vis the rest of creation relates back to the creation of both male and

---

5. Hart, "Genesis 1:1—2:3 as a Prologue." See also McBride, "Divine Protocol." McBride's work related more to the relation of Genesis 1:1—2:3 to the various covenants in the Pentateuch.

6. Hart, "Genesis 1:1—2:3 as a Prologue," 315.

7. Hart, "Genesis 1:1—2:3 as a Prologue," 322.

8. Hart, "Genesis 1:1—2:3 as a Prologue," 333–36.

female in the *imago Dei* in Genesis 1:27.⁹ Genesis 5:2 echoes nearly verbatim the description of male and female creation in the *imago Dei*, thus demonstrating a continuity between Genesis 5:2 and Genesis 1:27.¹⁰

THE *IMAGO DEI* AS AN EVALUATIVE CONCEPT IN GENESIS 1

Given the evidence that shows Genesis 1:1—2:3 functions as a prologue, the question arises, what purpose does the prologue serve? Is Genesis 1:1—2:3 a simple introduction, merely establishing the setting and characters for the unfolding narrative? Or does it provide the reader with something more? The following section argues that the prologue of Genesis 1:1—2:3 does not merely introduce the setting and characters, but also provides readers concepts by which the reader can *evaluate* the characters and events that unfold.

God made a divine evaluation of the goodness (טוֹב) of creation on each day, with the exception of day 2. Following the creation of humanity in the *imago Dei* in Genesis 1:26–28, God's preliminary evaluations culminate in a final evaluation where he proclaims creation was "very good" (טוֹב מְאֹד). Notably, God himself was the one who provided the evaluations. In stark contrast to God's positive evaluations in Genesis 1, Genesis 2:18 records God's negative evaluation of the man's state apart from the woman: "And God said, 'It is not good for the man to be alone'" (וַיֹּאמֶר יְהוָה אֱלֹהִים לֹא־טוֹב הֱיוֹת הָאָדָם לְבַדּוֹ).

Given the craftsmanship, rhythm, and structural precision of Genesis 1:1—2:3, the reader must ask the question, why does the author provide these evaluations and what is their purpose? The author need not have provided God's evaluations to the reader, yet he chose to do so. Thus, the decision to include these evaluations was intentional and, like the other descriptions of creation, does much more than provide bare facts.

As the reader considers the timing and placement of God's evaluations, it becomes clear that the evaluations occur *after* God had established

---

9. See the argument in Fried, "Image of God." Fried argued that Genesis 1 and Genesis 2–3 also link together through the act of naming. Whereas God named objects in Genesis 1, Fried argued that God intentionally gave Adam the prerogative to name in Genesis 2–3. Fried, "Image of God," 215.

10. See chapter 3 for an extensive discussion of the relationship between Genesis 1:26–28 and Genesis 5:1–3.

and indicated the purpose of his creative work. John Walton, for instance, showed that God not only created the world, but he endowed the various elements of creation with a specific function.[11] God not only brought into being objects, plants, and animals, but he also established the function and purpose of the things that he created. God not only created the world, but he divided (בדל) between light and darkness, the waters and the waters, and the land and sea. In Genesis 1:14, God created heavenly lights in the firmament. Beyond merely creating the lights, God explained his reason for creating them: to divide between the day and the night (לְהַבְדִּיל בֵּין הַיּוֹם וּבֵין הַלָּיְלָה) to mark the seasons, days, and years (וּלְמוֹעֲדִים וּלְיָמִים וְשָׁנִים) and to provide light on the earth (לְהָאִיר עַל־הָאָרֶץ). In Genesis 1:11–12 and 20–25, God purposefully created and ordered animal and plant life according to its kind (מִין). God not only created animals, but he also described their allotted environments and habitats in creation. Fish teemed in the waters, birds filled the skies, and the earth brought forth creatures and creeping things, each according to its kind (Gen 1:20–25). These statements provide the reader not only with a bare description of creation, but with a clear sense of God's purpose and order in creation. Accordingly, God provided his positive evaluations only after he had established and clarified his creative purposes (Gen 1:4, 10, 12, 18, 21, 24, 31).

Considering the purpose and order of God's creation, and that God's evaluations follow descriptions of order and purpose, the reader can infer that God's evaluation is tied to the proper function of creation. God's evaluations therefore establish a normative standard and govern how the reader should evaluate what is or is not good in creation, both in Genesis 1 and beyond. To the extent that God's purpose in creation remains unchanged, creation is good, and God's evaluation still applies. Conversely, to the extent God's original description and purposes do not hold, the reader should evaluate the events or circumstances as not good (Gen 2:18). God's description and evaluation function as the standard by which the reader evaluates the unfolding narrative.

The function and significance of the *imago Dei* in Genesis 1 fits within this evaluative framework. As argued in chapter 3, the structural pattern of Genesis 1 indicates that the creation of humanity in the *imago Dei* is the climactic act of the six-day creation pattern. As with his other acts of creation, God explained his purposes for humanity. In Genesis 1:26, God created

---

11. Walton, *Lost World*, 21–70. For a detailed argument regarding the specific functions of each creation day, see Walton, *Genesis 1 as Ancient Cosmology*, 122–92.

humanity to rule (רדה) over the created order, including all the animals God had previously created (Gen 1:26). God's description of humanity as his צֶלֶם and דְּמוּת suggests that humans exercise authority as God's royal sons.[12] After stating this purpose, the author majestically and emphatically described the creation of humanity in the *imago Dei* in Genesis 1:27. In Genesis 1:28, God blessed humanity and reiterated his purposes by giving humanity commands to be fruitful and multiply, fill the earth, and subdue it. God's commands in Genesis 1:28 align with his expressed purpose in Genesis 1:26. In Genesis 1:28, God used the same verb (רדה) as an imperative and repeated the same list of animals that appears in 1:26. Thus, the creation of humanity in the *imago Dei*, and their commission to rule over the created order, constitutes God's expressed purpose for his creation of humanity.

In Genesis 1:29–30, God provided humanity with the food they needed to fulfill his purposes. Finally, God gave a culminative evaluation in Genesis 1:31: "And God saw all that he had made, and behold, it was very good" (וַיַּרְא אֱלֹהִים אֶת־כָּל־אֲשֶׁר עָשָׂה וְהִנֵּה־טוֹב מְאֹד). Importantly, just as God's evaluation of other elements of creation follows statements of God's purposes, so, too, does God's description of humanity as his image bearers. That God would provide a superlative evaluation after the creation of humanity in the *imago Dei* underscores the importance of humanity's place in the order of creation.

One major difference, however, in the evaluative aspects of humanity's creation in the *imago Dei* and the other evaluations is that humanity alone among the created order is given both the privilege and responsibility of willingly submitting to the rule of God. Humanity's royal status and relationship with God set it apart from the firmament, sun, moon, stars, earth, plants, and animals, who do not have a choice in their submission to the purposes of God. Just as the description of humanity's creation is unique, so, too, is their responsibility and freedom. God's commands in Genesis 1:28 imply the possibility of obedience or disobedience. Humanity's creation in the *imago Dei*, and the commands God gave, entail a responsibility for humanity to submit to God and live within the relational construct God established. God's final evaluation, then, occurred in the context of humanity *accepting* its status as royal sons and living within God's vision for the created order.

---

12. See chapter 2 for argumentation regarding the interpretation of צֶלֶם and דְּמוּת as "royal sons."

In sum, Genesis 1:1—2:3 functions as a prologue that not only establishes the setting, categories, and concepts the reader must have to understand the unfolding story of Genesis 1–11, but also establishes the purposes, standards, and framework the reader should use to evaluate the story. God established and described what was good in Genesis 1, and in doing so provided the readers with necessary categories to evaluate the unfolding actions, events, characters, and decisions in Genesis 2–11. At the pinnacle of the evaluative framework of Genesis is humanity's creation in the *imago Dei*. While this argument rests upon an analysis of Genesis 1:1—2:3 alone, the test of its accuracy will be to analyze Genesis 2–11 to determine whether the *imago Dei*, in fact, functions as an evaluative concept. This chapter will now turn to examine the narrative of the remaining chapters of Genesis 2–11 to analyze whether such a function is evident in the text.

THE *IMAGO DEI* AND THE *TOLEDOT* OF THE HEAVENS AND THE EARTH

Genesis 2:4–4:26

Genesis 2:4 records the first *toledot* section of Genesis: the *toledot* of the heavens and the earth. This *toledot* section consists of Genesis 2:4—4:26 and includes the story of humanity's creation and placement in the garden of Eden, the temptation and fall, the expulsion of humanity from the garden, the spread of sin through Cain, and the line of Cain and development of civilization in the context of a fallen world. The story begins with a picture of perfect union without shame and ends with a family growing in oppression and bloodshed, even as they grow in wealth, power, and skill.

From the perspective of plot analysis, the linkages between Genesis 1:1—2:3 and Genesis 2:4–25, as well as the additional detail provided in the narrative of Genesis 2, suggest that Genesis 2 is building on and expanding upon Genesis 1.[13] Thomas Keiser catalogued several scholars who articulated the similarities and links between Genesis 1 and 2. Richard Hess, for example, examined the similarities between the genealogies of Genesis 4–5 and Genesis 10–11 and argued that Genesis 1–2 acts as a focusing doublet in similar ways to the genealogies.[14] Umberto Cassuto pointed to

13. Keiser, "Genesis 1–11," 28–34.
14. Hess, "Genesis 1–2." See also Shea, "Unity of the Creation Account."

the duplication and elaboration of Marduk's initial creation and his fate in the Babylonian creation story as a parallel to the initial creation story of Genesis 1 and the subsequent expansion of Genesis 2.[15]

Robert Alter likewise saw literary intentionality and development between the two stories of creation.[16] Alter argued that the more detailed presentation of Genesis 2, especially when considered against the backdrop of the unfolding narrative of Genesis 3 and beyond, created a much more satisfying and full account of the relationship between God, humanity, and creation. Alter concluded:

> A similar encompassing of divergent perspectives is achieved through the combined versions in the broader vision of creation, man, and God. God is both transcendent and immanent (to invoke a much later theological opposition), both magisterial in His omnipotence and actively, emphatically involved with His creation. The world is orderly, coherent, beautifully patterned, and at the same time it is a shifting tangle of resources and topography, both a mainstay and a baffling challenge to man. Humankind is the divinely appointed master of creation and an internally divided rebel against the divine scheme, destined to scrabble a painful living from the soil that has been blighted because of man.... The creation story might have been more "consistent" had it begun with Genesis 2:4b, but it would have lost much of its complexity as a satisfying account of a bewilderingly complex reality that involves the elusive interaction of God, man, and the natural world. It is of course possible, as many scholars have tended to assume, that this complexity is the purely accidental result of some editor's pious compulsion to include disparate sources, but that is at least an ungenerous assumption and, to my mind, an implausible one as well.[17]

To separate Genesis 1 and Genesis 2, an interpreter would have to propose that the commonalities between the two were mere coincidence. Yet, such a conclusion is highly improbable. Nahum Sarna pointed out the narrative of Genesis 2 presupposes an awareness of the narrative of Genesis 1, as the latter story involves many of the "leading ideas" of the former.[18] Indeed, Genesis 2 is in many ways unintelligible when considered in isolation

---

15. Cassuto, *Genesis, Part One*, 91.
16. Alter, *Art of Biblical Narrative*, 141–47.
17. Alter, *Art of Biblical Narrative*, 146–47.
18. Sarna, *Genesis*, 16.

from Genesis 1.[19] For instance, Genesis 2 assumes the reader is aware of the existence of God, the cosmos, light, darkness, the firmament, the seas, and the earth itself. Without the account of Genesis 1:1—2:3, the reader has no information regarding cosmic origins, the existence of one creator God as opposed to many gods, or the unquestioned supremacy of God's rule.

For those who read the text as a unified story with a continuous plot, the driving interpretive question is how precisely the story of Genesis 2 reveals and continues the author's purposes. How does the author connect Genesis 2 with Genesis 1, and for what purpose? To understand the logical flow of the narrative, and thus the author's intentions in crafting the text, it is necessary to examine the similarities between the two texts, as well as the differences between them.

Genesis 2 connects at several points to the prologue in Genesis 1, yet it also expands upon the prologue in important ways. Genesis 2:4 begins with the introductory statement "these are the generations of the heaven and the earth" (אֵלֶּה תוֹלְדוֹת הַשָּׁמַיִם וְהָאָרֶץ). The reference to the "heavens and the earth" obviously alludes to Genesis 1:1.[20] Immediately after the *toledot* formula, the author used similar language to the creation week with the adverbial phrase "in the day the Lord God created the earth and the heavens" (בְּיוֹם עֲשׂוֹת יְהוָה אֱלֹהִים אֶרֶץ וְשָׁמָיִם). After reading Genesis 1, the reader is familiar with the language of creative days. By referencing the "day" the Lord God created the earth and the heavens, the author brings the reader's attention back to the story of creation before its completion.[21] Also, by echoing the prior section, the *toledot* formula functions as a narrative

---

19. Keiser, "Genesis 1–11," 31.

20. Cassuto, *Genesis, Part One*, 99.

21. The combined appellation of *Yahweh Elohim* in this pericope has fascinated and puzzled commentators for centuries. While a solution to this problem is beyond the scope of the current project, Sarna presented a satisfying solution in saying, "The absolutely transcendent God of Creation ('elohim) is the same immanent, personal God (YHVH) who shows concern for the needs of human beings." Sarna, *Genesis*, 17. Given the very personal act of creation described in Genesis 2, as well as the intimate act of breathing into the nostrils of the man and building the woman from the rib of the man, God's personal name is more appropriate in this pericope. Yet, since these are still creative acts, the name *Elohim* is appropriate. Indeed, it is possible that the unique combined use of the name in this pericope provides further evidence that the story of Genesis 2 takes place within the creation week. Whereas Genesis 3 switches to the use of the personal name of God, the transitional passage of Genesis 2 shows both God's creative power and purpose, as well as the intimacy of God's creation of humanity.

seam, indicating the beginning of a new section, but also showing that the new section links to the events that precede it.

Genesis 2:4 forms a chiasm, as C. John Collins argued, that links it with the preceding section and introduces new material for the narrative to follow.[22] In the second half of the chiasm, the author reverses the order of the reference to heaven and earth. By referring first to the earth, the text seems to bring the earth into the foreground, which is appropriate given the role the earth will play in the unfolding narrative.[23]

As the story unfolds, Genesis 2:4–25, like the prologue in Genesis 1:1—2:3, presents the completion of the heavens and the earth with an anthropocentric climax. The introduction of Genesis 2:4 describes a state prior to God's creation of man. Genesis 2:5–6 provides further details regarding the timing, circumstances, and purpose of God's creation of humanity. Genesis 2:5 states that humanity's creation took place before any bush or plant had yet sprung on the earth. Importantly, the text provides the reason that nothing had yet grown: "For God had not yet caused rains to fall upon the earth and there was not a man to work the ground" (כִּי לֹא הִמְטִיר יְהוָה אֱלֹהִים עַל־הָאָרֶץ וְאָדָם אַיִן לַעֲבֹד אֶת־הָאֲדָמָה). The detail about

---

22. Collins, *Genesis 1–4*, 109. Collins went further and argued that, given the statement in Genesis 2:18 that it was not good for man to be alone, the story in Genesis 2 takes place on the sixth day of creation. Collins, *Genesis 1–4*, 110. Cassuto, *Genesis: From Adam to Noah*, 99. Sarna, *Genesis*, 16.

23. Waltke and Fredricks, *Genesis*, 79. Sarna, *Genesis*, 16–17. Van Wolde made a compelling case for seeing the earth itself as an important literary element in Genesis 1–11. Van Wolde noted that the text of Genesis 1–11 often describes the earth in anthropomorphic terms. Six times the author described the earth (הָאָרֶץ) as having a face (1:29, 7:3, 8:9, 11:4, 8, 9), eight times the land (הָאֲדָמָה) as having a face (2:6, 4:14; 6:1, 7; 7:4, 23, 8:8, 13), and once the earth as having a mouth (4:11). Van Wolde, "Facing the Earth," 46. Van Wolde offered a model of "dominion" and "dependency" whereby humanity rules over the earth but is also dependent upon it. Van Wolde wrote, "As sovereigns of the earth and the animals, people are at the same time dependent on the sun, the air, the waters and the plants of the earth. Dominion and dependency go hand in hand." Van Wolde, "Facing the Earth," 28. In addition to the earth's anthropomorphic features, Genesis 1–11 thematically portrays God acting on the earth's behalf as its protector given the failure of humanity to exercise their role as vice-regents and humanity's defilement of the land by violence (Gen 6:11–12). Van Wolde, "Facing the Earth," 38. While certain elements of Van Wolde's argument do not fully convince, she succeeded in demonstrating that the earth is more than a simple backdrop upon which the events of the plot take place. The earth is both the setting and, in some sense, a participant, even if a passive and non-living one, who is subject to both the success and the failure of humanity's vocation as image bearers of God. The New Testament resonates with the idea of the earth itself being caught up in the failure of humanity and awaiting the wrongs of the world to be made right (Rom 8:20–22).

the rain is consistent with God's desire to create a world conducive to humanity's service and dominion, yet also dependent upon God's provision. Victor Hamilton noted that for plant life to grow, God had to send rain *and* humanity had to work the ground. Both divine provision and human effort are necessary for the land to flourish.[24] The author, then, implies that because God had not yet created man, He refrained from sending rain. Some argue that, at this point in creation, wild plant life existed, but cultivated plant life did not.[25] Collins offered the helpful insight that plant life not yet growing is not the same as plant life not being created, and thus there is no discrepancy between the timeline of Genesis 1 and Genesis 2.[26] Against those who see the climate as arid due to lack of rain, Derek Kidner described the setting as a "watery waste" given the reference to mist (אֵד) coming up from the earth.[27] Whatever interpretation one finds compelling regarding the state of the land, the text clearly sets the stage for and anticipates the creation of humanity.

Genesis 2:7 uses two different statements to describe God's intimate formation of the man. First, God formed (יצר) the man from the dust of the ground. The choice of יצר rather than the more general עשׂה gives the reader a sense of the uniqueness of God's creation. God, as a potter fashions clay, formed man from the dust of the ground.[28] God shaped and crafted humanity in a way that was unlike anything else he had made.

In addition to the pictorial analogy implied by the verb choice יצר, the text describes the material from which the man was formed. The man (הָאָדָם) was formed "from the dust of the ground" (עָפָר מִן־הָאֲדָמָה). The wordplay between "the man" and "the land" is clear. Other texts in the Old Testament reiterate the creation of humanity from dust, and other cultures of the ancient Near East held similar views.[29] John Calvin noted that humanity's creation from the dust was a reminder of his frailty and humility, a theme picked up in Psalm 103:14.[30]

---

24. Hamilton, *Genesis*, 138.

25. Hamilton, *Genesis*, 154. Wenham, *Genesis 1–15*, 58.

26. Collins, *Genesis 1–4*, 111. Collins compared the arid climate described in Genesis 2:5 with the arid climate of the Levant in the summer.

27. Kidner, *Genesis*, 60.

28. Hartley, *Genesis*, 59. Wenham, *Genesis 1–15*, 59. Hamilton argued the context of Genesis 2 does not quite allow for the imagery of God as potter, but he does conclude some type of craftsmanship is in view. Hamilton, *Genesis*, 156.

29. Wenham, *Genesis 1–15*, 59–60.

30. Calvin, *Genesis*, 32. Psalm 103:14 also uses a noun form of יצר to describe the

The Charge of God's Royal Children

God not only formed humanity from the dust, but he also breathed into his nostrils the breath of life. Catherine McDowell's work on ancient Near Eastern rituals involving divine images provided important background on the significance of humanity's creation and animation in Genesis 2.[31] McDowell detailed how the Babylonian *mīs pî pīt pî* ritual describes the creation, animation, purification, and installation of divine images in sacred temples.[32] McDowell wrote:

> In ancient Mesopotamia, the creation, animation, and installation of a divine statue in its temple was a complex task requiring a skilled set of craftsmen and priests. The materials used to manufacture the image and the ritual spaces in which the creative activity took place had to be prepared and purified according to strict, confidential guidelines. After the image was created it had to be "brought to life" through the appropriate incantations and rituals, dressed, adorned with the proper insignia, installed in its temple, and fed its first meal before it could be effective.[33]

In the *mīs pî pīt pî* ritual, craftsman would create an image in a workshop. After the craftsmen completed the image, priests would perform the "vivifying acts" to animate the image's eyes, ears, organs, and mouth.[34] The ritual would often take place in a temple garden.[35] The priest would then install the newly animated image in its temple home.[36] These aspects of the *mīs pî pīt pî* ritual find an obvious parallel in Genesis 2:8–9 with God crafting the man from the dust of the ground, breathing into the man's nostrils the breath of life, and placing him in the garden of Eden. Regarding God crafting and animating the man in Genesis 2:7, McDowell wrote, "The notion that his ears, mouth, and eyes were opened is not stated but it is implied by the fact that God spoke to him about what he could and could not eat, that he named all the animals paraded before him, and by his exclamation of delight at the creation of Eve."[37] McDowell noted that in Genesis 2:15 the author used the *hiphil* form of נוח to describe God placing or installing the

---

frame of humanity.

31. McDowell, *Image of God*.
32. McDowell, *Image of God*, 43–116, 142–52, 157–58.
33. McDowell, *Image of God*, 43–44.
34. McDowell, *Image of God*, 43–45, 142–44.
35. McDowell, *Image of God*, 143.
36. McDowell, *Image of God*, 156.
37. McDowell, *Image of God*, 150.

first man in the garden.³⁸ *Hiphil* forms of נוח occur in several other biblical passages describing the installation or placement of images (2 Chr 4:8; 2 Kgs 17:29; Isa 46:7; Zec 5:11 in the *hophal*).³⁹

Given the parallels between the description of Genesis 2 and the *mīs pî pīt pî* and *wpt-r* rituals, the narrative of Genesis 2 likely describes God's creation and establishment of a divine image in the garden. While Genesis 2 does not explicitly reference the creation of humanity in the *imago Dei*, McDowell's work helps provide context for how Genesis 2 continues the thought of Genesis 1. McDowell herself concluded that Genesis 1 and Genesis 2–3 both describe the same phenomenon of humanity being created in the *imago Dei*, although she did not reach a conclusion regarding the compositional relationship of the two texts.⁴⁰

McDowell's examination of the parallels between *mīs pî pīt pî* and *wpt-r* rituals and their similarity to Genesis 2–3 corroborates a straightforward interpretation of the narrative logic of the text. Given the structural and compositional intentionality of Genesis 1, and given the emphasis on the creation of humanity in the *imago Dei* as the climax of the created order in Genesis 1, the reader naturally expects that humanity's creation in the *imago Dei* will be an important part of the unfolding narrative. That McDowell identified specific ways in which the language of Genesis 2–3 related to rituals in the ancient Near East does not come as a surprise, but rather as a verification and corroboration of a linear narrative reading.

After the description of humanity's creation, Genesis 2:8–14 includes vivid details of the man's home. The garden of Eden, described somewhat ambiguously as planted in the East, flourished with plant life that would

---

38. McDowell, *Image of God*, 157–58.

39. McDowell, *Image of God*, 158. McDowell saw other potential parallels at work as well. She noted that the *mīs pî pīt pî* and *wpt-r* both speak of an image being clothed and crowned. While McDowell recognized that Adam and Eve were naked in the garden, she pointed to Psalm 8 as an example of humanity being crowned in glory. McDowell, *Image of God*, 159–68. She also noted there is a parallel between eyes being opened in the Babylonian and Egyptian rituals and the eyes of Adam and Eve being opened after sinning. McDowell, *Image of God*, 168–70. With reference to "opening of the eyes," McDowell wrote that the biblical depiction represents "perhaps the most significance difference" between the parallels because the eyes of the Adam and Eve were opened independently of their animation and installation. McDowell, *Image of God*, 169. The desire to have opened eyes may have been "an attempt by Adam and Eve at divinization." McDowell, *Image of God*, 169. McDowell did not suggest a genetic theory between the *mīs pî pīt pî* and *wpt-r* rituals and the description of Genesis 2–3.

40. McDowell, *Image of God*, 199–202.

provide all the newly-fashioned man would need for food. Included in the garden were two special trees, the tree of life at the center of the garden, and the tree of the knowledge of good and evil. Genesis 2:10–14 describes the four-headed river that flowed from Eden, as well as the branches of the river and the environs and contents of the lands associated with those rivers.

The imagery of the garden continues to captivate commentators and garner significant attention. Richard Davidson catalogued an impressive list of similarities between the garden of Eden and a heavenly temple/sanctuary, as well as a list of scholars who advocate for the view that creation/Eden is a cosmic temple/sanctuary.[41] Davidson claimed there are more than forty "lines of biblical evidence" to suggest the garden of Eden "constituted earth's original sanctuary/temple,"[42] among which are the garden's eastward orientation, God's planting of Eden, a river flowing from Eden, its placement on a high place or mountain as implied by four rivers flowing out of it, and the presence of precious metals.[43] McDowell articulated the possibility that the garden of Eden is garden-temple, although she acknowledged the text does not directly express this idea.[44] Wenham, who defended the view that the garden is a temple, noted that the tree of life shares characteristics with the golden lampstand in the tabernacle, and therefore the lampstand is likely intended to be a "stylized tree of life."[45] Whereas other ancient Near Eastern stories included something like the tree of life, the tree of the knowledge of good and evil is without parallel in comparative literature.[46] Davidson argued that the earthly Eden reflects a heavenly counterpart that existed before sin.[47]

Building on the idea of creation/Eden as a temple/sanctuary, John Swann offered a book-length argument for seeing the *imago Dei* as primarily a reference to humanity's priestly calling.[48] Swann argued that the

---

41. Davidson, "Earth's First Sanctuary"; Beale, *Temple and the Church's Mission*, 66–80; and Beale, "Eden, the Temple," 7–10.

42. Davidson, "Earth's First Sanctuary," 89.

43. Davidson, "Earth's First Sanctuary," 89.

44. McDowell, *Image of God*, 151.

45. Wenham, *Genesis 1–15*, 63.

46. Cassuto, *Genesis, Part One*, 109–10. For a helpful study on the significance of the tree metaphor in the Old Testament, as well as the relationship of trees and kingship in the Prophets, see Osborne, *Trees and Kings*.

47. Davidson, "Earth's First Sanctuary," 66.

48. Swann, Imago Dei: *A Priestly Calling*.

temple-building imagery and priestly terminology of Genesis 1 is so pervasive that humanity's creation in the *imago Dei* must be understood through the lens of temple imagery.[49] Swann sought to show how God's creative activity performed a priestly function. Among God's priestly activities, according to Swann, are God's dividing between elements of creation, God protecting against chaos by the creation of a curtain/firmament, God creating a sanctuary schedule by the appointment of heavenly lights, and the establishment of temple order including Sabbath and sanctification.[50] While Swann did not deal in-depth with Genesis 2 and the garden of Eden as a sanctuary, he argued that God placed humanity in a "holy place" and therefore Genesis 1 and the *imago Dei* relate to a "priestly motif rather than a royal one."[51]

The similarities between Genesis 1–2 and later descriptions of the tabernacle/temple are indeed impressive. Yet, for the following reasons, the arguments of those who see these correlations as the interpretive key for understanding Genesis 1–2, and therefore understanding the *imago Dei*, do not convince.

First, those who identify connection points between the tabernacle/temple and the creation/garden have not succeeded in demonstrating that later allusions function in the reverse order. The fact that later references to the tabernacle/temple use similar language, imagery, and symbolism as Genesis 1–2 shows only that the tabernacle/Temple reflect the imagery of the garden. It does not prove anything about the garden reflecting the tabernacle/temple.

Davidson, aware of this problem, argued that Ezekiel 28:13 referred to the heavenly garden of Eden, and that the earthly garden of Eden "was created as the counterpart of the heavenly sanctuary," in a similar way that "the later earthly tabernacle ... was built as a copy of the heavenly original."[52] Davidson argued that the cherub described in Ezekiel 28 was present in Eden *before* he sinned and was cast down to the earth, and therefore the reference in Ezekiel 28 must be to a heavenly Eden "before the planting of the garden of Eden sanctuary on earth."[53] Davidson's interpretation faces serious difficulties. If a heavenly Eden/sanctuary already existed, and

---

49. Swann, Imago Dei: *A Priestly Calling*, 24.
50. Swann, Imago Dei: *A Priestly Calling*, 54–86.
51. Swann, Imago Dei: *A Priestly Calling*, 90.
52. Davidson, "Earth's First Sanctuary," 68.
53. Davidson, "Earth's First Sanctuary," 68.

awareness of its existence is key to understanding the setting and characters of Genesis 2–3, why is there no mention of the heavenly Eden in Genesis 1–2? One possibility, as Cassuto articulated, is that the narrative of Genesis 2 assumed the readers had knowledge of an "epic tradition" of the garden of Eden that predated the authorship of the Pentateuch.[54] Yet, in other instances where the Bible describes earthly copies of heavenly realities (Exod 25:9, 40), the author explicitly stated that the earthly copies derived from a heavenly original. For the author to describe the creation of an earthly copy of a heavenly sanctuary and not explicitly reference the existence of a heavenly sanctuary seems strange.

Second, Davidson's use of Ezekiel 28 to interpret Genesis 2 leaves questions unanswered. For instance, if the earthly Eden is a copy of the heavenly Eden, why would God expel Satan from the heavenly Eden only to allow him access to the earthly Eden? And why would such an important event receive such an opaque explanation in the Scriptures, in a text that is poetic?

Third, the curse of the serpent in Genesis 3 does not reference a prior sin on the part of the serpent. Rather, the references in both Genesis 3 and Ezekiel 28 seem to imply that the curse/expulsion of the serpent is tied to his temptation of the man and the woman. Even in Ezekiel 28, the reference to the guardian cherub's expulsion from the garden follows a similar timeline as the creation described in Genesis 1–2 (Ezek 28:13, 15) and clearly assumes a human and terrestrial (Ezek 28:17) context for the cherub's expulsion.[55]

Fourth, while God dwelt and walked in the garden (Gen 3:8), and in that basic sense the garden functioned as sanctuary/temple, what strikes the reader is how, in a pre-fall context, such descriptions as God forming the

---

54. Cassuto argued that the use of the definite article to describe the tree of life and the tree of the knowledge of good and evil, as well as a reference to a guardian cherub in Genesis 3, shows that the readers had knowledge of a prior tradition. Cassuto, *Genesis: From Adam to Noah*, 72–75.

55. Ezek 28:13, 15 both use a phrase similar to Genesis 2:4 (בְּהִבָּרְאָם בְּיוֹם) to describe God's creation of the cherub in Ezek 28. Ezek 28:13 reads, "In the day you were created/of your creation" (בְּיוֹם הִבָּרַאֲךָ), and Genesis 28:15 reads, "from the day you were created/of your creation" (מִיּוֹם הִבָּרַאֲךָ). Ezek 28:17 states that the cherub was thrown upon the earth (אֶרֶץ) and speaks of his humiliation before kings. Therefore, at the time of the cherub's expulsion, Ezekiel seems to presuppose the existence of the earth and of people. While the interpreter must be aware of the peril of reading too much literal reference in poetic and apocalyptic texts, Rev 12:7–12 also seems to assume the existence of people and the creation of the earth at the time of Satan's expulsion.

man and woman, God walking in the garden, and God speaking directly to the man and the woman, are unremarkable. Indeed, in a world before sin, such categories as temple, sanctuary, and priesthood do not carry the same level of significance as they do in a post-fall world where access to God must be mitigated and protected. For instance, Genesis 2 does not mention anything about clean or unclean spaces, rituals required for worship, or any other ritual requirements associated with later temples and sanctuaries. So, while it may be true in the most basic sense that God's presence renders the garden/cosmos a kind of temple, the descriptions of Genesis 1–2 point to a time when such designations as temple/sanctuary or clean/unclean were not necessary. Indeed, the idea of humanity fulfilling a priestly vocation does not seem to fit the context of a pre-fall world, for in what sense would a priest or priesthood be necessary in a world without sin? What seems more likely is that the later references point back to a time of perfect innocence, fellowship, and relationship—a time when later realities such as mediation, purification, and atonement were unnecessary and perhaps even unintelligible. In sum, the impulse to describe the original creation or the garden with later descriptions and categories is not warranted and may even inadvertently undermine, rather than elucidate, the purposes of the author.[56] The impulse to interpret *imago Dei* as a priestly function is unnecessary if the creation/garden does not function as a temple.

As the reader considers Genesis 2:9–14, the description creates a sense of familiarity yet dissimilarity with the world the Israelites knew. Genesis 2:9 states that God caused many trees to come up that were "pleasing to the sight and good for food" (נֶחְמָד לְמַרְאֶה וְטוֹב לְמַאֲכָל). By planting trees, God provided food for the man and the woman. Of the many trees in the garden, the tree of life and the tree of the knowledge of good and evil grew in the midst (בְּתוֹךְ) of the garden. Most commentators have given attention

---

56. See also the argument in Block, "Eden: A Temple?" Block concluded, "The question is, should we read Gen 1–3 in light of later texts, or should we read later texts in the light of these? If we read the accounts in the order given, then the creation account provides essential background to primeval history, which provides background for the patriarchal, exodus, and tabernacle narratives. By themselves and by this reading the accounts of Gen 1–3 offer no clues that a cosmic or Edenic temple might be involved. However, as noted above, the Edenic features of the tabernacle, the Jerusalem temple, and the temple envisioned by Ezekiel are obvious. Apparently their design and function intended to capture something of the original creation, perhaps even to represent in miniature the original environment in which human beings were placed. However, the fact that Israel's sanctuaries were Edenic does not make Eden into a sacred shrine. At best this is a nonreciprocating equation." Block, "Eden: A Temple?," 21.

to the ancient Near Eastern parallels of the two trees. For instance, Wenham, Cassuto, Westermann, and Hamilton all pointed out that the tree of life finds parallels in other ancient Near Eastern stories.[57] Yet, as Hamilton noted, Genesis 2:9 underscores the fact that God *himself* planted both trees and, therefore, the gift of life comes from God, not from any inherent or magical quality of the tree.[58] Indeed, God planted both trees in the garden intentionally, which indicates that their existence somehow ties into God's purposes in creating humanity.

Genesis 2:10–14 describes the four heads (רָאשִׁים) that flow from the unnamed river of Eden. Of the four river heads mentioned in Genesis 2:10–14, two rivers and regions were familiar to the Israelite readers.[59] The Tigris and Euphrates were well known and played an important role in the events of Israel, whereas the physical location of the Pishon and Gihon rivers remains unclear.[60] Strangely, the two unfamiliar rivers flow through the lands of Havilah and Cush, respectively, which the Israelites would have known. Cassuto argued that the descriptions of gold, bdellium, and onyx in the land of Havilah show they are natural substances without magical significance.[61]

Taken together, the description of the trees and the rivers paints a picture of a world like the world of the first readers in many ways, yet with enough difference to remind them of the world's fallen state (e.g., no access to the tree of life or the immediate presence of God). The world of the garden was a world full of God's provision. In this setting, God placed the newly formed man.

Genesis 2:15 recounts God giving the man the task to work (עבד) and keep (שמר) the garden. Both verbs are very common, and in the context of Genesis 2 they most naturally take on the sense of tilling, working, and maintaining the garden. A form of עבד occurs later in Genesis 4:2 to describe Cain as "worker of the land" (עֹבֵד אֲדָמָה). שמר has a wide range of use

---

57. Wenham, *Genesis 1–15*, 62. Hamilton, *Genesis*, 162. Westermann, *Genesis 1–11*, 213–14. See also Westermann's argument that the tree of the knowledge of good and evil and the tree of life are two descriptions for the same tree. Westermann, *Genesis 1–11*, 212–13.

58. Hamilton, *Genesis*, 163.

59. Of course, the possibility remains that the ancient Israelites knew the location of the Gihon and Pishon rivers, but modern readers are simply not aware of the Israelites' knowledge or designations.

60. See the discussion in Cassuto, *Genesis, Part One*, 115–19.

61. Cassuto, *Genesis, Part One*, 119.

and most often means "to guard, keep," but also at times takes on the nuance of "to take care of, save, retain," or "to watch over."[62] The word can be used to describe guarding or keeping flocks (Gen 30:31), protecting locations (2 Kgs 9:14), watching over food (Gen 41:35, 1 Sam 9:24), or carefully keeping commandments (Deut 4:6, 7:12, 16:12). As is appropriate when analyzing any word usage, the context of the passage is essential in understanding the intended nuance. As noted by Wenham, elsewhere in the Pentateuch the combination of these two verbs describes the work of priests in the tabernacle (e.g., Lev 18:5; Num 1:53; 3:7–8).[63] Yet, the use of these verbs in later texts does not necessarily mean their priestly connotations apply in the garden. Indeed, given the agricultural realities of the garden, the state of innocence Adam and Eve experienced in the garden, and the overall harmony of creation described in Genesis 1 and confirmed in Genesis 2, the priestly connotations do not seem appropriate.[64] The simple task of tilling, working, and maintaining the garden best fits the context.

Having created the man and commissioned him to work and keep the garden, God then gave the man a warning in Genesis 2:17. God's warning constitutes the first prohibition: "But from the tree of the knowledge of good and evil, you shall not eat from it, for on the day you eat from it you will surely die" (וּמֵעֵץ הַדַּעַת טוֹב וָרָע לֹא תֹאכַל מִמֶּנּוּ כִּי בְּיוֹם אֲכָלְךָ מִמֶּנּוּ מוֹת תָּמוּת). While the prohibition is obviously dietary in nature, its placement in the narrative helps shed light on God's intention. Genesis 2:15–25 describes God's order and design for the garden, including humanity's dominion over the animals and the harmonious and fruitful relationship of male and female. God's command not to eat from the tree of the knowledge of good and evil comes in the context of God establishing humanity's place in the order of creation. Therefore, God's command is a literal prohibition with a symbolic significance. To know good and evil is a prerogative reserved for God (Gen 3:22). By creating the tree, giving humanity access to it, and commanding the man not to eat of it, God required humanity to recognize and respect God's created order and the supremacy of God in creation.[65] Indeed, given God's immediately prior command for the man to work and keep the garden, the implication is that the man and woman were called to take care of the garden, *including the tree of the knowledge of good and*

---

62. Koehler et al., *HALOT*, 4:1581–84.
63. Wenham, *Genesis 1–15*, 67. Waltke, *Genesis*, 87.
64. Block, "Eden: A Temple?," 12.
65. Waltke and Fredricks, *Genesis*, 87.

evil, and yet not eat of its fruit. By taking care of the tree, yet recognizing the prohibition to eat from it, the man and woman acknowledge their own place in the created order: exalted above all creation, yet subservient to God.

In Genesis 2:18, God once again provided an evaluation that echoed the creation week of Genesis 1:1—2:3: "it is not good for the man to be alone" (לֹא־טוֹב הֱיוֹת הָאָדָם לְבַדּוֹ). By invoking the same evaluative language, the author reminded the reader that God's evaluation in Genesis 1:31 comes only after both male and female are made in the *imago Dei*. In Genesis 2:18, God declared that he would make a helper corresponding to the man (עֵזֶר כְּנֶגְדּוֹ). Both descriptors עֵזֶר and נֶגֶד elevate the status of the woman above that of the animals, as the narrative fleshes out in Genesis 2:19–20. עֵזֶר, translated "help" or "assistance," most often refers to the function of God himself (Exod 18:4; Deut 33:7, 29; Pss 20:3; 115:9–11; 121:2; 124:8; 146:5; Dan 11:34). Given God's description that it was not good for the man to be alone, the word describes an essential, not a diminutive, function.[66] Furthermore, the idea that the man would need a helper only makes sense in light of the commissioned task described in Genesis 1:26–28, 2:14. Just as in Genesis 1:28 God commanded both male and female to rule, so, too, Genesis 2 describes the necessity of both male and female in being fruitful, working, and keeping the garden. Without the woman, the task God gave the man would be impossible to fulfill.

Similarly, the word נֶגֶד speaks to the position of the woman as a complement equal to the man, over and against the subordinate position of the animals who do not correspond to the man (Gen 2:20).[67] נֶגֶד often carries a connotation of physical proximity in space: "That which is opposite, that which corresponds."[68] For the woman to correspond physically to the man is for her to share an equality of honor in the order of creation. Unlike the animals, the woman is a counterpart necessary for the completion of the man's God-given tasks.

Genesis 2:19–20 continues to establish the created order of the garden in a way that both subordinates the animals and elevates the woman. The man named the animals in an act that solidified his difference and superiority over them, as described in Genesis 1:26–28.[69] As Hamilton pointed

---

66. Koehler et al., *HALOT*, 3:666–67.
67. Koehler et al., *HALOT*, 3:811–12.
68. Koehler et al., *HALOT*, 3:811–12.
69. Hamilton, *Genesis*, 176.

out, "the animals are creatures, but they are not helpers."[70] The animals are not active participants in ruling over creation, but rather the man rules over them. Cassuto went further and contended that God's purpose in having the man name the animals was so the man "would become conscious of his loneliness and would yearn for one who could be his life-companion and a helper fit to be his soul-mate in the full sense of the words, and, in consequence, he would be ready to appreciate and cherish the gift that the Lord God was to give him."[71] Indeed, given God's stated intention in 2:18, the reader is already aware of God's purpose and anticipates the creation of the woman. The reader, in a sense, is aware of God's intention for the man before the man himself is aware. The naming of the animals thus creates a pregnant pause and a sense of suspense.

After the man named all the animals and no suitable helper was found for him, God caused him to fall into a deep sleep. From the man's rib, his own flesh, God built (בנה) a woman. Upon seeing the woman, the man exclaimed emphatically that the woman was like him, bone of his bone and flesh of his flesh (עֶצֶם מֵעֲצָמַי וּבָשָׂר מִבְּשָׂרִי). The man explicitly stated, "because of this" (לְזֹאת), that is, because of the woman's likeness to the man (אִישׁ), she will be called woman (אִשָּׁה). The wordplay between אִישׁ and אִשָּׁה is conspicuous. The man emphasized the essential similarity of the man and woman over and against the animals (e.g., the homophonic similarity of אִישׁ and אִשָּׁה), yet also recognized a distinction between himself and the woman (e.g., the words are similar and correspond, but are not the same).[72] The man's naming of the woman אִשָּׁה is thus his recognition of her equality with him in the created order God had established and her difference from him as woman.

Genesis 2:24–25 switches perspectives from the man to the narrator. The narrator ends the account with an explanation of the proper relationship vis-à-vis a man, his parents, and his wife in future marriages. Of course, the first human pair did not have biological parents, but the narrator explained that the relationship between the first man and woman set an abiding precedent. Just as the first man and first woman came together in a harmonious and shameless one-flesh union, so a man would leave his father and mother, cleave to his wife, and the two would become one flesh.

70. Hamilton, *Genesis*, 176.
71. Cassuto, *Genesis, Part One*, 128.
72. For additional discussion on the significance of the naming, see Ramsey, "Is Name-Giving an Act."

The reference to becoming one flesh (וְהָיוּ לְבָשָׂר אֶחָד) refers to the creation of the woman from the flesh of the man. Sarna remarked that "the fashioning of the woman from the man's body explains why his bond to his wife takes precedence over his ties to his parents."[73] Gerhard von Rad went so far as to describe Genesis 2:24 as "the primary purpose toward which it [the narrative] was oriented toward the beginning."[74]

Genesis 2:25 continues the voice of the narrator and states, "And the two were naked, the man and his wife, and they knew no shame" (וַיִּהְיוּ שְׁנֵיהֶם עֲרוּמִּים הָאָדָם וְאִשְׁתּוֹ וְלֹא יִתְבֹּשָׁשׁוּ). While Genesis 2:24 describes etiological realities, as well as a statement of harmonious relations, the verse also reverses God's negative evaluation that it was not good for the man to be alone (Gen 2:18). Rather than repeating the language of "good" or "not good," the narrator artfully described the creation of the woman and the harmony between the woman and the man. The statement "and the two were naked, the man and his wife, and they knew no shame" acts as an evaluative exclamation mark, as it were, in a similar way as God's statement in Genesis 1:31 that creation was "very good." As the scene ends in Genesis 2:25, the man and his wife dwell in harmony with one another, are provided for by God in a perfect environment, and have no reason to experience need, want, or shame.

The final evaluation in Genesis 2:24–25 also brings into the fore another aspect of the man and woman's relationship that finds an echo in Genesis 1: fruitfulness. The act of becoming one flesh, and the explicit reference to a father and mother whose son will leave them to cling to his wife, point to the natural product of the man and the woman's union. While Genesis 1 includes God's command to be fruitful, Genesis 2 describes an environment and a relationship where the command is not burdensome or painful, but rather a natural outworking of joyous union.

Having examined Genesis 2, it is possible to identify and bring together several similarities between the texts of Genesis 1 and Genesis 2. Table 10 shows connections between the two passages.

As the reader considers these similarities, it becomes clear that the narrative description in Genesis 2 relates not only to Genesis 1 in general, but to humanity's creation in the *imago Dei* in particular. The connection points occur in the following ways.

---

73. Sarna, *Genesis*, 23.
74. Von Rad, *Genesis*, 82.

First, in both passages, God gave humanity authority over animals. In Genesis 1, God commanded humanity to rule over the animals in conjunction with their creation as *imago Dei*. As "royal sons" over creation, their authority over animals is explicit. In Genesis 2, God brought the animals to the man to see what he would name them, and thus the authority is implicit.

TABLE 10
LINKS BETWEEN GENESIS 1 AND GENESIS 2

Links between Genesis 1 and Genesis 2		
Genesis 1–2:3	Similarity	Genesis 2:4–25
Gen 1:26–28. God commanded humanity to rule over the fish of the sea, the birds of the sky, and everything that crawls upon the earth.	Humanity's authority over animals	Gen 2:19–20. God brought the beasts of the field and the birds of the heavens to the man to see what he would name them.
Gen 1:3–25. Before God created humanity, God prepared the land.	Preparation of the land for humanity	Gen 2:4b–6. Before God created humanity, God prepared the land.
Gen 1:29–30. God provided every seed-bearing plant and tree to provide for humanity.	God's provision for humanity	Gen 2:8, 16. God caused trees to grow that were pleasing in appearance and good for food.
Gen 1:26–28. God created humanity in his image, after his likeness.	God's special creation of humanity	Gen 2:7, 21–22. God formed the man from the dust of the ground, breathed into his nostrils the breath of life, and built the woman from the rib of the man.
Gen 1:27. God explicitly created both male and female in his likeness, and in doing so emphasized the man and woman's similarity to one another and their uniqueness vis-à-vis the rest of creation.	Creation of male and female	Gen 2:7, 21–23. God himself created both the male and the female. In the man's response, he emphasized the man and woman's similarity to one another and their uniqueness vis-à-vis the rest of creation.

Gen 1:28. God commanded humanity to be fruitful and multiply.	Humanity's procreation	Gen 2:24. A man leaves his father and mother, implying procreative continuity. The man joins with his wife and becomes one flesh, also implying procreative continuity.
Gen 1:26, 28. God declared humanity would rule over the whole earth.	Humanity's responsibility with reference to the earth/land	Gen 2:5, 15. God created humanity to till and keep the land and the Garden.
Gen 1:31. God saw all that He had made and, behold, it was very good.	Evaluative language	Gen 2:18. God stated that it was not good for the man to be alone. Gen 2:25. Both the man and his wife were naked, yet felt no shame.

Second, both Genesis 1 and Genesis 2 present a setting where God had prepared the earth for humanity's inhabitation and rule. Genesis 1 describes the various acts of creation and builds to the creation of humanity as the climactic act. Similarly, Genesis 2 presents creation in a raw, undeveloped state, awaiting humanity to work the ground (Gen 2:5).

Third, in the accounts of both Genesis 1 and Genesis 2, God provided humanity with everything needed to fulfill the tasks he had given them. He provided food for humanity in Genesis 1 and Genesis 2.

Fourth, both Genesis 1 and Genesis 2 underscore the special creation of humanity. In Genesis 1, the author carefully crafted the description of the sixth day to emphasize the creation of humanity in the *imago Dei*. In doing so, the author presented the creation of humanity as distinct from all other creatures. In Genesis 2, the author described God forming the man from the ground, as a potter fashions clay (Gen 2:7). God then breathed into the nostrils of the man the breath of life. Furthermore, God built the woman from the flesh of the man. These descriptions set the man and woman apart from the animals. As McDowell demonstrated convincingly, the animation of the man, his placement in the garden, among other factors, all relate directly to humanity's creation in the *imago Dei*, as evidenced by similar descriptions of image rituals in the ancient Near East.[75]

---

75. See McDowell, *Image of God*, 203–8, for a summary of her findings and conclusions.

Fifth, both Genesis 1 and Genesis 2 describe the creation of both male and female. Genesis 1 speaks of the creation of both male and female in the image and likeness of God, and God gave commands to both male and female. In Genesis 2, the author provided a more detailed account of the special creation of the woman. The account of Genesis 2 emphasizes the woman's likeness to and derivation from the man. Even as the man emphasized the sameness yet distinction between himself and his wife, the story ended with a statement of their oneness (Gen 2:25).

Sixth, and related to oneness, both Genesis 1 and Genesis 2 indicate the necessity and reality of human procreation. Genesis 1 presents human procreation as a command from God (Gen 1:28), whereas Genesis 2 strongly implies the goodness of procreation in stating that a man leaves his father and mother and becomes one flesh with his wife. Indeed, the reference to a mother and a father is out of place in Genesis 2, except to indicate the procreative realities of the man and woman coming together.

Seventh, both Genesis 1 and Genesis 2 tie the creation of humanity with ruling over the land. In Genesis 1:26, God declared that humanity would rule over the animals of the earth and over all the earth (וּבְכָל־הָאָרֶץ). In Genesis 1:28, God commanded humanity to fill the earth, subdue it, and rule it (וּמִלְאוּ אֶת־הָאָרֶץ וְכִבְשֻׁהָ וּרְדוּ). Genesis 2 likewise ties humanity's purpose and commission to the land. God created the man in order to work (לְעָבְדָהּ) and keep (וּלְשָׁמְרָהּ) the land (Gen 2:5, 15). While the vocabulary differs in the passages, the connection between humanity's creation and humanity's vocational objectives vis-à-vis the land is evident. That connection, in turn, flows from humanity's creation in the *imago Dei*, as demonstrated by God's statements and commands in Genesis 1:26–28.

Finally, both texts use evaluative language and statements. Genesis 1 repeatedly uses the evaluative language of creation being "good" and, following the creation of humanity in the *imago Dei*, God described the totality of the created order as very good (Gen 1:31). Genesis 2:18 uses the same language negatively, saying that it is "not good" for the man to be alone. Yet, after the creation of the woman, the text describes the two being naked and knowing no shame. The language of Genesis 2:25 speaks to the goodness of God providing a woman for the man and obviously remedying the situation in Genesis 2:18. Perfect harmony exists between the man and the woman in their one flesh union, and thus what was once "not good" is now good.

As the reader considers these similarities, the reader may justifiably conclude not only that Genesis 2 expounds on Genesis 1 in general, but that Genesis 2 intentionally expounds on humanity's creation in the *imago Dei* in particular. Genesis 2 provides a more detailed picture of God's designs in Genesis 1. The reference to animals, land, male and female, work, preparation, provision, procreation, and evaluation all flesh out the description of Genesis 1:26–28. While Genesis 1 describes the creation of humanity from God's perspective, Genesis 2 describes the lived reality of the *imago Dei* from the perspective of the man and the woman. Humanity enjoys an intimate relationship with God and a harmonious relationship with one another in an environment of perfect provision.

Genesis 3

The author set the stage of creation in Genesis 1 and expanded the backdrop in Genesis 2. Genesis 3:1 shifts the narrative flow, both by breaking the *wayiqtol* pattern that wove through Genesis 1–2 and by introducing a new character into the story. The serpent, the reader finds out in the opening explanatory statement, was "craftier than any other creatures of the field that the Lord God had made" (עָרוּם מִכֹּל חַיַּת הַשָּׂדֶה אֲשֶׁר עָשָׂה יְהוָה אֱלֹהִים). This introductory statement characterizes the serpent in two ways. First, the author described the serpent as crafty. The word עָרוּם, though often used in a positive way to describe wisdom or prudence (Prov 12:16, 23, 13:16, 14:8, 15, 18, 22:3, 27:12), also can imply a devious use of wisdom (Job 5:15, 15:5).[76] Given the serpent's actions, the latter nuance better fits the context. Furthermore, the word עָרוּם seems to be a wordplay on עָרוֹם, the word used in the previous verse to describe the nakedness of the man and the woman.[77] Second, the serpent is one of the creatures the Lord God had made, indicating the subordination of the serpent to God.

What strikes the reader is the rather minimal background given about the serpent and the immediacy of the conversation between the woman and the serpent. Cassuto argued that the serpent represents the internal cunning of humanity and the serpent's conversation with the woman is an internal dialogue.[78] The problem with this interpretation, apart from positing an inexplicable shift from narrative to allegory, is that God curses the

---

76. Koehler et al., *HALOT*, 3:883.
77. Wenham, *Genesis 1–15*, 72.
78. Cassuto, *Genesis, Part One*, 142.

serpent (Gen 3:14). It makes little sense to claim that God would curse a symbol of internal conflict.[79]

Interestingly, the serpent is aware of God's original commands, prohibition, and the reality of what would occur if the human pair were to partake of the fruit. Regarding the identity of the serpent, Christian interpreters have long followed the identification in Revelation 12:9 and 20:2 of the serpent with Satan. Even accepting this identification, it is notable that nowhere does Genesis 3 describe the serpent as evil or unclean. Yet, as noted by Stephen Dempster, the presence of the serpent relates to Genesis 1–2 in that humanity is explicitly given authority over all creatures. Dempster argued, "The snake is a bizarre aberration in the garden, with its ability to do what only humans and God can do (namely speak) and its attempt to rule the rulers."[80] Even so, the text provides no indication that the serpent appeared in any way evil or impure to the woman or the man. The woman seemed blissfully and woefully unaware of the serpent's intentions.

The serpent's cunning is evident in his ability to tempt and deceive the woman. The serpent began by asking the woman about God's prohibition of eating, and he framed the prohibition broadly, asking whether the man and woman were not allowed to eat from any tree in the garden. The woman's reply went beyond the actual words of God to the man in Genesis 2:16–17. The woman stated that they may not even touch the fruit lest they die. The serpent then replied in 3:4 with an outright denial of God's decree: "you shall not surely die" (לֹא־מוֹת תְּמֻתוּן). He went on to tell the woman that when she ate the fruit, her eyes would be opened and she would be like God/as gods (כֵּאלֹהִים), knowing good and evil. The woman, believing the serpent and seeing that the food was pleasing and desirable for obtaining wisdom, ate of the tree and gave some to her husband, who was with her (Gen 3:6). Upon eating the fruit, the eyes of both were opened, and they sewed fig leaves for themselves to cover their nakedness.

In the small span of a few verses, the beauty and harmony of creation in Genesis 1–2 shattered. As the reader considers this tragic scene, the temptation and deceit of the serpent comes into focus. Two important points emerge in considering the temptation. First, the temptation regards the tree of the knowledge of good and evil, which, as discussed above, God planted as a symbol of his order and authority. Thus, the temptation to eat

---

79. Curiously, Cassuto did not mention this problem in his comment on Genesis 3:14–15. *Genesis, Part One*, 158–60.

80. Dempster, *Dominion and Dynasty*, 67.

from the tree was, at its root, a temptation to disregard God's established order and thereby subvert God's authority. Second, the serpent intentionally framed the opening of the woman's eyes as becoming *like God*. J. Gordon McConville directly connected the temptation of Genesis 3 to humanity's position as *imago Dei* and their willingness to submit to God's authority. Given the description of Genesis 1:26–27, the reader already knows that the man and woman are like God, made in the *imago Dei*. Yet, the serpent tempts them with a new "godlikeness." Regarding the serpent's temptation for humanity to be like God, McConville wrote:

> The point depends on the recognition that Genesis 2:4b–3:24 should indeed be read as part of an integrated whole along with Genesis 1:1–2:4a. But the echo is unmistakable and forcefully demonstrates the theological danger that is courted by the notion of godlikeness. The aspiration to it, at least under the conditions in play in Genesis 3, is shown here to be at the root of the human experience of alienation and of mortality itself. Behind the desire for godlikeness lurk the ever-present possibilities of tyranny and idolatry. The sequel to Genesis 1:1–2:4a in 2:4b–3:24 highlights precisely this dilemma of the human condition—namely, how to understand and inhabit godlikeness in a properly human way.[81]

The serpent, then, led the woman to question whether she should be content with her current state as an image bearer and royal participant in God's rule over creation, or whether it was possible for her to be "like God" to a greater degree. Given these realities, the serpent's temptation related directly to humanity's creation in the *imago Dei*.

After eating the fruit, the man and woman reacted in a way that highlighted their loss of harmony and shamelessness. Not only were their eyes opened to good and evil, but they were immediately aware of the end of their shamelessness *vis-à-vis* one another and God. Genesis 3:8 records God walking (מִתְהַלֵּךְ) in the garden, something the text portrays as a rather normal occurrence.[82] That the man and woman hid themselves (וַיִּתְחַבֵּא) from God, in whose presence they had stood shameless, who had formed and crafted them both, whose voice they had heard, and whose hand had provided them with all good things, is a dark foreshadowing of the events

---

81. McConville, *Being Human in God's World*, 17–18.

82. On the possible interpretations of the meaning of the unique phrase, לְרוּחַ הַיּוֹם, see Cassuto, *Genesis, Part One*, 151–54.

A Literary Analysis of the Imago Dei in Genesis 1–11

to unfold. The deep harmony of creation, both between the man and the woman, and between humanity and God, was broken.

God's response to the man and woman in Genesis 3:9–19 stressed their breach of authority and their rebellion against God's created order. God questioned the man in Genesis 3:12 and described the tree as the tree "I commanded you not to eat from it" (צִוִּיתִיךָ לְבִלְתִּי אֲכָל־מִמֶּנּוּ). God's question reminded the man and woman of God's authority and implied that the man and woman had defied God's authority in ignoring the prohibition. As the scene unfolds, the man blamed the woman that God had given him. The man's shift of blame to the woman is a stark contrast to his exclamatory statement in Genesis 2:23, and it reversed the harmony of Genesis 2:25 regarding the essential oneness of the man and the woman. Similarly, when God turned to the woman, the woman stated that the serpent "deceived me" (הִשִּׁיאַנִי). God did not interview the serpent, but rather moved directly into a state of judgment.

The punishments God meted out fit the crimes, as it were, in a way where each judgment relates to God's original commission of humanity as the *imago Dei*. God cursed the serpent and relegated him to the position of eating dust (Gen 3:14). God also declared that he would put hostility between the offspring (זֶרַע) of the woman and the offspring of the serpent. Since no literal offspring of the serpent appear in later texts, God's statement regarding the seed of the serpent implies that certain human offspring would choose the way of the serpent and so act as his progeny. While Genesis 3:15 uses the root שׁוּף to describe both the serpent's attack on the human and the human's attack on the serpent, the seed of the woman would have the advantage of being able to crush the head (רֹאשׁ) of the serpent, whereas the serpent may only crush the heel (עָקֵב).[83] The struggle between the seed of the woman and the seed of the serpent would take place in perpetuity.[84] Yet, even the statement of perpetual enmity implied a promise of fruitfulness that harkened back to humanity's commission as the *imago Dei*. The offspring of humanity will continue, albeit in a condition of continuous discord with the seed of the serpent. The prospect of fruitfulness remained despite the reality of the curse.

Similarly, in Genesis 3:16, God's judgment on the woman related to her fruitfulness, and thus to her creation in the *imago Dei*. She would bear children, but the labor would be full of painful effort. God's punishment

---

83. Cassuto, *Genesis, Part One*, 161.
84. Wenham, *Genesis 1–15*, 79.

The Charge of God's Royal Children

did not nullify his original command (Gen 1:28), but rather changed the context in which obedience would be possible. The same is true for the man's punishment in Genesis 3:17. God explicitly stated the man's punishment stemmed from his decision to ignore God's prohibition. God thus reminded the man of God's supremacy in the created order, and the man's failure to submit to God's command. As with the woman's punishment, the curse of the ground in Genesis 3:17b–19 relates to humanity's creation in the *imago Dei*. God did not alter his command for humanity to rule the earth and subdue it (Gen 1:28) or to work and keep it (Gen 2:5, 15). The command and responsibility remained intact. Whereas the harmony and perfection of creation in Genesis 1–2 made the tending of the garden a job of relative ease, the disruption caused by Adam's sin rendered the stewardship and responsibility of dominion much more difficult. The land would yield its fruit only by pain, by the sweat of Adam's brow. Furthermore, Genesis 3:19 states that the man would indeed return to dust, a statement that anticipated death in the genealogies to come. The decision of the man and the woman to pursue an alternate godlikeness than they were originally given, to defy God's authority, and to usurp an authority that did not rightly belong to them fundamentally changed the environment in which they would live. But it did not negate humanity's responsibility as royal children.

Genesis 3:20–24 is an epilogue that tragically reverses the harmonious conclusion of the epilogue of the previous episode in Genesis 2:24–25. The beauty and harmony of the man's relationship with his wife, and the perfect intimacy they enjoyed with one another and with God, was gone. The man named his wife Eve, "because she was the mother of all living." (כִּי הִוא הָיְתָה אֵם כָּל־חָי). Adam's act of naming Eve echoed back to the naming of the animals (Gen 2:19),[85] but also demonstrated Adam's faith that God's blessing would culminate in offspring.[86] In an act of mercy and provision, God clothed their nakedness and shame (Gen 3:21). Cassuto noted that in providing clothing and in promising that humanity's fruitfulness would continue, albeit with great pain, God acted as a father who made sure his children would have what they needed in the new environment of a hostile world.[87] God acted as a benevolent father even after his son and daughter had rebelled. God's provisions amidst punishment corresponds to God's

---

85. Cotter, *Genesis*, 35.
86. Hamilton, *Genesis*, 206–7.
87. Cassuto, *Genesis, Part One*, 163–64.

original provision in Genesis 1:28.[88] Once again, God's commands and commission for his image bearers remained unchanged.[89]

Having provided for their needs, in Genesis 3:22–23 God sent (שׁלח) the man and woman out from the garden to prevent them from eating from the tree of life. God's decision is an apparent act of mercy, as both the man and the woman knew good and evil, and eternal life would bring eternal misery.[90] Genesis 3:24 describes God casting out (גרשׁ) the man from the garden, a stronger statement that perhaps relates to humanity's sin as an act of defilement. God appointed cherubim to guard the way to the tree of life (Gen 3:24). Thus, the man and the woman would have to fulfill their calling as royal sons in a world distant from God and hostile to God's purposes for them.

Genesis 4

As is the case with the narratives in Genesis 2–3, the narrative of Genesis 4 uses the *imago Dei* as a governing concept that enables the reader to evaluate the actions of the characters and the flow of the plot. Genesis 4:1–2 describes Adam knowing his wife, Eve, and her giving birth to two sons, Cain in Genesis 4:1 and Abel in Genesis 4:2. In these verses, the reader sees the first fulfillments of God's command in Genesis 1:28. Yet, very quickly the narrative reveals Cain's rebellious attitude, as well as his refusal to submit to God and maintain a proper relationship with his brother. Whereas Genesis 2–3 focused on the relationship of the man and woman vis-à-vis God and creation, Genesis 4 adds the proper relationship of brothers.

Genesis 4:3–4 describes both Cain and Abel offering a gift (מִנְחָה) to God. At the outset, by offering a gift directly to God, the author showed that humanity still enjoyed a relationship with God. Ostensibly, Cain and Abel both recognized God's lordship over creation and thus recognized the order God established in Genesis 1–2. God still reigned supreme and was worthy of worship. He was still the High King, and Cain and Abel both recognized his authority.

After God accepted Abel's offering, but did not accept Cain's, Cain's response betrayed the true state of his heart. God came to Cain, in a similar way as he came to Adam and Eve, and asked him a series of questions:

---

88. Cassuto, *Genesis, Part One*, 164.
89. Hamilton, *Genesis*, 206–7.
90. Waltke, *Genesis*, 96, described death as "both a judgment and a release."

The Charge of God's Royal Children

"Why are you furious and why has your face fallen?" (לָמָּה חָרָה לְךָ וְלָמָּה נָפְלוּ פָנֶיךָ). In Genesis 4:7, God encouraged Cain with the possibility of Cain being exalted if he did what was good (הֲלוֹא אִם־תֵּיטִיב שְׂאֵת). God also warned Cain that sin lay in wait and its desire was for him (חַטָּאת רֹבֵץ וְאֵלֶיךָ תְּשׁוּקָתוֹ), and that Cain must master it (וְאַתָּה תִּמְשָׁל־בּוֹ). By personifying sin with desires and the ability to lie in wait, God related to Cain the power and danger of sin's temptation. Here, as with Adam and Eve in Genesis 3, the temptation was for Cain to act rashly, succumb to his own desires rather than submitting to God's direction, and step outside his proper authority. As in Genesis 3, sin threatened to undermine humanity's God-ordained dominion.

Tragically, rather than heeding God's warning, Cain did not exercise proper dominion and rule over sin, but rather allowed sin to master him. The story of Genesis 4 follows a similar pattern as the story of Genesis 3, with both highlighting the fragmentation of human relationships and humanity's denial of God's authority. In the story of Cain and Abel, the familial relationship between Cain and Abel comes to the fore. The author referred to Abel as a "brother" (אָח) a total of seven times in the passage. In his rebuke and punishment of Cain, God referred to Abel as "your brother" (Gen 4:9) and twice referred to "your brother's blood" (דְּמֵי אָחִיךָ, Gen 4:10, 11). The emphasis on brotherhood serves at least two purposes. First, Cain's act of murder was that much more heinous because of his brotherhood with Abel. Clearly, God intended for the brothers to live in harmony with one another and with God. Second, the family ties pointed back to the family connection inherent in humanity being made in the likeness of God (Gen 5:1). Royal sonship entails royal brotherhood. As royal sons, Cain and Abel had a responsibility to God *and* to one another. Cain's refusal to listen to God's warning culminated in his denial of his responsibility vis-à-vis God and vis-à-vis his brother. Cain's decision thus represented an abject denial of an essential aspect of royal sonship and responsibility.

The reader may detect an ironic reference in Cain's retort to God. Similar to God asking the man where he was (Gen 3:9), God asked Cain, "Where is your brother, Abel?" (אֵי הֶבֶל אָחִיךָ). Cain lied and retorted with a question of his own: "Am I my brother's keeper?" (הֲשֹׁמֵר אָחִי אָנֹכִי). Genesis 4:2 describes Cain as a "worker" (עֹבֵד) of the ground, using the same root God used to describe the man's responsibility to work the garden in Genesis 2:15. Cain's question uses שמר, the other verbal root that occurred in Genesis 2:15, where God created the man to "keep" or "maintain" the garden. Cain's retort might have subtly referenced God's original purpose and implied that God intended for Cain to work and keep the land, not to protect or guard his brother. In that sense, Cain suggested he had no authority over Abel and no responsibility for his well-being. Yet, the author's repetition of the word "brother" implies that Cain *did* have a responsibility that he refused to recognize or accept.[91] God was not adding a new responsibility to Cain, but rather pointing him back to the original intention for harmony within the family of God. By not recognizing Abel's creation in the *imago Dei*, and by denying his responsibility under God and as Abel's brother, Cain fell prey to his own sinful desires and received a curse as a punishment.

God's punishment was in keeping with Cain's rebellious heart and actions. To this point in the narrative, God had cursed (ארר) only the serpent (Gen 3:14) and the ground (Gen 3:17). In Genesis 4:11, God extended a curse to Cain himself. God's cursing of Cain speaks to the seriousness of the crime, and the similarity of Cain's punishment with the punishment of the serpent may reference God's statement that the serpent would have offspring who would live at enmity with the offspring of the woman (Gen 3:15). God also intensified the curse of the ground for Cain, stating that it would never again provide its yield (Gen 4:12). Once again, God's curse of the ground related to the original dominion that royal sons were to exercise over the land (Gen 1:26, 28, 2:5, 15). Whereas Adam and Eve could no longer dwell in the garden, Cain must now live as a vagrant with no home on the earth.

Cain's response in Genesis 4:13–14 echoes back to the story of Genesis 3. Cain declared that he must hide (סתר) from God. Whereas Adam and Eve hid from God momentarily (Gen 3:10), Cain's hiding would be a perpetual reality. Furthermore, Cain expressed fear that whoever found him would kill him (Gen 4:15). In response, God protected Cain from capital punishment and stated that whoever killed him would suffer vengeance, apparently from God himself, seven times over (שִׁבְעָתַיִם יֻקָּם).[92] Interestingly, God's statement in Genesis 4:15 seems to be in direct contrast to God's statement in Genesis 9:5–6 regarding capital punishment, a text that also references the killing of a brother and the creation of humanity in the *imago*

---

91. Keiser, "Genesis 1–11," 144, hinted at the significance of Cain's remark and its relation to his responsibility toward his brother.

92. Wenham, *Genesis 1–15*, 109.

Dei.[93] After God placed a mark on Cain, Cain left the presence of God and lived in the land of Nod, east of Eden. Cain's expulsion from God's presence once again mirrored the expulsion of Adam and Eve from the garden.

As the reader compares Genesis 2–3 and Genesis 4:1–15, several similarities emerge. Both stories describe a tranquil and harmonious beginning. Both texts describe the temptation to undermine God's created order and defy God's warning and prohibitions (Gen 2:17, 4:7).[94] Both texts describe the temptation to undermine and repudiate God's rightful authority. Both texts culminate in shame, burdens, and curses. Both texts conclude with the expulsion of the main characters from the presence of God. The main difference between the stories is the increase in severity of the sin in Genesis 4, as well as Cain's awareness and deliberation over sin. Thus, the story of Genesis 4 is like Genesis 3 in that it features rebellion against God's created order, a rupture in human familial relationship, and the limitation and increased difficulty of human dominion that results. As the severity of sin increases, so God's curse and punishment increases with it. What began as eating a piece of forbidden fruit grows into a murderous appetite for vengeance. The context of growing defiance, sin, and punishment then sets the stage for the next pericope, the line of Cain and the defiance of Lamech.

Genesis 4:17–24 recounts a seven-generation genealogy that culminates in the taunt of Lamech. The new section begins with a similar statement as Genesis 4:1. Cain knew his wife and she bore a son, Enoch. Cain, in a possible act of defiance of God's curse, built a city and named it after his son (Gen 4:17).[95] As the line of Cain continued, sin and rebellion found a new embodiment in the person of Lamech.

Before Lamech's taunt, the author described Lamech's two wives and four children. Lamech's offspring appear as important figures in the development of civilization and the arts.[96] Since the text presents Lamech in a negative light, the question arises as to why the author described cultural progress in this passage. In answer, Hart wrote:

---

93. Cassuto, *Genesis, Part One*, 221, argued that the reason God did not take Cain's life is that the purpose of capital punishment was to provide an example and warning to others. As Adam and Eve were the only other people, God had no reason to make an example of Cain, according to Cassuto.

94. While Genesis 4:7 does not provide a prohibition in the grammatical sense, God's warning functions in the story with a similar force of prohibition.

95. Hamilton, *Genesis*, 237–38.

96. See Lowery, *Toward a Poetics*, 7, for an analysis of the genre of Genesis 4:17–22.

By placing this technical and cultural progress within the genealogy of Cain, the biblical writer is certainly suggesting that all of human culture is in some way tainted by sin, a taint emphasized by the ferocity of Lamech (vv. 23–24), but he is fundamentally favorable to these advances in man's rule over the natural world.[97]

The development of civilization is not inherently evil, and even seems to hold potential for good. Yet, the sin of Cain and its culmination in Lamech looms as a shadow over the entire enterprise of civilization. Just as Cain built a city for his son, and Lamech's life was self-centered, so the other civilizational achievements are oriented toward the glory of humanity rather than the glory of God. The text does not describe repentance, offerings, or any other indications that the line of Cain turned back to God. Thus, the description in Genesis 4:20–21 provides a grim and negative portrait of the relationship with humanity God intended from the beginning.

The appalling nature of human rebellion finds voice in Lamech's taunt. First, Lamech defied the created order by having two wives. While nowhere does the author explicitly condemn Lamech's polygamy, by associating polygamy with a person who demonstrated an oppressive, murderous appetite, the text presents it as a negative development. Furthermore, considering God's precedent in Genesis 2, the text presents polygamy as rebellion against God's created order. God brought the gift of one woman to the man in Genesis 2:22, and Genesis 2:24 clearly states that a man will leave his father and mother to join with his wife, singular. Furthermore, given God's intention for humanity to be fruitful and multiply, God could have easily expedited the process of multiplication by creating and presenting multiple women to the man. But God did not. By establishing and blessing the precedent of one man and one woman, God clearly intended for monogamy to be the model for future generations.

As Lamech launched into his poetic taunt, he identified the audience as his two wives, Adah and Zillah (Gen 4:23). That Lamech would address his aggressive taunt toward his wives indicates that the harmonious relationship between the man and woman in the garden (Gen 2:24–25) had completely deteriorated. Lamech boasted about killing a young man (יֶלֶד) for striking him.[98] In boasting about his own murderous appetites, his exponential increase in rage and defiance, and his unrestrained and indiscriminate vengeance for only a slight injury, Lamech celebrated his

---

97. Hart, "Genesis 1:1—2:3 as a Prologue," 335.
98. See the brief but sound argument in Miller, "*Yeled* in the Song."

sovereignty and challenged anyone who would defy him. Lamech asserted an illegitimate form of authority over his wives and anyone weaker than he. Furthermore, rather than succumbing to sin as Adam, Eve, and Cain had, Lamech exalted in his rebellion.[99] Thus, the final picture of the line of Cain is one of oppressive, murderous, and unrestrained evil. Lamech was a man who taunted his wives, killed children, and did so in high-handed defiance of God. He overturned every part of God's mandate for humanity and, in that sense, was the antithesis of a submissive royal son.

Despite the severity of Lamech's sin, Genesis 4:25–26 ends the *toledot* of the heavens and the earth with a note of hope. Adam once again knew his wife, and she gave birth to a son. Eve named the boy Seth and explicitly stated that God had provided Adam and Eve with another seed (זֶרַע) in place of Abel. The statement draws the reader's attention back to the enmity between the seed of the serpent and the seed of the woman in Genesis 3:15, and the promise that Genesis 3:15 contains. The line of Seth continues through Enosh in a way that creates a narrative seam between the current section and the new *toledot* that begins in Genesis 5:1. Genesis 4:26 ends the section with the positive statement, "At that time people began to call on the name of the Lord" (אָז הוּחַל לִקְרֹא בְּשֵׁם יְהוָה). By ending the section with a positive statement and associating it with the line of Seth, the author leads the reader to see a hint of promise against the dark backdrop of sin.[100] By calling on the name of God, at least some royal sons expressed a desire to walk under God's authority and follow his expressed purposes for humanity.

In sum, the *toledot* of the heavens and the earth portrays a tragic picture of royal sons who, though given the opportunity to live in perfect harmony with God and each other, were not content with their royal responsibility and position. Rather than submitting to God's lordship, they allowed sin to establish its mastery over them. What began as a seemingly minor infraction in a matter of a few generations grew into fratricide and high-handed rebellion against God's created order. The section ends with a ray of hope that comes through the line of Adam through Seth, to which the next episode turns.

---

99. Kidner, *Genesis*, 78.
100. Cassuto, *Genesis, Part One*, 246–48.

A Literary Analysis of the Imago Dei in Genesis 1–11

THE *IMAGO DEI* AND THE *TOLEDOT* OF ADAM

Compared to the *toledot* of the heavens and the earth, the *toledot* of Adam is much shorter, yet it shares obvious similarities. As discussed in Chapter 3, the opening verses of Genesis 5 harken back to Genesis 1 with many intentional echoes. Among these are the reference in Genesis 5 to the "day" God created humanity, the threefold use of the verb ברא, the reference to God creating Adam in his likeness, the creation of humanity male and female, and God's blessing of humanity. Furthermore, the references to Adam being made in the likeness of God in Genesis 5:1, and the reference to Seth being made in the image and likeness of Adam in Genesis 5:3, show that the *imago Dei* continues to function as a governing category by which the reader should understand the narrative and evaluate the characters and events.

Genesis 5:3 provides a concrete example of Seth being made in the likeness of Adam, and the example helps shed light on the significance of Genesis 5:1. Just as Adam beget a son in his likeness, the description of God's creation of humanity in his likeness seems to emphasize God's divine parentage. Additional evidence for the divine parentage of God is God's naming of humanity in Genesis 5:2. Naming progeny is an act reserved for parents, as shown by Eve's naming of Seth (Gen 4:25), Seth's naming of Enosh (Gen 4:26), Adam's naming of Seth (Gen 5:3), and Lamech's naming of Noah (Gen 5:29). Also significant is the reversal of the two nouns used to describe the *imago Dei* in Genesis 1:26, דְּמוּת and צֶלֶם. דְּמוּת occurred alone in Genesis 5:1 and first in the word pair in Genesis 5:3. The introduction to the *toledot*, then, seems to emphasize the continuation of God's parental relationship with humanity, as well as the continuation of humanity's responsibilities as royal sons and daughters of God.[101]

Yet, alongside the continued reality of humanity's status as sons and daughters of God, the reality of death permeates Genesis 5. Adam and Eve, following the blessing of God (Gen 5:2), were indeed fruitful and began to multiply. In addition to the linear genealogy, the text emphasizes that Adam and his offspring had other "sons and daughters" (וַיּוֹלֶד בָּנִים וּבָנוֹת). Thus, God's blessing found immediate fulfillment in the genealogy.[102]

---

101. For additional arguments on the divine parentage of God, see Crouch, "Genesis 1:26–27 as a Statement," and Ortlund, "Image of Adam," 678–80, as well as chapter 3 of this volume.

102. Hamilton, *Genesis*, 255. Waltke, *Genesis*, 113–14. Wenham, *Genesis 1–15*, 126. Westermann, *Genesis 1–11*, 348.

Several features of the genealogy of 5:3–32 merit attention. First, the genealogy features ten generations from Adam to the sons of Noah. Each generation follows a similar formula, with the author giving information on the father's age at the time of a son's birth, the father's total age, and the death of each generation.[103] Second, in Genesis 5:24, the seventh generation in the genealogy features an aberration with Enoch, who walked with God and "was no more, for God took him" (וְאֵינֶנּוּ כִּי־לָקַח אֹתוֹ אֱלֹהִים). Enoch's close relationship with God indicates that obedience and fellowship with God is possible, even on the other side of the curse.[104] Third, the long lifespan of the antediluvian patriarchs presents a marked difference when compared to the normal lifespan of the reader. Hamilton suggested that the long lifespan could be a sign of God's blessing upon the Sethites.[105] While the lifetime of the antediluvian patriarchs greatly eclipsed the lifespan of the later patriarchs (Gen 47:9) and first readers, death still held sway due to sin. Fourth, another unique feature of the genealogy is the description of Noah's name. In Genesis 5:29, Lamech gave his son the name Noah, saying, "This one will bring comfort from the work and toil of our hands because of the ground which the Lord has cursed" (זֶה יְנַחֲמֵנוּ מִמַּעֲשֵׂנוּ וּמֵעִצְּבוֹן יָדֵינוּ מִן־הָאֲדָמָה אֲשֶׁר אֵרְרָהּ יְהוָה). The word עִצָּבוֹן is the same word used to describe the pain of childbearing in Genesis 3:14. Thus, despite the blessing of humanity's longevity and fellowship with God, the land remained cursed and the toil of working the land lingered.

The genealogy brings the unfolding narrative to the unusual story of the sons of God procreating with the daughters of man. Wenham provided an excellent overview of the various interpretations regarding the identity of the "sons of God."[106] Among these are the beliefs that "sons of god" refers to ancient kings, angels, the Sethite line, or the Cainite line. While the purpose here is not to adjudicate between all the possible theories, it is possible that an understanding of God's parentage and the creation of humanity in the *imago Dei* may shed light on the identity of the sons of God.

Meredith Kline, for instance, argued that "sons of God" is an idiomatic expression that describes despotic kingship. Kline pointed out that ancient

---

103. With the obvious exception of Noah and his sons.

104. See Cassuto, *Genesis, Part One*, 283, who said that "'walking with God' signifies walking God's ethical ways and cleaving to the virtues of a wholly righteous man."

105. Hamilton, *Genesis*, 256.

106. Wenham, *Genesis 1–15*, 138–41.

Near Eastern kings were often referred to as sons of gods.[107] He adduced the Sumerian Deluge account and the introduction to the Sumerian King List as evidence in favor of seeing kingship in Genesis 6:1–4. In both cases, "kingship was lowered from heaven" prior to the flood described.[108] According to Kline, these parallels suggest that the "sons of God" were kings who exercised despotic authority, evidenced by polygamy, which drew the just condemnation of God in the flood.[109] Kline concluded, "By this simple literary stroke the author at once caught the spirit of ancient paganism and suggested darkly the satanic shapers that formed the background of the human revolt against the King of kings. For these 'sons of the gods' were of all the seed of the serpent most like unto their father."[110] Kline believed the despotic kings referred to the Cainite line.[111]

Kline's view, however, unnecessarily limited the despotic kingship to the line of the Cainites, especially since the *toledot* section focuses on the line of Seth. Additionally, although Enoch and Noah walked with God (Gen 6:9), none of the other Sethites received favorable descriptions. According to Genesis 6:5, God saw that wickedness was widespread on the earth. Thus, there is no indication that there was an righteous line (e.g., Sethites) over and against the unrighteous line (e.g., Cainites). Rather, among the Sethites, a single family (e.g., Noah's) found favor with God despite the ubiquity of wickedness and violence in the world.

Against the interpretation of seeing the sons of God as fallen angels, Keiser argued convincingly that the "sons of God" must refer to human beings. Considering God's statement in Genesis 6:5 regarding human wickedness, Keiser argued that it is incongruous to claim that nonhuman or partially human creatures are involved. In Genesis 8:21, God explicitly stated his punishment was due to *humanity's* sin.[112] Additionally, Keiser pointed out that any interpretation that supposes divine or semidivine beings breaks dramatically with the larger context of the unfolding narrative,

---

107. Kline, "Divine Kingship," 191–92.

108. Kline, "Divine Kingship," 196–99.

109. Kline also drew a parallel between the sons of God in Genesis 6:1–4 and Nimrod in Genesis 10. Nimrod is described as a Gibborim (Gen 10:8; cf. Gen 6:4) whose kingdom was in the land of Shinar (Gen 10:10) where the tower of Babel was built (Gen 11:2). Thus, there is a textual connection between kingship and the mighty progeny of the sons of God. See Kline, "Divine Kingship," 199–204.

110. Kline, "Divine Kingship," 192.

111. Kline, "Divine Kingship," 195.

112. Keiser, "Sons of God," 108.

where such beings are never described.¹¹³ Instead, Keiser argued that the phrase "sons of God" sarcastically invokes the glory and authority humanity claimed for itself in the antediluvian world.¹¹⁴ The expression "sons of God" is an ironic description of humanity's high self-opinion. While Keiser did not believe kingship was directly in view, his argument is not mutually exclusive with Kline's.

A solution exists that builds upon the observations regarding God's divine parentage in Genesis 5:1–3 and combines the views of Keiser and Kline. As shown above, in the genealogical line of Seth, the author uses דְּמוּת to describe the relationship of Adam to Seth, and the relationship between Adam and God. Seth is made in the דְּמוּת of Adam and is his son. Adam is made in the דְּמוּת of God, and God exercised the parental prerogative of naming him Adam. In this light, the expression "sons of God" may be an idiomatic way of expressing the same relationship described in Genesis 5:1–3. This is especially possible given that the story of the "sons of God" occurs in the same *toledot* section as humans who are made in God's דְּמוּת, and this interpretation would make sense of the immediate context without introducing new characters into the story. Although it is true that elsewhere angelic beings are referred to as "sons of God" (Job 1:6; 38:7; Ps 29:1), this designation never refers to angels elsewhere in the book of Genesis.

If the author were trying to tie the two passages together, the emphasis of humanity's creation in the דְּמוּת of God in Genesis 5:1–3 provides narrative continuity. By underscoring the creation of humanity in the דְּמוּת of God, the author may be intentionally preparing the way for the reader to understand humanity's sin in Genesis 6:1–4. This interpretation coincides with Keiser's argument that the phrase "sons of God" idiomatically

---

113. Keiser, "Sons of God," 106.

114. Keiser, "Sons of God," 115–20. Keiser's argument was based on several observations: (1) the decline unfolding in the narrative from creation to the flood; (2) the comparative language of the sons of God "seeing" that which is "good," yet exploiting what they saw for their own lusts; (3) the sin of male domination in Genesis 6:2 (Keiser saw polygamy as a possibility, but saw the larger problem as the exploitation of women at the hands of powerful men. He saw possible significance in the description that men "took" wives for themselves rather than a man "clinging" to his wife, as described in Genesis 2:24. The harsher term of a man "taking" his wife, Keiser argued, echoes the curse of Genesis 3:16 where the husband rules [e.g., harshly] over his wife); and (4) the exploitation of women, he argued, explains why the text uses the subtle but important distinction between "sons of God" and "daughters of man." The guilt lies primarily with those who had seen themselves as "sons of God" and therefore exercised illegitimate prerogatives over women.

described humanity, as well as Kline's argument that humanity's failure to rule God's creation as he intended is the reason for humanity's punishment. Also, considering the functional hendiadys formed by צֶלֶם and דְּמוּת, the reference to "sons of God" as royal sons provides interpretive cohesion to the entire *toledot* section.[115]

If the "sons of God" are human beings who exercised illegitimate authority, the question arises as to what grievous sin would lead to such a strict and widespread punishment. As Kline's argued, the text likely points to widespread polygamy as the sin. Genesis 6:2 states that the sons of God took for themselves "wives from all they chose" (נָשִׁים מִכֹּל אֲשֶׁר בָּחָרוּ). Two features of the text indicate that this refers to polygamy. First, the text uses the plural of women or wives, נָשִׁים. Given the fact that the last model of human sinfulness was Lamech, who disregarded God's created order by taking two wives, the reoccurrence of polygamy is very possible. By tying the sin of the sons of God to the sin of Lamech, the author framed their action in a negative light.

The second feature, which points in a similar direction, is the statement that the sons of God took wives "from among all which they chose" (מִכֹּל אֲשֶׁר בָּחָרוּ). While it is true, as Cassuto and Wenham noted, that the language of "taking" a wife is common,[116] the text modifies this normal phrase in a way that emphasizes the plurality (מִכֹּל) and the choice (בחר) of the sons of God. While it is possible, as Cassuto argued, that the prefixed מִן functions in a partitive sense, "from among all," the emphasis on the *beauty* of the women and the *choice* of the men works against this interpretation.[117] Similarly, if an interpreter adopted the view that the sons of God are angelic rebels, it would be exceedingly strange to claim that fallen angels, driven by lust, would choose to enter into monogamous marriages. As Donat Poulet contended, "The Hebrew expression 'took to themselves wives' is inappropriate to transient intercourse, and indicative of a stable union with women, into which angels could not be supposed to enter."[118] If it is the case that the sons of God lusted after the daughters of men because of their beauty, why would they limit their lustful appetites to only one woman? Already a

---

115. See chapter 2 for argumentation on interpreting צֶלֶם and דְּמוּת as a hendiadys meaning "royal sons."

116. Cassuto, *Genesis, Part One*, 294, and Wenham, *Genesis 1–15*, 141, both argued that the phrase is a common description of marriage.

117. Cassuto, *Genesis, Part One*, 294.

118. Poulet, "Moral Causes of the Flood," 297.

human had disregarded God's divine precedent of one man for one woman, so why would angelic beings refrain from taking multiple wives?

The point is not to suggest that angelic beings are in view, but to show that, whatever the identity of the sons of God, their appetites were likely insatiable. On this interpretation, the sin of the sons of God continued in the vein of the sin of Lamech. Whereas Lamech only took two wives, the sinfulness of humanity continued to escalate in the indiscriminate choosing of wives based upon the external beauty of women and the internal lust of men. Again, the plural נָשִׁים certainly allows for this interpretation, and the statement that the sons of God took wives "from all they chose" points in that direction. Similarly, as the next pericope will show, the violence that began with Cain filled the earth (Gen 6:11), and thus there is additional evidence to read Genesis 6 in the light of the events of Genesis 4.

Indeed, it is possible to see the reference to "sons of God" as a sad irony. As those made in the *imago Dei*, God created humanity to rule under God as royal sons. Following their own appetites, the royal sons gave up their high calling for the fallen cravings of the flesh. Whereas even Lamech limited his lusts to two women, these sons of God chose from all that they saw, letting their lusts lead them. As with Lamech, the total abandonment of God-given responsibility led to the sons of God arrogating forbidden rights. Whether or not the sons of God were considered kings *per se* is not nearly as important as the fact that they were not properly exercising their authority as God's royal sons.[119]

On this view, the description of the progeny as הַנְּפִלִים and הַגִּבֹּרִים is also satirical. They were "mighty and notorious men."[120] Ironically, they are "men of name" (אַנְשֵׁי הַשֵּׁם) who are *not* named in the text. Indeed, given the judgment that follows in the flood, it seems almost impossible to understand this expression as a positive description. Furthermore, the reference to "men of name" is similar to the description of the men of Babylon who sought to make a name for themselves (Gen 11:4) in an act of blatant rebellion against God.

If the "sons of God" refers to the Sethite line, or perhaps to all the sons of Adam, God's evaluation in Genesis 6:5–8 comes into full relief. The Sethite line had fallen into the same sin as the Cainite line. What was true of Lamech is true of all the sons of God. Genesis 6:5 records that God saw that

---

119. The proposed interpretation also helps to explain why Deuteronomy 17:17 prohibits the king from having multiple wives.

120. Keiser, "Sons of God," 117.

the "evil of humanity was great on the earth" (רַבָּה רָעַת הָאָדָם בָּאָרֶץ). Seeing the evil of the human heart, God was grieved he had made humanity and declared that he would wipe humanity off the face of the earth, along with all the animals (Gen 6:7). God's reference to animals once again points back to Genesis 1:26–28 and humanity's failure to exercise proper dominion as those made in the *imago Dei*.

While this interpretation of Genesis 6:1–8 does not answer every interpretive question, the identification of the sons of God in Genesis 6:1–4 with the description in Genesis 5:1–3 may help shed light on the text. If not, Genesis 6:1–8 remains an interpretive crux. If, however, the proposed interpretation is not far off the mark, it provides a consistent narrative thread with the preceding chapters.

As in the final refrain of the *toledot* of the heavens and the earth, in the final refrain of the *toledot* of Adam, the author provided a glimpse of hope. Despite the widespread presence of human sin and failure of humanity to act as God's royal sons, Noah found grace in the eyes of the Lord (Gen 6:8).

THE *IMAGO DEI* AND THE *TOLEDOT* OF NOAH

Genesis 6:9—9:29

The *toledot* of Noah, as with the *toledot* of the heavens and the earth and the *toledot* of Adam, begins with a positive statement. Genesis 6:9 records that Noah was "a righteous and blameless man in his generation. Noah walked with God" (אִישׁ צַדִּיק תָּמִים הָיָה בְּדֹרֹתָיו אֶת־הָאֱלֹהִים הִתְהַלֶּךְ־נֹחַ). The statement that Noah was righteous "in his generation" assumes the reader is aware of the condemnation of Noah's generation in Genesis 6:5–8. That Noah walked with God aligns him with his forefather Enoch, who also walked with God and whom God also preserved (Gen 5:23).

Genesis 6:11–12 provides additional insight into God's reason for sending the flood. Genesis 6:11 records, "The earth was corrupted before God, and the earth was filled with violence" (וַתִּשָּׁחֵת הָאָרֶץ לִפְנֵי הָאֱלֹהִים וַתִּמָּלֵא הָאָרֶץ חָמָס). P. J. Harland argued that the verb שחת as well as the noun חָמָס both specify the nature of humanity's sin.[121] In the *niphal*, as שחת occurs in Genesis 6:11, the word takes on the nuance of being "ruined" or "spoiled."[122] Rather than the world being "very good," as God described it in

---

121. Harland, *Value of Human Life*, 29–40.
122. Koehler et al., *HALOT*, 4:1469–72.

The Charge of God's Royal Children

Genesis 1:31, the world had become corrupt and defiled because of human sin, particularly the sin of חָמָס. Cassuto, who saw the reference to חָמָס as a reference to general wickedness, stated that "there is no reason to suppose that the text speaks of a particular kind of wrongdoing."[123] However, in an extensive study of the word, Harland made a compelling case that a more nuanced meaning of "violence" is in view in Genesis 6:11.[124] Harland noted that חָמָס is often associated with the spilling of blood and other crimes whereby one person violates the rights and/or dignity of another.[125] This nuance of חָמָס fits well with the specific sins of violence already described in Genesis 4:1–16 and 4:23–24, as well as the possible forceful violation of women by the sons of God in Genesis 6:1–4. Importantly, Harland tied this violence to humanity's failure to live out its calling as the *imago Dei*. He wrote,

> Violence is a deliberate breach of the way ordained by God in Gen. 1:26ff, since God does not permit the oppression of one's fellows. The function of the *imago Dei* is corrupted, because instead of faithfully exercising his role as God's representative (צלם) and vice-gerent, man grasps at powers which are not rightfully his. Instead of using the dignity and power which is entrusted to the image at creation for the benefit of the world, humanity assumes an arbitrary false authority, which brings evil. The world is not just corrupt, but it is corrupted by violence. It can then be seen why the image of God is given such prominence both in the creation and in the flood. Having severed himself from God by the sin of חמס, man has made himself liable for drastic punishment by death. Humanity which commits חמס destroys itself.[126]

Harland's interpretation finds support in two further considerations. First, following the flood narrative, God spoke directly to the sin of violence and bloodshed, and did so in a way that explicitly invoked the *imago Dei* (Gen 9:6). That God would directly address the shedding of blood after the flood suggests that shedding of blood was part of his reason for sending the flood.

Second, if the sins of the sons of God in Genesis 6:1–4 does refer to polygamy, then the reference to violence in Genesis 6:11 ties together

---

123. E.g., Cassuto, *Genesis, Part Two*, 52.

124. Harland, *Value of Human Life*, 32–37.

125. Harland, *Value of Human Life*, 32–36. See also Wilson, "Blood Vengeance," 268–69.

126. Harland, *Value of Human Life*, 38.

the sin of the Sethite line with the sin of the Cainite line in another way. The Cainites, as exemplified through Cain and Lamech, fell into violence and indiscriminate bloodshed. If חָמָס in Genesis 6:12 refers to violent bloodshed, then all humanity—both Sethites and Cainites—had fallen into the same kind of violence that Cain and Lamech exemplified. That is, the world was full of those who, in the spirit and mold of Lamech, ignored God's created order, asserted their own authority, and did so in such a way that denied any kind of concern for the well-being of their fellow humans. Humanity had totally repudiated its royal responsibility, rejected God's authority, distorted God's model of marriage, and defied its duty to be fruitful and multiply. Rather than multiplying, humans were violently destroying human life. God's warning to Cain in Genesis 4:7 fell on deaf ears, and eventually all the sons of Adam succumbed to sin's temptation in the same manner as Cain and Lamech.

If the above interpretation is correct, God's decision to destroy the world becomes more explicable. Both the Sethites and the Cainites had fallen into indiscriminate violence and had become slave to their appetites for lust, power, and bloodshed. Noah and his sons alone in their generation found favor in God's eyes.[127]

Another salient feature of the account is God's call for Noah to preserve two kinds of every animal (Gen 6:19–20) and seven pairs of clean animals (Gen 7:2–3). In Genesis 6:20, God described the animals in the same way he had described them in Genesis 1:20–24, both in terms of their order of creation (e.g., birds, cattle, and creeping things) and their creation "according to their kind."[128] Westermann noted that, even in this fallen context, the relationship between humanity and the animal world remained, including the prohibition of humans to eat meat in Genesis 1:29.[129] In Genesis 6:21, God commanded Noah to bring food for himself and for the animals, implying that Noah should not use the animals on the ark for food. Thus, God's command for Noah to save the animals harkened back to humanity's responsibility and original commission in Genesis 1:26–28. As the story unfolded, Noah obeyed God, and God preserved Noah's family and the animals in the ark. When the waters finally receded,

---

127. Another piece of evidence that polygamy was a grievous sin of Noah's generation is that Noah and his sons, the only ones who found favor in God's eyes, each had only one wife (Gen 6:18; 1 Pet 3:20).

128. Wenham, *Genesis 1–15*, 179.

129. Westermann, *Genesis 1–11*, 423.

God commanded Noah and his family to come out of the ark (Gen 8:15) and then proceeded to make a covenant with Noah that consisted of both similarities and differences with the original arrangement between God and humanity at creation.

The conclusion of the flood story consists of three sections as demonstrated by the three times God spoke to Noah: Genesis 8:15–22, Genesis 9:1–7, and Genesis 9:8–17. Each section relates to humanity's relationship to God, to fellow human beings, and to creation. Together, the sections show how the postdiluvian environment was much different than the antediluvian world.

In Genesis 8:21, after God accepted the pleasing aroma of Noah's sacrifice, God stated that, despite the continuing and pervasive evil of the human heart, he would not destroy the world again as he had done in the flood. In this light, Genesis 9:1–7 represents an alteration of the previously established order. Echoing the original commandment and blessing in Genesis 1:28 and Genesis 5:2, God once again blessed Noah and his sons and commanded them to be fruitful and multiply.[130] While God's blessing remained, humanity's relationship to animals and to one another underwent a significant change in Genesis 9:2–6. In Genesis 9:2, the very animals that humanity had been called to rule and subdue as benevolent masters would be filled with the fear and terror of man. Before the flood, God had given humanity plants and fruit for food (Gen 1:29). After the flood, God gave humanity animals for food (Gen 9:3). Thus, in Genesis 9:1–4 God adjusted the scope of humanity's rule over animals. God's only prohibition for humanity was from eating food with its lifeblood still in it (Gen 9:4).

In Genesis 9:5, God transitioned from humanity's rule over animals to humanity's relationship with fellow humans. God said in Genesis 9:5 that he would require the lifeblood of any creature or human who took the life of a human. God specifically references bloodshed from "the hand of each man's brother" (מִיַּד אִישׁ אָחִיו). Genesis 9:5, then, connects God's statement to the episode with Cain, where all three features of bloodshed, brotherhood, and the possibility of capital punishment are also in view. In Genesis 4:15, God explicitly denied any person the authority to take Cain's life. Unlike the example of Cain in Genesis 4:15, God stated that he *would* now require the lifeblood of one's brother.

---

130. On the connection points between Genesis 9:1–7 and the account of creation, see Mulzac, "Genesis 9:1–7."

Genesis 9:6 continues by way of explanation of the previous verse: "Whoever sheds the blood of man, *by man* his blood shall be shed, for in the image of God he made man" (שֹׁפֵךְ דַּם הָאָדָם בָּאָדָם דָּמוֹ יִשָּׁפֵךְ כִּי בְּצֶלֶם אֱלֹהִים עָשָׂה אֶת־הָאָדָם). The narrative raises a natural question: how could God claim in Genesis 9:5 that *he* would require the blood of man, but in Genesis 9:6 claim that a *human* would carry out the sentence? The answer comes in the second half of verse 6: "For in the image of God he made humanity." Human agents, as royal sons, were originally called to act on God's behalf and by God's commission. Just as God commissioned humans in Genesis 1:26–28, human agency is justified because humanity is made in the *imago Dei*. Before the flood, humanity's rule extended only over animals and the land, but not over their fellow humans (Gen 1:26–28). In the postdiluvian world, the structure and scope of authority changed. Because of sin, particularly the bloodshed perpetuated by Cain, Lamech, and the ubiquitous violence of all humanity, God granted his royal sons a new prerogative that he had previously denied (Gen 4:15). Just as the scope of humanity's rule is in view in Genesis 1:26–28, and in Genesis 9:1–4, so the scope of humanity's is in view in Genesis 9:5–6. Given the violence that led to the flood, God no longer allowed bloodshed to occur with impunity. God granted his royal sons permission to execute capital punishment in an extension of God's own rule.[131] Yet, the new authority God granted to humanity was not indiscriminate. Later laws would detail exactly what situations merit such punishment, and God placed severe limitation upon capital punishment to prevent unjust killing (Deut 17:6, 19:15).

Genesis 9:8–17 goes on to record God's gracious covenant with Noah, his sons, and every living creature. Once again, in Genesis 9:10, the text lists all the living creatures in an echo of Genesis 1:24–30. In his mercy, God declared that he would place his bow in the sky. In doing so, he provided humanity a sign that his judgment was complete (Gen 9:12–16). The new order of creation, though similar in that humanity continued to live under God's blessing to be fruitful and multiply, would take place under both the shadow of sin and the promise of God's faithfulness.

The final story in the *toledot* of Noah (Gen 9:18–29) involves the action of Noah and his sons in this new environment. Genesis 9:19 showed that the blessing of God quickly took effect as Noah's three sons repopulated the earth. Verse 20 describes Noah, like Adam, as a "man of the land"

---

131. Wilson noted that the punishment of blood violence is often the responsibility of the king, as shown in 1 Kings 2 and 2 Kings 9. Wilson, "Blood Vengeance," 270.

(אִישׁ הָאֲדָמָה). In the new environment, the text story pits Noah as a kind of new Adam.[132] Just as Adam's consumption led him to experience grief and nakedness, so Noah's consumption led to his exposure and shame.

Noah planted a vineyard and became drunk from its wine (Gen 9:20). Noah was naked in his tent. When Ham, the father of Canaan (Gen 9:18), saw Noah's nakedness, Ham told his two brothers.[133] The two brothers responded honorably, made sure to turn their face away, and covered their father's shame (Gen 9:23). Noah's response to Ham resulted in Canaan being cursed (Gen 9:25) and the other sons being blessed (Gen 9:26). In cursing the future nation of Canaan, the author anticipated the shift to come in later chapters of Genesis and, indeed, in the Pentateuch. Not only did Canaan receive a curse, but Shem received a blessing that explains why his line becomes the focus of the narrative from that point. The section ends in Genesis 9:28–29 with the familiar pattern of the genealogy of Genesis 5, stating Noah's age at his death. Once again, the author intentionally wove the *toledot* sections together.

Genesis 10:1—11:9

The *toledot* of Noah's sons, as already discussed, begins in Genesis 10:1 and connects to the previous section with a conjunctive *waw*. The conjunction indicates that the section is not a major break, but rather a subsection of the larger *toledot* of Noah. The subordinate section spans from Genesis 10:1—11:9 and includes the genealogy of Noah's sons, often referred to as the Table of Nations, as well as the final narrative of Babel.

Unlike the genealogies of Genesis 4–5, the genealogy of Genesis 10 follows all three sons of Noah and expands significantly on the offspring of each child and the nations that arose from them. In this sense, the genealogy provides a detailed record of the fulfillment of God's command in Genesis 1:28, and the blessings he gave in Genesis 1:28, 5:2, and 9:1. As Robert Robinson noted, "The genealogy serves notice, after the flood, that the intention of God in creation has not been revoked; the command to

---

132. See Keiser, "Genesis 1–11," 173, for a list of ways the text presents Noah as a new Adam.

133. Hamilton, *Genesis*, 322–23, discussed the position that sees the sin of Ham as incest, but rightly concluded that this interpretation "is almost impossible to square with the biblical story." Hamilton, *Genesis*, 323.

be fruitful and multiply is renewed."[134] The genealogy, however, follows a strange order, starting with Japheth, moving to Ham, and finally ending with Shem. Yet, the order makes sense considering the focus on Shem in Genesis 11:10, and the fact that the remainder of Genesis will follow the line of Shem. The focus on Shem also ties in with the one narrative in this subsection, the narrative of Babel. In Genesis 11:4, the builders of Babel sought to make a name (שֵׁם) for themselves. As Robinson noted, by making a play on this word, the author highlighted "the ludicrous spectacle of humanity attempting to create by its own exertions a counterfeit of what God already provided."[135]

The narrative of Genesis 11:1–9 consists of a story of human foolishness and the continuation of humanity's sinful rebellion. The narrative, which harkens back to an undisclosed time, describes several elements of human rebellion against God's desires for those made in the *imago Dei*. Rather than filling the earth (Gen 1:28, 9:1), the builders of Babel desired to live in one place, lest they be dispersed (Gen 11:4). Rather than submitting to God, they desired to make a name for themselves (וְנַעֲשֶׂה־לָּנוּ שֵׁם). Cassuto pointed out that the builders ironically succeed, but only in making a "name of derogatory significance."[136] Rather than recognizing their proper place on the earth and their submission to God, they sought to build a tower with its "head in the heavens" (וְרֹאשׁוֹ בַשָּׁמַיִם). Ironically, God came down to see the city (וַיֵּרֶד יְהוָה לִרְאֹת אֶת־הָעִיר), confused their language, dispersed the people, and ended the pathetic attempt of humanity to grasp for godlikeness once again. In dispersing the people, God achieved his purpose in spreading humanity across the whole earth (Gen 11:9). Tragically, God had to do so over and against the rebellion of the people. Once again, the foolishness and rebellion of humanity is on display.

As the reader considers the sad state of affairs at the end of the Babel narrative, the contrast between the perfect world of Genesis 1–2 could not be more drastic. Rather than living in a state of perfect harmony with God and one another, and rather than embracing their relationship with God as blessed royal sons, humanity continuously rebelled and made their home in a new world of death, bloodshed, and rebellion. Far from the presence of God in Eden, humanity obstinately refused to comply with God's expressed will and instead tried to reach the heavens through their own devices. The

---

134. Robinson, "Literary Functions," 602.
135. Robinson, "Literary Functions," 603.
136. Cassuto, *Genesis, Part Two*, 242–43.

toledot of Noah, then, does not end with a note of hope as do the other *toledot* sections, except perhaps that despite the rebellion of humanity, God's purposes continued to unfold (Gen 11:9).

CONCLUSION

Genesis 1 presents the *imago Dei* as a governing evaluative category by which the reader should understand God's purposes for humanity and evaluate the actions of human beings. The above considerations show, even if briefly, that in each *toledot* section, the author tied the actions of the characters to the *imago Dei* in a way that affirms its evaluative function in the story. By explicitly referencing the *imago Dei* at crucial junctures in the narrative (Gen 1:26–28; 5:1–3; 9:6), the author showed that God's commission of humanity remained the standard by which humanity would be judged. Although humanity continued to choose rebellion over obedience, sin corrupted the earth, and the earthly environment changed drastically, God's creation of humanity in the *imago Dei* remained the constant by which the reader understands, analyzes, and evaluates the actions of the characters. Despite the failure of humanity to embrace and uphold God's plan in creation, God's calling of humanity as the *imago Dei* continues to progress and unfold in the narrative of Genesis 1–11.

Chapter 5

Analysis of Authorial Aims and Conclusion

THIS WORK PRESENTED A methodology for literary analysis in chapter 1, examined critical questions regarding the corpus material in chapter 2, performed a structural analysis of the *imago Dei* texts in chapter 3, and completed an examination of the literary function of the *imago Dei* in Genesis 1–11 in chapter 4. Building on that foundation, the study will now examine the authorial aims regarding the *imago Dei* in Genesis 1–11. Finally, the author will offer a conclusion to the study.

THE AUTHORIAL AIM OF THE *IMAGO DEI* IN GENESIS 1–11

As discussed in chapter 1, the goal of literary analysis is to make "purposive sense" of a text.[1] In analyzing the author's aims, or the illocutionary purpose of the text, the reader considers how a text "shape[s] the beliefs, practices and disposition of the target communities."[2] As Meir Sternberg stated, "Our primary business as readers is to make purposive sense of it [the text], so as to explain the *what's* and the *how's* in terms of the *why's* of communication."[3] Therefore, as the reader considers the *imago Dei* in

---

1. Sternberg, *Poetics of Biblical Narrative*, 1.
2. Collins, *Reading Genesis Well*, 44.
3. Sternberg, *Poetics of Biblical Narrative*, 1.

The Charge of God's Royal Children

Genesis 1–11, the operative question is not only how the concept of the *imago Dei* functions within the narrative, but what the *imago Dei* reveals about the author's aims and purposes.

In order to ascertain how the author intended for the *imago Dei* to shape the worldview, beliefs, and behaviors of the reader, it is helpful to summarize the key exegetical findings of the previous chapters.

Genesis 1:26–28 introduces the concept of the *imago Dei* in the most emphatic terms. The six-day pattern of creation in Genesis 1 climaxes in the creation of humanity in Genesis 1:26–28. The author presented the two words used to describe the *imago Dei*, צֶלֶם and דְּמוּת, as a functional hendiadys meaning "royal sons." Furthermore, the author tied humanity's creation in the *imago Dei* to God's purposes for humanity, in the same way that God created other parts of creation with an expressed purpose. After creating humanity in the *imago Dei*, God issued a summative and cumulative evaluation that creation was "very good" (Gen 1:31). Thus, the creation of humanity in the *imago Dei*, and humanity's willing and continued submission to God, function as a governing standard by which the reader should evaluate the events, characters, and actions that unfold.

Given the emphasis on humanity's creation in the *imago Dei* in Genesis 1, the reader should expect that the *imago Dei* will play an important role in interpreting Genesis 2–11. As the events of Genesis 2–4 unfold, the evaluative role of the *imago Dei* continues. The failure of Adam and Eve to submit to God's authority, the desire for godlikeness apart from God's provision, and the Cainite rejection of the responsibilities entailed in royal brotherhood, all relate to humanity's creation in the *imago Dei*. Humanity's failure to live out its calling as the *imago Dei* led to a disastrous descent into high-handed rebellion against God.

The second explicit referent to the *imago Dei*, Genesis 5:1–3, ties to Genesis 1:26–28 in a series of echoes, allusions, and quotations. Yet, Genesis 5:1–3 also utilizes intentional variation with Genesis 1:26–28. Both poles of the conceptual hendiadys "royal sons" are still present in Genesis 5:1–3, but the focus shifts to God's fatherhood and humanity's sonship, in keeping with the emphasis of the genealogy and unfolding narrative of the *toledot* of Adam/humanity. By invoking the *imago Dei* at the beginning of a new section, the author indicated its continued function as a governing evaluative concept through which the reader should judge the narrative. The actions of the "sons of God," in turn, showed that the line of Seth fell into the same sins (e.g., polygamy and violence) as the sons of Cain. Beholding the

Analysis of Authorial Aims and Conclusion

ubiquity of human sin (Gen 6:5–6), God judged humanity by sending the flood. Yet, Noah found grace in the eyes of the Lord, and God preserved Noah, Noah's family, and the creatures he had made. After the flood, God (re)established the created order, albeit with changes necessitated by the dark realities of the fallen world (Gen 9:1–6).

The third explicit reference to the *imago Dei*, Genesis 9:6, simply invokes the *imago Dei* as justification for punishment in cases of murder. The invocation of the *imago Dei* in this instance, along with the changes recorded in Genesis 9:1–6, represents a tragically necessary alteration to the original arrangement in Genesis 1:26–28. Because of humanity's sin, the intended harmony between God, humanity, and animals no longer pertained. God altered humanity's dominion over the animals as the fear and dread of humanity fell upon them (Gen 9:2). God gave animals over to humans as food (Gen 9:3). In light of the murderous reality between brothers (Gen 9:5; cf. Gen 4:1–16), God provided a limited authority for humans to act on God's behalf to take the life of their fellow humans. Importantly, even against the dark backdrop of the postdiluvian world, God's blessing and commission of his royal sons remained (Gen 9:1, 7).

Throughout Genesis 1–11, the author presented humanity's creation in the *imago Dei* as a reality that functions within the narrative as an evaluative ideal. As such, humanity's creation in the *imago Dei* is a conceptional cornerstone of the narrative of Genesis 1–11.

Considering the function of the *imago Dei* within the narrative of Genesis 1–11, the author's presentation of the *imago Dei* suggests the following aims:

(1) *The author presented humanity's creation in the* imago Dei *as the basis for understanding humanity's relationship with God, fellow human beings, and creation, both before and after the fall.*

The author of Genesis 1–11 presented humanity's creation in the *imago Dei* as a paradigm by which the reader should understand human relationship with God, fellow humans, and creation.[4] Because God created humans in the *imago Dei*, humanity related to God in a fundamentally different way than the rest of creation. Humanity related naturally and integrally to God as royal sons, and God acted as a benevolent Father who supplied all humanity's needs. Even after the tragic fall of humanity into sin, the author carefully articulated humanity's creation in the *imago Dei*

---

4. Hoekema, *Created in God's Image*, 75–82.

(Gen 5:1–3) and the reality of humanity's continued relationship with God as Father. After the flood, humanity's creation in the *imago Dei* grounded the ethical imperatives of the postdiluvian order (Gen 9:6). Humanity's creation in the *imago Dei* is the basis of humanity's unique relationship with God among all of creation, including humanity's moral responsibility.

Humanity's relationship to God as "royal sons" entails a familial relationship with fellow human beings. Cain's failure to recognize the responsibilities inherent in brotherhood led to sin having mastery over him (Gen 4:7). Not only did the author of Genesis link the biological relationship of all humans to Adam and Eve, but he also linked human brotherhood back to the fatherhood of God (Gen 5:1–3; 9:5–6). Human failure to live out the calling of the *imago Dei* resulted in family strife, including the failure to treat fellow human beings as brothers or sisters (Gen 4:1–16, 23–24; 9:5).

Humanity's creation in the *imago Dei* also included responsibilities vis-à-vis humanity and creation. As a part of humanity's commission as the *imago Dei*, God called upon humans to steward the earth and rule over the animals. Just as humanity's sin resulted in devastation for fellow humans, so also humanity's disobedience plunged the created world into the decay of death. As almost helpless bystanders, the earth and animals reap the consequences of humanity's failure to live out their calling as image bearers. Yet, God continued to remember humanity and the animals even amidst the flood (Gen 8:1), and his covenant after the flood included Noah, his descendants, all living things (Gen 9:9–11), and the earth (Gen 9:13). Humanity's responsibility for animals and creation is a key feature of both Genesis 1:26–28 and Genesis 9:1–6.

(2) *The author used the concept of the* imago Dei *to ground human purpose, establish expectations, and provide evaluations of human behavior in a way that provides a foundation and rationale for the Law.*

As an evaluative concept, the *imago Dei* provided the standard by which the reader should evaluate the events and characters in the unfolding narrative of Genesis 1–11. By invoking the *imago Dei* before and after the fall, the author indicated that this evaluative standard remained beyond the events of Genesis 1–11. In Genesis 9:6, the *imago Dei* relates to the later Law in at least two ways. First, Genesis 9:6 provides the first clear statement of humans ruling or rendering judgment over fellow human beings. God's original mandate in Genesis 1:26–28 included humanity's authority over

Analysis of Authorial Aims and Conclusion

animals and the earth, but it did not include rule over fellow humans. In Genesis 4:15, God prohibited anyone from taking Cain's life, despite his obvious guilt. The author presented Lamech as a defiant man who killed with impunity (Gen 4:24). Both the murderous aggression of Lamech and the violence that filled the earth (Gen 6:5) occurred in a context where God had given no explicit sanction for one human to limit the violence of others. By authorizing humans to render judgment on God's behalf in Genesis 9:5–6, the author established a new paradigm of human justice. Genesis 9:5–6 showed that God, in certain cases, was willing to delegate his governing authority to human beings. The delegation of authority is legitimate, according to Genesis 9:6, because human beings were created in the *imago Dei*. Thus, the principle of delegated authority is directly related to humanity's creation in the *imago Dei*. Just as God altered and expanded the dominion of animals in light of sin (Gen 9:1–4), God also expanded human authority over fellow human beings. While Genesis 9:6 spoke directly to capital punishment, God's permission to allow humans to act on his behalf underlies human governance in general.[5] Therefore, humanity's creation in the *imago Dei*, and the invocation of the *imago Dei* in Genesis 9:6, provides a basic rationale upon which the law rests; namely, the creation of humanity in the *imago Dei* provides the justification for why human beings may govern one another under the authority of God.[6]

Second, Genesis 1–11 transitions from the original environment, where God's commands and prohibitions were few, to a fallen world where additional laws were necessary. C. John Collins described the Pentateuch as a "constitution" for the people of Israel.[7] Following this analysis, the narrative of Genesis 1–11 functions as a kind of preamble to the Pentateuch that grounds and explains its purposes. Later passages in the Pentateuch present human obedience to the law as imitation that flows from a relationship with God.[8] In particular, Israel functioned as a son (Ex 4:22) who reflects

---

5. Tigay connected the Noachian laws to human governance. He stated, "The flood story testifies that man's failure to perform his Godlike role upon himself is what most disturbs God about man. Seen in this light, it is no accident that the rabbis inferred that the Noachide laws required man to establish courts of justice in every human settlement." The rabbinic tradition Tigay cited was Sandhedrin 56a–56b. Tigay, "Image of God," 178.

6. See McKeating, "Development of the Law," 65–67. Rather than seeing Genesis 9:6 as a rationale for the law, McKeating saw Genesis 9:6 as an exilic text that illustrates the later development of Israel's sacral laws.

7. Collins, *Reading Genesis Well*, 131–34.

8. McDowell, "In the Image of God," 43.

the holiness of God to the world. God grounded his desire for Israel to be holy as a mimetic imperative: "You shall be holy, for I, the Lord your God, am holy" (Lev 19:6). Immediately before giving the law, God expressed his desire for Israel to function as a kingdom of priests (Exod 19:6).[9] Israel's obedience to God should flow from a loving relationship (Deut 6:5). By describing humanity's relationship as those made in the *imago Dei*, the author of Genesis 1–11 established the relationship upon which the obedience to the Law is based (e.g., sonship), explained the necessity of the law (e.g., human sin and rebellion), and explained the rationale for human beings acting on God's behalf (e.g., human governance).

(3) *Humanity's creation in the* imago Dei *entails the ability of humans to carry out God's commands and requirements.*

As those made in the *imago Dei*, human beings possess certain capacities that allow them to fulfill their calling as royal sons. To claim that humans are "royal sons" is to implicitly make a claim about their qualities and capacities, since it would be nonsensical for God to give humanity the right and responsibility to rule but not endow humans with the qualities necessary to fulfill their mandate. Evidence of humanity's unique capacities as those made in the *imago Dei* abounds in Genesis 1–11. The author of Genesis 1–11 portrays human ability to reason (Gen 4:6–7), build (Gen 4:17, 11:4), play music (Gen 4:21), craft (Gen 4:22), choose (Gen 4:7, 6:2), speak (11:4–9), and obey (Gen 6:22). In a world marred by sin, human

---

9. God's description of Israel as a "kingdom of priests" in Exodus 19:6 raises the question whether priesthood is also important in understanding the *imago Dei*. John Swann argued that Exodus 19:6 is the interpretive crux of the Pentateuch and wrote that "if a central aspect for understanding the Pentateuch as a whole can be discerned, it is reasonable to use that same central aspect in the understanding of Genesis 1." Swann, Imago Dei: *A Priestly Calling*, 42. One problem with Swann's analysis is that it does not account for the evident differences between the context of Genesis 1–3 and Exodus 19:6. Reading Exodus 19:6 as an interpretive crux may inadvertently impose the tragic realities of a sinful world (e.g., priesthood) onto a sinless context where such requirements do not pertain. By reading Genesis 1 through the lens of Exodus 19:6, Swann failed to account for the tragic change of environment that followed humanity's failure to uphold the original commission as the *imago Dei*. Against Swann's interpretation, God's intent from the beginning was for all humanity to live in his presence as royal sons, not for a single nation to mediate his presence to the world (Gen 1:26–28). Indeed, such priestly mediation was unnecessary in a sinless world. Arguably, had humanity lived according to God's original intent, the priestly function of Israel would never have been necessary, in the same way that the law would not have been necessary had the first human beings obeyed God's original commands (Gal 3:9). See chapter 4 for additional discussion.

beings may use these capacities either for good or for evil. By portraying human actions in these ways, the author of Genesis 1–11 artfully depicted the abilities God gave to those made in his image. These abilities are not constitutive of the *imago Dei*, but rather are an entailment of humanity's creation as royal sons. God equipped humanity with everything needed to rule the earth, including rational, emotional, and relational capacities similar to God's own.

(4) *The author anchored human purpose and dignity in humanity's creation in the* imago Dei.

Rather than grounding human purpose and value in an abstract quality, the author of Genesis 1–11 grounded human value in the concrete reality of royal sonship. Human beings find their value precisely in their innate relationship to God. To claim that humans are royal sons and daughters of God is to make a claim regarding their purpose (e.g., live in relationship and submission to God), as well as their value (e.g., innate worth as sons and daughters). Regarding the debate about a so-called "functional" or "spiritual" interpretation of the *imago Dei*, the dichotomy between function and ontology is not present in the biblical text.[10] As evidenced by the descriptions before and after the fall, humanity's fundamental identity and worth remained despite humanity's sinful choices. Therefore, human value is not a by-product of obedience or even derived from the ability to obey.[11] By describing human beings as the *imago Dei*, both before and after sin, the author of Genesis 1–11 skillfully portrayed purpose and inherent value as royal sons and daughters of God.

EVALUATION OF THE EXPLANATORY POWER OF THE PRESENT STUDY

In chapter 1, the study proposed explanatory power as a measure of success in literary analysis. Although explanatory power inevitably involves a degree of subjectivity, interpretations that have a high degree of explanatory power are much more likely to compel other interpreters of their veracity. Five questions were proposed to help evaluate the explanatory power of a

---

10. See Hoekema, *Created in God's Image*, 66–73, for a helpful discussion of the "structural/functional" aspects of humanity's creation in the *imago Dei*.

11. For an excellent study on the implications of the doctrine of *imago Dei* for those with severe cognitive disabilities, see Hammond, *It Has Not Yet Appeared*.

proposed literary interpretation. At the conclusion to the study, it is possible to offer tentative answers to these five questions.

(1) *Does the proposed interpretation provide greater evidence of cohesion and unity within a given text (e.g., within Genesis 1–11)?*

This book has analyzed how the *imago Dei* functions within the narrative of Genesis 1–11, and the analysis has demonstrated that the *imago Dei* underlies and weaves through the various stories of Genesis 1–11. While much evidence already exists for the unity of Genesis 1–11, this present project has provided additional corroboratory evidence by showing how otherwise disparate events in the plot all relate to humanity's creation in the *imago Dei*.[12] For instance, the proposed interpretations of the *imago Dei* showed how the sins described in Genesis 1–11 relate to humanity's failure to live out its calling as royal sons. In addition, the analysis demonstrated links between passages (e.g., the sins of Cain and Lamech and the sin of the "sons of God") that otherwise seem unrelated. By identifying structural and plot links between the *imago Dei* passages, the analysis demonstrates a high degree of intentionality in the repetition of the *imago Dei*. In light of these findings, the study provides additional evidence of cohesion and unity in the text of Genesis 1–11.

(2) *Does the proposed literary reading create a greater sense of unity between a textual unit and the larger text of which the unit is a part (e.g., the relationship between Genesis 1–11 and Genesis 12–50)?*

This diagnostic question goes beyond the scope of this study, but further research might lead an interpreter to answer the question in the affirmative. Even a cursory reading of Genesis demonstrates that kingship is an important part of the unfolding narrative. For instance, Joseph functions as vice-regent of Pharaoh and is a favored son who experiences the blessing of his father. Furthermore, the analysis has shown how references to the *imago Dei* (e.g., Gen 9:6) lay a foundation and rationale for the Law. In light of their creation in the *imago Dei*, humans received authorization to act on God's behalf. After the flood, God expanded human authority, albeit in a limited way, so that humans could also govern fellow humans. Thus, further study might show that the interpretations offered by this literary analysis provide a greater sense of unity between Genesis 1–11, Genesis, and the Pentateuch as a whole.

---

12. See chapter 2 for argumentation and evidence for the unity of Genesis 1–11.

Analysis of Authorial Aims and Conclusion

(3) *Does the proposed literary reading utilize literary methods that are clearly discernible in other texts?*

This diagnostic question seeks to ensure that a proposed literary interpretation is not an arbitrary invention of the reader's imagination. Thus, if a literary analysis of the *imago Dei* in Genesis 1–11 is built upon well-established literary techniques (e.g., repetition and plot), it is more likely to convince. The present project has sought to use structural analysis and plot analysis, including an examination of inter-textual echoes and the repetition of the *imago Dei* in the beginning (Gen 1:26–28), middle (Gen 5:1–3), and end (Gen 9:6) of the story of Genesis 1–11. The analysis was not based on new techniques of literary analysis.

(4) *Does the proposed literary reading shed light on other grammatical, historical, or theological insights of the text?*

This diagnostic question highlights the interplay of narrative readings and other exegetical procedures. If a proposed literary reading completely overthrows the historical, grammatical, and theological findings of centuries of research, it is obviously less likely to be the correct reading. Conversely, if a proposed narrative reading illuminates independently corroborated grammatical, historical, and theological insights, it is more likely to be true. Thus, if a narrative reading of the *imago Dei* in Genesis 1–11 helps to explain other exegetical insights of the text, it is more likely to convince.

The current project helps shed light on features of Genesis 1–11 that would otherwise remain opaque. For instance, understanding the *imago Dei* as royals sons helps to explain the word choice and reversal of governing prepositions between Genesis 1:26–28 and Genesis 5:1–3, illuminates the identity of the sons of God in Genesis 6:1–4, ties together the sins of the Cainite line (Gen 4:1–26) and the Sethite line (Gen 5:1—6:8) in a way that makes sense of God's judgment (Gen 6:5–7), explains the interlinkage of the Cain and Abel narrative and the reference to the killing of a brother in Genesis 9:5, and shows the possibility of Genesis 9:6 representing a tragic expansion of humanity's authority over fellow human beings. Thus, the interpretations offered in this dissertation comport with and potentially shed light on other grammatical and historical findings.

(5) *Does the proposed literary reading help to explain later allusions to a text (e.g., other teachings on the* imago Dei *in the Old Testament)?*

The Charge of God's Royal Children

Outside of Genesis 1–11, no other Old Testament passage explicitly references the *imago Dei*. Although the phrase itself does not occur, Psalm 8 seems to interpret humanity's creation in the *imago Dei*. Thus, if a narrative analysis of the *imago Dei* in Genesis 1–11 can be shown to comport with the teaching of Psalm 8, it is more likely to be compelling.

The invocation of God's covenant name in Psalm 8:1, along with the reference to God as "our Lord" (אֲדֹנֵינוּ), sets the Psalm within the context of the corporate worship of God's covenant people.[13] The opening verse of Psalm 8 extols the "magnificence" (אַדִּיר) of God's name and the "majesty" (הוֹד) of God through the earth (Ps 8:1–2). הוֹד is often associated with royalty and is used in Psalm 21:6 to describe the majesty God bestowed upon a king, as well as in Psalm 45:4 to describe the majesty of the warrior king.[14] Likewise, אַדִּיר refers to the magnificence or might of a king in Psalm 136:18.[15] The descriptions of Psalm 8:1–3 present God as a "Creator king" who created and rules over the world.[16] In light of God's majesty and magnificence in creation, the psalmist marveled that God is mindful of or would care for the sons of man/Adam (וּבֶן־אָדָם, Ps 8:3–4). Translations render וּבֶן־אָדָם variously as "son of man" (e.g., NASB, ESV), "human being" (e.g., CSB), or "mankind" (e.g., NET, NIV). The reference to the "son of man" likely refers to humanity's lowly origins as those made from the dust.[17] Given the clear echo of Genesis 1:26–28 in Psalm 8:6–8, "son of man" may also point back to Adam, the first man.

Despite humanity's lowliness, especially compared to the magnificence of God, God crowned humanity with glory (כָּבוֹד) and honor (הָדָר). In both Psalm 21:6 and Psalm 45:4, הוֹד occurs with הָדָר to form a hendiadys that describes the fullness of a king's glory. In Psalm 8:6, the writer stated that God made humans to rule (משל) over the work of his hands. Psalm 8:7–8 includes a list of animals that echoes the list in Genesis 1:26–28.[18]

---

13. Jacobson described the reference to אָדוֹן as a "royal title." Jacobson, "Psalm 8," 122.

14. Koehler et al., *HALOT*, 1:241.

15. Koehler et al., *HALOT*, 1:241.

16. Jacobson, "Psalm 8," 123.

17. Shaefer, *Psalms*, 24.

18. Psalm 8:6 uses an enigmatic and oft debated phrase, וַתְּחַסְּרֵהוּ מְּעַט מֵאֱלֹהִים. The phrase most woodenly reads, "You have lowered him a little from God/gods." Most English translations supply a verb of creation for clarity (cf. NASB, "made him a little lower than God"; ESV, "you have made him a little lower than the heavenly beings"; NET, "and make him a little less than the heavenly beings"). Although the discussion whether God

Analysis of Authorial Aims and Conclusion

As a whole, Psalm 8 describes the incomparable majesty of God, but also depicts humanity as those given a royal authority and assignment. While Psalm 8 does not fully flesh out the idea of "royal sonship," humanity's royal status and continued commission is obviously present. Psalm 8, however, reminds humans of their humble status as those who rule under the high kingship of God. Thus, the emphasis on the royalty of humanity in Psalm 8 is consonant with the analysis of the *imago Dei* in Genesis 1–11. The cohesion between Psalm 8 and the interpretations offered in the present analysis of Genesis 1–11 render the present analysis more compelling.

AREAS OF FURTHER RESEARCH

Using the tools of literary analysis, the following areas of continued research may bear fruit within *imago Dei* studies.

First, if the *imago Dei* functions as a governing evaluative concept in Genesis 1–11, how might the concept continue to function in the rest of Genesis? Does humanity's creation in the *imago Dei* bear on how the reader should judge the decisions and actions of Abraham, Isaac, Jacob, Joseph, and others?

Second, how do the findings of the present project relate to other thematic elements or features of Genesis 1–11 or later texts? For instance, Jason DeRouchie claimed that humanity's "blessing-commission" in Genesis 1:28 plays "a central role in understanding the development and narrowing in the book [of Genesis]."[19] DeRouchie related the blessing-commission to God's statement in Genesis 3:15 that a seed of the woman will crush the head of the serpent.[20] The insights offered in this analysis may provide evidence to support and elaborate upon DeRouchie's claims. DeRouchie focused more on God's command for humans to be fruitful and multiply than other aspects of humanity's creation in the *imago Dei* (e.g., ruling).[21] But, if the *imago Dei* refers more particularly to human beings' role as royal

---

or other heavenly beings is in view in Psalm 8:6 is interesting and important, it is sufficient for the purposes of this project to note that the preceding references to the lordship, majesty, and power of Yahweh in Psalm 8:1, and the reference to God crowning humanity and humanity's dominion in Palms 8:6–8, indicate that the comparison of humanity to God/gods is a reference to humanity's place in the created order.

19. DeRouchie, "Blessing-Commission," 226.
20. DeRouchie, "Blessing-Commission," 228.
21. DeRouchie, "Blessing-Commission," 226.

sons of God, the reader would expect that the seed of the woman who will crush the head of the serpent will do so as a royal son. Taking this insight further, the narrowing effect of the book may serve the purpose of identifying this royal seed.[22]

Third, further research is necessary to determine how understanding the *imago Dei* as "royal sons" relates to kingship in the rest of the Pentateuch. Is it possible that the analysis of this book might help explain the rationale for the kingship laws in the Pentateuch? For instance, Deuteronomy 17:14–20 details the laws of kingship and explicitly references both brotherhood (Deut 17:14, "one from among your brothers"; Deut 17:20, "his heart shall not be lifted up among his brothers") and polygamy (Deut 17:17, "he shall not acquire many wives"). Both elements are present in Genesis 1–11. More research could help shed light on the relationship of the *imago Dei* in Genesis 1–11 and later texts on kingship.

Fourth, although beyond the purposes of this study, a confessional Christian would desire to compare the results of the present study to relevant teachings in the New Testament. The author has begun to address this question in other work.[23] The New Testament presents Jesus Christ as the *imago Dei par excellence*. Christ is the perfect "royal son" whose divine nature and perfect obedience qualify him for worship (Phil 2:5–11). While humanity is made *in* the image of God, Christ *is* "the image of the invisible God, the firstborn over all creation" who rules over all authority in heaven and on earth (Col 1:15–20). God predestined his sons and daughters to be conformed to the image of his Son so that he might be the "firstborn among many brethren" (Rom 8:28–29). James stated that "with the tongue we bless our Lord and Father, and with it we curse people who are made in God's likeness" (Jas 3:9). James thus related humanity's "likeness" (ὁμοίωσιν) to God with God's Fatherhood. More research is necessary to show how elements in Genesis 1:26–28, 5:1–3, and 9:6 find parallels in New Testament descriptions of Jesus Christ as the *imago Dei*.

Finally, while the present study examined Genesis 1–11 as a coherent literary unit, further research might fruitfully consider the implications of literary studies of Genesis 1–11 for source criticism. To the extent an interpreter can convincingly demonstrate narrative coherence in sources

---

22. DeRouchie noted that the final narrowing of Genesis focuses on the kingly line of Judah (Gen 49:10), but he did not connect this to any kind of royal connotation in the seed of the woman as an image bearer of God. DeRouchie, "Blessing-Commission," 229.

23. Howe, "God's Cosmic King."

Analysis of Authorial Aims and Conclusion

believed to be of different origin, the hypothesis that multiple sources exist is undermined. One might examine how the analyses of the present study cut through sections from purportedly different sources. While the goal of the study was not to undermine text critical assumptions, narrative considerations continue to assay the conclusions of much of modern Old Testament scholarship regarding multiple authors.

CONCLUSION

The project has shown that the *imago Dei* in Genesis 1–11 link together in a web of intertextual echoes and narrative allusions. The *imago Dei* provides a standard by which the reader should evaluate the events, characters, and actions that unfold in the narrative of Genesis 1–11. Indeed, the unfolding plot of Genesis 1–11 is explicable only in reference to God's original creation of humanity in the *imago Dei* and humanity's failure to fulfill God's design. The sins of Genesis 1–11 relate directly to humanity's failure to live under God as royal sons and daughters. In Genesis 5:1–3 and Genesis 9:6, the author references the *imago Dei* to point the reader back to God's original purpose, as well as to point the reader forward to God's continued purposes for humanity in a fallen world. If one were to remove the references to humanity's creation in the *imago Dei* in Genesis 1:26–28, Genesis 5:1–3, and Genesis 9:6, it would be difficult, if not impossible, to understand the author's evaluation of the events and characters. Given the description of humanity's creation in the *imago Dei*, the reader comes to understand the author's perspective on humanity's proper role vis-à-vis God, fellow humans, and creation.

The study of the *imago Dei* will no doubt continue as it has for thousands of years, and the mountain of material written on the *imago Dei* will continue to grow. And it should. The present study has sought to add a small pebble to the mountain by analyzing the explicit references to the *imago Dei* in the narrative context of Genesis 1–11. The author of Genesis 1–11 articulated humanity's creation in the *imago Dei* in explicit statements and portrayed it with artistic mastery. As the reader of Genesis 1–11 considers the perfection and beauty of God in creation and the abysmal fall of humanity from glory to sin—yet also beholds the continued mercy and blessing of God on humanity as his royal sons (Gen 1:28; 5:2; 9:1)—the reader comes to understand both the nature of humanity and the heart of God. By anchoring the story of Genesis 1–11 in the *imago Dei*, the author sealed in the minds of the reader the glory inherent in humanity as royal sons and daughters and the tragic outcome of humanity's rejection of its God-given purpose. The author's depiction of humanity's creation in the *imago Dei*, and humanity's tragic failure, launches the story forward into the continued work of God to redeem his royal sons and daughters so that they might live in his presence once more.

As a final word, for those who see it as their calling to serve the church, the study of the *imago Dei* remains an absolute imperative, as humanity's creation in the *imago Dei* is the irreducible essence of God's call on human life. Christ himself is described as the image of God, perfectly displaying God's invisible qualities as his royal son (Col 1:15–20). By beholding the One in whose image we are made, we come to see the reality God intended for us in the beginning, as well as the model by which God is shaping us for eternity. Only by understanding the glory of human creation and the grievous consequence of human sin—a glory and grief that is portrayed most poignantly in Genesis 1–11—can we come to understand the full richness of the Gospel. The claim that Christ would die to bring many sons to glory is explicable only in the terms first recorded in Genesis 1–11: the creation of humanity in the *imago Dei*. Those who claim to be for the church must embrace the calling inherent in our creation and seek to live, by the power of the Spirit, as the royal sons and daughters God created us to be.

Bibliography

Aejmelaeus, Anneli. "Function and Interpretation of כי in Biblical Hebrew." *Journal of Biblical Literature* 105.2 (1986) 193–209.

Alexander, T. Desmond. "Genealogies, Seed and the Compositional Unity of Genesis." *Tyndale Bulletin* 44.1 (1993) 255–70.

Alexander, T. Desmond, and David W. Baker, eds. *Dictionary of the Old Testament Pentateuch: A Compendium of Contemporary Biblical Scholarship*. Downers Grove: InterVarsity, 2003.

Alter, Robert. *The Art of Biblical Narrative*. New York: Basic, 1981.

Baker, David W., and Bill T. Arnold, eds. *The Face of Old Testament Studies: A Survey of Contemporary Approaches*. Grand Rapids: Baker Academic, 1999.

Bar-Efrat, Shimon. *Narrative Art in the Bible*. New York: T&T Clark, 2004.

———. "Some Observations on the Analysis of Structure in Biblical Narrative." *Vetus Testamentum* 30.2 (1980) 154–73.

Barr, James. "The Image of God in the Book of Genesis: A Study of Terminology." *Bulletin of the John Rylands Library* 51.1 (1968) 11–26.

Beale, G. K. "Eden, the Temple, and the Church's Mission in the New Creation." *Journal of the Evangelical Theological Society* 48.1 (2005) 5–31.

———. *The Temple and the Church's Mission: A Biblical Theology of the Dwelling Place of God*. New Studies in Biblical Theology, vol. 17. Downers Grove: InterVarsity, 2004.

Bechtold, William K., III. "An Introduction to the Hermeneutics of Old Testament Narrative." *Midwestern Journal of Theology* 15.2 (2016) 51–73.

Bentzen, Aage. *Introduction to the Old Testament*. 3rd ed. Vol. 1. Copenhagen: G. E. C. Gad, 1957.

Berlin, Adele. *Poetics and Interpretation of Biblical Narrative*. Winona Lake, IN: Eisenbrauns, 1994.

Bird, Phyllis A. "'Male and Female He Created Them': Gen 1:27b in the Context of the Priestly Account of Creation." *Harvard Theological Review* 74.2 (1981) 129–59.

Block, Daniel I. "Eden: A Temple? A Reassessment of the Biblical Evidence." In *From Creation to New Creation: Biblical Theology and Exegesis*. Edited by Daniel M. Gurtner and Benjamin L. Gladd. Peabody, MA: Henrickson, 2013.

Botterweck, G. Johannes, and Helmer Ringgren, eds. *Theological Dictionary of the Old Testament*. Vol. 2. Grand Rapids: Eerdmans, 1975.

Botterweck, G. Johannes, et al., eds. *Theological Theological Dictionary of the Old Testament*. Vol. 12. Grand Rapids: Eerdmans, 2003.

Bibliography

Brichto, Herbert Chanan. *Toward a Grammar of Biblical Poetics: Tales of the Prophets.* New York: Oxford University Press, 1992.

Brown, Francis, et al. *The Enhanced Brown-Driver-Briggs Hebrew and English Lexicon.* Oxford: Clarendon, 1977.

Bullinger, E. W. *Figures of Speech Used in the Bible: Explained and Illustrated.* Reprint, Grand Rapids: Baker, 1968 (1898).

Byron, John. *Cain and Abel in Text and Tradition: Jewish and Christian Interpretations of the First Sibling Rivalry.* Themes in Biblical Narrative Jewish and Christian Traditions vol. 14. Leiden: Brill, 2011.

Calvin, John. *Genesis.* The Crossway Classic Commentaries. Edited by Alistair McGrath and J. I. Packer. Wheaton, IL: Crossway, 2001.

Carr, David M. "Biblos Geneseōs Revisited: A Synchronic Analysis of Patterns in Genesis as Part of the Torah." *Zeitschrift für die alttestamentliche Wissenschaft* 110.2 (1998) 159–72.

Cassuto, Umberto. *A Commentary on the Book of Genesis, Part One: From Adam to Noah.* Translated by Israel Abrahams. Jerusalem: Magnes, 1961.

———. *A Commentary on the Book of Genesis, Part Two: From Noah to Abraham.* Translated by Israel Abrahams. Jerusalem: Magnes, 1964.

Chambers, Nathan J. "Genesis 1.1 as the First Act of Creation." *Journal for the Study of the Old Testament* 43.3 (2019) 384–94.

Childs, Brevard S. *Introduction to the Old Testament as Scripture.* Philadelphia: Fortress, 1979.

Clines, David J. A. "The Image of God in Man." *Tyndale Bulletin* 19 (1968) 53–103. https://legacy.tyndalehouse.com/tynbul/Library/TynBull_1968_19_03_Clines_ImageOfGodInMan.pdf.

Collins, C. John. *Genesis 1–4: A Linguistic, Literary, and Theological Commentary.* Philipsburg, NJ: P&R, 2006.

———. *Reading Genesis Well: Navigating History, Poetry, Science, and Truth in Genesis 1–11.* Grand Rapids: Zondervan, 2018.

Cotter, David W. *Genesis.* Berit Olam: Studies in Hebrew Narrative and Poetry. Edited by David W. Cotter et al. Collegeville, MN: Liturgical, 2003.

Crouch, C. L. "Genesis 1:26–27 as a Statement of Humanity's Divine Parentage." *Journal of Theological Studies* 61.1 (April 2010) 1–15. https://academic.oup.com/jts/article/61/1/1/1673983.

Davidson, Richard M. "Earth's First Sanctuary: Genesis 1–3 and Parallel Creation Accounts." *Andrews University Seminary Studies* 53.1 (2015) 65–89.

Dempster, Stephen G. *Dominion and Dynasty: A Theology of the Hebrew Bible.* New Studies in Biblical Theology, vol. 15. Downers Grove: InterVarsity, 2006.

DeRouchie, Jason S. "The Blessing-Commission, the Promised Offspring, and the *Toledot* Structure of Genesis." *Journal of the Evangelical Theological Society* 56.2 (2013) 219–47.

Dorsey, David A. *The Literary Structure of the Old Testament: A Commentary on Genesis-Malachi.* Grand Rapids: Baker Academic, 1999.

Dozeman, Thomas B., et al., eds. *The Pentateuch: International Perspectives on Current Research.* Forschungen zum Alten Testament 78. Tübingen: Mohr Siebeck, 2011.

Driver, S. R. *The Book of Genesis.* Westminster Commentaries. 4th ed. London: Methuen, 1904.

Bibliography

Fishbane, Michael A. *Biblical Text and Texture: A Literary Reading of Selected Texts*. Oxford: Oneworld, 1998.

Fokkelman, J. P. *Narrative Art and Poetry in the Books of Samuel*. Vol. 2. Assen: Van Gorcum, 1986.

Fried, David. "The Image of God and the Literary Interdependence of Genesis 1 and Genesis 2–3." *Jewish Bible Quarterly* 47.4 (2019) 211–16.

Garr, W. Randall. "'Image' and 'Likeness' in the Inscription from Tell Fakhariyeh." *Israel Exploration Journal* 50.3/4 (January 2000) 227–34.

———. *In His Own Image and Likeness: Humanity, Divinity, and Monotheism*. Culture and History of the Ancient Near East, vol. 15. Boston: Brill, 2003.

Garrett, Duane. *Rethinking Genesis: The Sources and Authorship of the First Book of the Pentateuch*. Grand Rapids: Baker, 1991.

Gentry, Peter J. "Humanity as the Divine Image in Genesis 1:26–28." *Eikon* 2.1 (Spring 2020) 56–69. https://cbmw.org/2020/06/10/humanity-as-the-divine-image-in-genesis-126-28//.

Gentry, Peter J., and Stephen J. Wellum. *Kingdom through Covenant: A Biblical-Theological Understanding of the Covenants*. Wheaton: Crossway, 2012.

Gunnlaugur, A. Jónsson. *The Image of God: Genesis 1:26–28 in a Century of Old Testament Research*. Translated by Lorraine Svendsen. Revised by Michael S. Cheney. Coniectanea Biblica Old Testament Series, vol. 26. Stockholm: Almqvist & Wiksell, 1988.

Hamilton, Victor P. *The Book of Genesis: Chapters 1–17*. The New International Commentary on the Old Testament. Grand Rapids: Eerdmans, 1990.

Hammond, George C. *It Has Not Yet Appeared What We Shall Be: A Reconsideration of the* Imago Dei *in Light of Those with Severe Cognitive Disabilities*. Phillipsburg, NJ: P&R, 2017.

Harland, P. J. *The Value of Human Life: A Study of the Story of the Flood (Genesis 6–9)*. Supplements to *Vetus Testamentum*, vol. 64. Boston: Brill, 1996.

Harrison, R. K. *Introduction to the Old Testament*. Grand Rapids: Eerdmans, 1969.

Hart, Ian. "Genesis 1:1—2:3 as a Prologue to the Book of Genesis." *Tyndale Bulletin* 46.2 (1995) 315–36.

Hartley, John E. *Genesis*. New International Biblical Commentary. Edited by Robert L. Hubbard Jr. and Roberk K. Johnston. Peabody, MA: Hendrickson, 2000.

Hasel, Gerhard F. "Meaning of 'Let Us' in Gn 1:26." *Andrews University Seminary Studies* 13.1 (1975) 58–66.

Hehn, Johannes. "Zum Terminus 'Bild Gottes.'" In *Festschrift Eduard Sachau zum siebzigsten Geburtstage*, edited by Gotthold Weil, 36–52. Berlin: G. Reimer, 1915.

Hendel, Ronald S. *The Text of Genesis 1–11: Textual Studies and Critical Edition*. Oxford: Oxford University Press, 1998.

Hess, Richard S. "Genesis 1–2 in Its Literary Context." *Tyndale Bulletin* 41.1 (1990) 143–53.

Hoekema, Anthony A. *Created in God's Image*. Carlisle, UK: Paternoster, 1994.

Howe, Timothy M. "God's Cosmic King: The Image of God in Paul." Paper presented at the Annual Meeting of the Evangelical Theological Society, Denver, CO, November 2018.

Jacobson, Rolf A. "Psalm 8." In *The Book of Psalms*, edited by Nancy L. deClaissé-Walford et al., 120–28. The New International Commentary on the Old Testament. Grand Rapids: Eerdmans, 2014.

BIBLIOGRAPHY

Jenni, Ernst, and Claus Westermann, eds. *Theological Lexicon of the Old Testament.* Peabody, MA: Hendrickson, 1997.

Joüon, S. J. Paul. *A Grammar of Biblical Hebrew.* Subsidia Biblica, vol. 14.1–14.2. Translated by T. Muraoka. Rome: Editrice Pontificio Istituto Biblico, 1991.

Kaiser, Walt. "The Literary Form of Genesis 1–11." In *New Perspectives on the Old Testament.* Edited by J. Barton Payne. Waco: Word, 1970.

Keiser, Thomas A. "Genesis 1–11: Its Literary Coherence and Theological Message." PhD diss., Dallas Theological Seminary, 2007.

———. "The 'Sons of God' in Genesis 6:1–4: A Rhetorical Characterization." *Westminster Theological Journal* 80.1 (Spring 2018) 103–20.

Kidner, Derek. *Genesis: An Introduction and Commentary.* Tyndale Old Testament Commentaries. Downers Grove: InterVarsity, 1967.

Kikawada, Isaac M., and Arthur Quinn. *Before Abraham Was: The Unity of Genesis 1–11.* Nashville: Abingdon, 1985.

Kilner, John F. *Dignity and Destiny: Humanity in the Image of God.* Grand Rapids: Eerdmans, 2015.

Kittel, Rudolf, and Wilhelm Rudolph. *Biblia Hebraica Stuttgartensia.* Stuttgart: Deutsche Bibelgesellschaft, 1997.

Kline, Meredith G. "Divine Kingship and Genesis 6:1–4." *The Westminster Theological Journal* 24.2 (May 1962) 187–204.

———. *Kingdom Prologue: Genesis Foundations for a Covenantal Worldview.* Overland Park, KS: Two Age, 2000.

Koehler, Ludwig, et al. *The Hebrew and Aramaic Lexicon of the Old Testament.* 5 vols. Leiden: E. J. Brill, 1994–2000.

Lemma, Mengistu. "Noachic Blessing and Covenant as Programmatic Divine Decrees in Genesis 9:1–17." PhD diss., Union Presbyterian Seminary, 2012.

LeMon, Joel M., ed. *Method Matters: Essays on the Interpretation of the Hebrew Bible in Honor of David L. Petersen.* Atlanta: Society of Biblical Literature, 2009.

Lichtheim, Miriam. *Ancient Egyptian Literature: A Book of Readings.* Vol. 2. Berkeley: University of California Press, 1976.

Longman, Tremper, III. "Literary Approaches to the Old Testament Study." In *The Face of Old Testament Studies: A Survey of Contemporary Approaches,* edited by David W. Baker and Bill T. Arnold, 97–115. Grand Rapids: Baker Academic, 1999.

Lowery, Daniel D. *Toward a Poetics of Genesis 1–11: Reading Genesis 4:17-22 in Its Near Eastern Context.* Bulletin for Biblical Research Supplement 7. Winona Lake, MI: Eisenbrauns, 2013.

Lust, Johan. "'For Man Shall His Blood Be Shed': Gen 9:6 in Hebrew and in Greek." In *Tradition of the Text: Studies Offered to Dominique Berthélemy in Celebration of His 70th Birthday,* edited by Gerard J. Norton and Stephen Pisano, 91–102. Göttingen: Vandenhoeck & Ruprecht, 1991.

McBride, S. Dean, Jr. "Divine Protocol: Genesis 1:1—2:3 as Prologue to the Pentateuch." In *God Who Creates: Essays in Honor of W. Sibley Towner,* edited by William P. Brown and S. Dean McBride Jr., 3–41. Grand Rapids: Eerdmans, 2000.

McConville, J. Gordon *Being Human in God's World: An Old Testament Theology of Humanity.* Grand Rapids: Baker, 2016.

McDowell, Catherine L. *The Image of God in the Garden of Eden: The Creation of Humankind in Genesis 2:5—3:24 in Light of the* mīs pî pīt pî *and* wpt-r *Rituals of*

Bibliography

Mesopotamia and Ancient Egypt. Siphrut: Literature and Theology of the Hebrew Scriptures 15. Winona Lake, IN: Eisenbrauns, 2015.

———. "'In the Image of God He Created Them': How Genesis 1:26-27 Defines the Divine-Human Relationship and Why It Matters." In *The Image of God in an Image Driven Age: Explorations in Theological Anthropology*, edited by Beth Felker Jones and Jeffrey W. Barbeau, 29-46. Downers Grove: InterVarsity, 2016.

McKeating, Henry. "The Development of the Law on Homicide in Ancient Israel." *Vetus Testamentum* 25.1 (1975) 46-68.

Merrill, Eugene. "Image of God." In *Dictionary of the Old Testament Pentateuch: A Compendium of Contemporary Biblical Scholarship*, edited by T. Desmond Alexander and David W. Baker, 441-45. Downers Grove: InterVarsity, 2003.

Middleton, J. Richard. *The Liberating Image: The Imago Dei in Genesis 1*. Grand Rapids: Brazos, 2005.

Miller, Patrick D., Jr. *Genesis 1-11: Studies in Structure and Theme*. Journal for the Study of the Old Testament Supplement Series 8. Sheffield, UK: JSOT, 1978.

———. "*Yeled* in the Song of Lamech." *Journal of Biblical Literature* 85.4 (1966) 477-78.

Muilenburg, James. "Form Criticism and Beyond." *Journal of Biblical Literature* 88.1 (1969) 1-18.

———. "The Linguistic and Rhetorical Usages of the Particle כי in the Old Testament." *Hebrew Union College Annual* 32.1 (1961) 135-60.

Mulzac, Kenneth D. "Genesis 9:1-7: Its Theological Connections with the Creation Motif." *Journal of the Adventist Theological Society* 12.1 (2001) 65-77. https://digitalcommons.andrews.edu/cgi/viewcontent.cgi?article=1284&context=jats.

Nicholson, Ernest W. *The Pentateuch in the 20th Century: The Legacy of Julius Wellhausen*. Oxford: Clarendon, 1998.

Niskanen, Paul. "The Poetics of Adam: The Creation of אדם in the Image of אלהים." *Journal of Biblical Literature* 128.3 (Fall 2009) 417-36.

Ortlund, Gavin. "Image of Adam, Son of God: Genesis 5:3 and Luke 3:38 in Intercanonical Dialogue." *Journal of the Evangelical Theological Society* 57.4 (2014) 673-88. https://etsjets.org/wp-content/uploads/2014/12/files_JETS-PDFs_57_57-4_JETS_57-4_673-88_Ortlund.pdf.

Osborne, William R. *Trees and Kings: A Comparative Analysis of Tree Imagery in Israel's Prophetic Tradition and the Ancient Near East*. Bulletin for Biblical Research Supplement 18. University Park, PA: Eisenbrauns, 2018.

Oseka, Matthew. "History of the Jewish Interpretation of Genesis 1:26, 3:5, 3:22 in the Middle Ages." *Scriptura* 117.1 (2018) 1-24.

Poulet, Donat. "The Moral Causes of the Flood." *The Catholic Biblical Quarterly* 4.4 (October 1942) 293-303.

Poythress, Vern S. "Genesis 1:1 Is the First Event, Not a Summary." *The Westminster Theological Journal* 79.1 (Spring 2017) 97-121. https://frame-poythress.org/wp-content/uploads/2017/05/PoythressVernGenesis1.1IsTheFirstEventNotASummary.pdf.

Preuss, Horst Dietrich. "דָּמָה, *dāmāh*; דְּמוּת, *demûth*." In *Theological Dictionary of the Old Testament*, vol. 2, edited by G. Johannes Botterweck et al., 260-65. Grand Rapids: Eerdmans, 2003.

Ramsey, George W. "Is Name-Giving an Act of Domination in Genesis 2:23 and Elsewhere?" *The Catholic Biblical Quarterly* 50.1 (January 1988) 24-35.

BIBLIOGRAPHY

Robinson, Robert B. "Literary Functions of the Genealogies of Genesis." *The Catholic Biblical Quarterly* 48.4 (1986) 595–608.

Rooker, Mark F. *Leviticus*. The New American Commentary, vol. 3a. Nashville: Broadman & Holman, 2000.

Routledge, Robin. *Old Testament Theology: A Thematic Approach*. Downers Grove: InterVarsity, 2012.

Ryken, Leland. *How to Read the Bible as Literature . . . and Get More Out of It*. Grand Rapids: Zondervan, 1984.

Sailhamer, John H. *The Meaning of the Pentateuch: Revelation, Composition, and Interpretation*. Downers Grove: InterVarsity, 2009.

———. *The Pentateuch as Narrative: A Biblical-Theological Commentary*. Grand Rapids: Zondervan, 1992.

Sarna, Nahum M. *Genesis*. The JPS Torah Commentary. Philadelphia: Jewish Publication Society, 1989.

Schmidt, W. H. *Die Schöpfungsgeschichte der Priesterschrift: Zur Überlieferungsgeschichte von Genesis 1:1—2:4a und 2:4b—3:24*. Wissenschaftliche Monographien zum Alten und Neuen Testament 17. Neukirchen-Vluyn: Neukirchener, 1964.

Shaefer, Konrad. *Psalms*. Berit Olam: Studies in Hebrew Narrative and Poetry. Edited by David W. Cotter. Collegeville, MN: Liturgical, 2001.

Shea, William H. "The Unity of the Creation Account." *Origins* 5.1 (1978) 9–38.

Simango, Daniel. "The *Imago Dei* (Gen 1:26–27): A History of Interpretation from Philo to the Present." *Studia Historiae Ecclesiasticae* 42.1 (2016) 172–90.

Smith, Gary V. "Structure and Purpose in Genesis 1–11." *Journal of the Evangelical Theological Society* 20.4 (1977) 307–19.

Sommer, Benjamin. "Dating Pentateuchal Texts and the Perils of Pseudo-Historicism." In *The Pentateuch: International Perspectives on Current Research*, edited by Thomas B. Dozema et al., 85–108. Forschungen zum Alten Testament 78. Tübingen: Mohr Siebeck, 2011.

Stendebach, F. J. "צֶלֶם, ṣelem," In *Theological Dictionary of the Old Testament*, vol. 12, edited by G. Johannes Botterweck et al., 385–96. Grand Rapids: Eerdmans, 2003.

Sternberg, Meir. *The Poetics of Biblical Narrative: Ideological Literature and the Drama of Reading*. Bloomington: Indiana University Press, 1985.

Strawn, Brent. "Comparative Approaches: History, Theory, and the Image of God." In *Method Matters: Essays on the Interpretation of the Hebrew Bible in Honor of David L. Petersen*, edited by Joel M. LeMon, 117–42. Atlanta: Society of Biblical Literature, 2009.

Swann, John. *The Imago Dei: A Priestly Calling for Humanity*. Eugene, OR: Wipf & Stock, 2017.

Tal, Abraham. *Biblia Hebraica: Quinta Editione cum Apparatu Critico Novis Curis Elaborato; Genesis*. Fascicle 1. Stuttgart: Deutsche Bibelgesellschaft, 2015.

Thomas, Matthew A. "These Are the Generations: Identity, Promise, and the *Toledot* Formula." PhD diss., Claremont Graduate University, 2006.

Tigay, Jeffrey H. "The Image of God and the Flood: Some New Developments." In *Studies in Jewish Education and Judaica in Honor of Louis Newman*, edited by Alexander M. Shapiro and Burton I. Cohen, 169–82. New York: Ktav, 1984

Tov, Emanuel. "The *Biblia Hebraica Quinta*: An Important Step Forward." *Journal of Northwest Semitic Languages* 31.1 (January 2005) 1–21.

Bibliography

———. "Criteria for Evaluating Textual Readings: The Limitations of Textual Rules." *Harvard Theological Review* 75.4 (October 1982) 429–48.

———. *Textual Criticism of the Hebrew Bible*. Minneapolis: Fortress, 2012.

Van Wolde, Ellen. "Facing the Earth: Primaeval History in a New Perspective." In *The World of Genesis: Persons, Places, Perspectives*, edited by Philip R. Davies and David J. A. Clines, 22–47. Journal for the Study of the Old Testament Supplement Series 257. Sheffield: Sheffield Academic, 1998.

———. "The Story of Cain and Abel: A Narrative Study." *Journal for the Study of the Old Testament* 52 (1991) 25–41.

Von Rad, Gerhard. *Genesis: A Commentary*. Rev. ed. Translated by John H. Marks. The Old Testament Library. Philadelphia: Westminster, 1972.

———. *Theology of the Old Testament*. Translated by D. M. G. Stalker. Vol. 1. New York: Harper & Row, 1962.

Waltke, Bruce K., and Cathi J. Fredricks. *Genesis: A Commentary*. Grand Rapids: Zondervan, 2001.

Waltke, Bruce K., and Charles Yu. *An Old Testament Theology: An Exegetical, Canonical, and Thematic Approach*. Grand Rapids: Zondervan, 2007.

Waltke, Bruce K., and M. O'Connor. *An Introduction to Biblical Hebrew Syntax*. Winona Lake, IN: Eisenbrauns, 1990.

Walton, John H. *Ancient Near Eastern Thought and the Old Testament: Introducing the Conceptual World of the Hebrew Bible*. Grand Rapids: Baker Academic, 2006.

———. *Genesis 1 as Ancient Cosmology*. Winona Lake, IN: Eisenbrauns, 2011.

———. *The Lost World of Genesis One: Ancient Cosmology and the Origins Debate*. Downers Grove: InterVarsity, 2009.

Weil, Gotthold, ed. *Festschrift Eduard Sachau zum Siebzigsten Geburtstage*. Berlin: G. Reimer, 1915.

Wenham, Gordon. *Genesis 1–15*. Word Biblical Commentary. Waco: Word, 1982.

Westermann, Claus. *Genesis 1–11: A Continental Commentary*. Translated by John J. Scullion. Minneapolis: Fortress, 1994.

Whybray, R. N. *The Making of the Pentateuch: A Methodological Study*. Journal for the Study of the Old Testament Supplement Series 53. Sheffield, UK: JSOT: 1987.

Wildeberger, H. "צלם, ṣelem, image." In *Theological Lexicon of the Old Testament*, edited by Ernst Jenni and Claus Westermann, 1080–85. Peabody, MA: Hendrickson, 1997.

Wilson, Stephen M. "Blood Vengeance and the *Imago Dei* in the Flood Narrative (Genesis 9:6)." *Interpretation: A Journal of Bible and Theology* 713 (2017) 263–73.

Wiseman, P. J. *Ancient Records and the Structure of Genesis: A Case for Literary Unity*. Nashville: Nelson, 1985.

Wurthwein, Ernst. *The Text of the Old Testament: An Introduction to the Biblia Hebraica*. 3rd ed. Rev. and exp. by Alexander Achilles Fisher. Translated by Erroll F. Rhoads. Grand Rapids: Eerdmans, 2014.

Zehnder, Markus. "Cause or Value? Problems in the Understanding of Gen 9, 6a." *Zeitschrift für die Alttestamentliche Wissenschaft* 122.1 (2010) 81–89.

www.ingramcontent.com/pod-product-compliance
Lightning Source LLC
Chambersburg PA
CBHW050817160426
43192CB00010B/1801